D1526423

KANT'S POLITICS

KANT'S POLITICS

provisional theory for an uncertain world

elisabeth ellis

yale university press / new haven and london

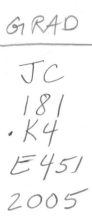
Set in Minion and Franklin Gothic types by The Composing Room of Michigan, Inc.

Printed in the United States of America.

Library of Congress Cataloging-in-Publication Data

Ellis, Elisabeth.

    Kant's politics : provisional theory for an uncertain world / Elisabeth Ellis.

        p. cm.

    Includes bibliographical references and index.

    ISBN 0-300-10120-1 (cloth : alk. paper)

    1. Kant, Immanuel, 1724–1804—Contributions in political science.

  2. Political science—Philosophy.   I. Title.

JC181.K4E45 2005

320′.092—dc22

                                   2004055299

10   9   8   7   6   5   4   3   2   1

For Susie

CONTENTS

PREFACE

I began thinking seriously about Kant's theory of the public sphere in 1993. Bill Clinton had just been elected to the presidency of the United States with a plurality (43 percent) of the popular vote. The conduct of the campaign was unprecedented in its degree of professionalism, and it cost an unprecedented amount of money.[1] Standard political analysis would predict that a new administration like Clinton's would be especially responsive to the interests of its best-organized constituencies, rather than to the preferences of diffuse majorities. In fact, in going about the business of the first hundred days of his administration, Clinton addressed the needs of many of the interest groups who had supported his candidacy. His cabinet, the most diverse in American history, included representatives from most major Democratic constituencies. In one of his first acts as president, Clinton complied with a campaign promise to end official discrimination against gays in the military.[2] He proposed to use an executive order to change the policy of dismissal on the basis of sexual orientation, an act that not only offered to right an existing injustice toward a large group of American citizens but also would have satisfied a significant and well-organized group of Clinton's campaign supporters.[3] The administration was surprised, however, by the level of opposition to the proposal. Faced with resistance from the military establishment, from members of both parties in Congress, and most important, from opinion polls showing popular disapproval of the measure, Clinton dropped his proposal. The final compromise policy of "don't ask, don't tell" satisfied no one.[4]

As I followed the early days of the new Democratic administration along with everyone else in 1993, I wondered why Clinton had conceded this part of his policy agenda so quickly. He did not face reelection for another three years, making his first hundred days the most opportune time to enact an unpopular policy to satisfy an important minority constituency. Conventional political science explains the outcome by pointing out that such unpopular policies require low visibility to succeed, but there was something about the administration's response to public opinion polls that ordinary policy analysis fails to capture. Perhaps because Clinton, as a centrist "new Democrat," was claiming a popular mandate, short-term poll results seemed to be driving policy decisions. Poll respondents lacked coercive sanctioning power over Clinton. In fact, the only sanctioning then imaginable in the electoral interim was via the checkbook, and Clinton's decision to backpedal on gay rights probably hurt rather than helped him among well-heeled Democrats.[5] The power of public opinion to determine executive policy should have been at its weakest three years from the next election, and yet in this case it seemed, paradoxically, all the more powerful for its lack of concrete sanctions to wield.

What does the Clinton administration's 1993 failure to enact a policy of nondiscrimination in the military have to do with my reading of Kant? The long answer will take the rest of this book to unfold. The short answer is that Kant, from his early essay on enlightenment through his late political works, develops an original theory of political transition that accounts for that part of political change driven by the concrete effects of common political ideals. As I emphasize later in the book, there are enormous and significant differences between the Kantian republic of letters and the modern public sphere. However, Kant's basic analysis of the power of political ideals, especially in opposition, remains as interesting as ever.

This book could not have been written without the constant and generous assistance of many other people, though I remain responsible for its shortcomings. It happened that I was attending graduate school at Berkeley just as the new Clinton administration was taking office. My teachers and fellow students there patiently listened to my preliminary ramblings about the power of the public sphere and followed up with tough questions that improved my work. Though I cannot list them all here, thanks are due to the many individuals who contributed to my project with conversations held in halls and seminar rooms in Berkeley, La Jolla, College Station, and elsewhere. I am especially grateful to Shannon Stimson, whose incisive questions, tough readings, and commitment to serious inquiry made this work possible for me. Paul Thomas's discussions of German philosophy and literature helped me formulate my problem and understand it as the project unfolded. Robert Holub's expertise on German social thought and his thoughtful comments on work in progress helped direct my thinking at a couple of critical junctures. Eric Santner's kind attention to my early interest in German culture, his thorough critiques of my work, and his series of excellent recommendations for reading first led me to think about pursuing a scholarly life; to him I am most grateful. Hanna Pitkin, Hubert Dreyfus,

Tracy Strong, and Henry Allison all asked me important questions that I was unable to answer at first, pushing me to improve my thinking at crucial moments. Without Henry Allison's Kant seminars in the Department of Philosophy at the University of California, San Diego, not to mention his lucid and indispensable books, I would have been unable to produce this work.

In the later stages of this project, I benefited enormously from the comments of my fellow students of Kant. Georg Cavallar's comments on chapter 4 were very useful and encouraging. I am deeply grateful for John Christian Laursen's generous contributions of time and expertise in reading large parts of the manuscript in progress. Chris's brilliant and humane example has been a constant inspiration to me. I have learned a great deal about how to read Kant, and why to read Kant, from Mika LaVaque-Manty's writings and from his comments on parts of this work; if only I had also learned to imitate his perfectly expressed formulations of political-philosophical problems, this book would have been much better than it is.

I am grateful to Ian Shapiro for his generous encouragement of this project, for spending time explaining his work and listening to me try to explain mine, and for asking tough questions about naturalism. Thanks also to James Booth, Doug Dow, Jeffrey Isaac, James Johnson, Felicitas Munzel, Sankar Muthu, and my graduate students, all of whom graciously spent time discussing parts of this work with me. I deeply appreciate the work of John Kulka, my editor at Yale University Press, and the extremely productive and enlightening comments of two anonymous readers for the press. I can hardly express my gratitude to these readers for bringing their formidable erudition and general thoughtfulness to bear on my manuscript; without their suggestions, large and small, this book would have been much the worse.

The Andrew W. Mellon Fellowships of the Woodrow Wilson National Fellowship Foundation, the Henry Robert Braden Fund of the Department of Political Science at the University of California, Berkeley, the Deutsche Akademische Austauschdienst, the Texas A&M University Office of the Vice President for Research, and the Texas A&M University College of Liberal Arts each supported this project financially, for which I am very grateful. The Center for European Studies at Harvard University invited me to a conference on civil society, where the excellent discussion and challenging questions of the participants, including especially John Keane, John Hall, and Frank Trentmann, led me to refine my project. An early version of some of the arguments in chapter 1 was published in a volume edited by Frank

Trentmann, as "Immanuel Kant's Two Theories of Civil Society" (*Paradoxes of Civil Society: New Perspectives on Modern German and British History* [New York and Oxford: Berghahn Books, 2000]). Thanks are due to the participants on panels at regional and national meetings of the American Political Science Association, whose invaluable questions about my work assisted its progress.

I am especially grateful to the theory faculty at Texas A&M University—Judith Baer, Cary Nederman, and Edward Portis—whose comments on my work both informally and as part of the theory convocation have been extremely helpful to me. I would like to thank the members and staff of the Department of Political Science at UC–San Diego, who generously provided office space and a wonderfully collegial atmosphere for a key stage of my writing. The staff of the Department of Political Science at UC–Berkeley made the impossible possible as a matter of course; I am especially grateful to Ellen Borrowman for her tireless and occasionally miraculous support. I would like to thank Steven Weber and Henry Brady for their patient and generous support of my studies. Thanks to Leon LeBuffe and his colleagues at the Southern California Chapter of the National Multiple Sclerosis Society for enormously generous help at a critical moment in the writing of this book. This project could not have been completed without the assistance of the staff at the Department of Political Science at Texas A&M University. For their help, and for the able research assistance provided by Phillip Gray, I am extremely grateful.

Finally, I would like to thank the friends and family who have sustained me throughout this effort of scholarship. I am especially grateful to my husband, Michael LeBuffe, for his natural reason and for his philosophical expertise, both of which he placed at the service of this project more often than I had any right to expect. I consider myself extremely lucky to be surrounded by people interested in investigating the world. Thanks to them, this work has been possible.

introduction

This book offers two things to its readers: first, a new reading of Immanuel Kant's political theory, and, second, an application of this reading to contemporary political problems. Kant himself was deeply interested in the day-to-day politics of late eighteenth-century Europe and followed them via printed reports, personal letters, and dinnertime conversation from his home in the remote Prussian city of Königsberg. While such issues as whether to educate poor children, the right to petition the king, or the long-term authority of church synods may seem obscure to us today, the general principles at stake in Kant's time are as contested at the outset of the twenty-first century as ever. Connecting all of Kant's political interests, the project of enlightenment—of escaping moral, intellectual, and political tutelage—moved Kant to think about what we now call regime change. The problem of how to escape absolute rule and make progress toward republican self-rule dominated Kant's political thought. These days we use the language of democracy to justify nearly every variety of political order, but our problems are still problems of transition. Instead of clashes between ostensibly perfect representatives of different regime types, we have a universe of in-betweens and halfway-to-who-knows-wheres cooperating and competing in unpredictable ways. Kant, among political theorists, is uniquely comfortable with the provisional and uncertain politics of transition.

While political theorists have been directing their attention elsewhere, political scientists have been using these sorts of Kantian insights to explain some of the world-transforming changes that have taken place over the past decade. Empirical work, such as that of Peter Haas, Margaret Keck, and Kathryn Sikkink, for example, is demonstrating the unexpected political efficacy of principled ideas transmitted by organized international actors.[1] As Jeffrey Isaac has pointed out, however, political theorists seem unable to address new political realities, such as the fall of the Soviet Union, with the resources currently available.[2]

In response to this problem, I argue here for a new Kantian political theory that refocuses scholarly attention away from stale debates over absolute principles and toward the kinds of politics that really matter: toward substantive rather than merely formal citizenship; toward dynamic theories of democratization rather than static models of constitutional perfection; and toward empirically disciplined recognition of the power of shared ideas in political change, rather than the currently available and equally unappetizing alternatives of liberal universalism and reductivist realism.

Political theorists of all stripes are beginning to call for such an alternative: Ian Shapiro writes that a "good deal of what passes for 'ideal' political theory carries with it a whiff of irrelevance"; Daniel Bell complains that Anglo-American political philosophy seems to be seeking its own "final solution."[3] *Kant's Politics* supplements these critiques with a historically grounded and empirically engaged positive contribution to the new debate on the scope of political theory. Kantian political theory takes the provisional nature of political institutions seriously, focusing less on ideal outcomes than on the places where citizens gain the capacities needed to bring the promise of democratic freedom closer to reality.

It is no longer necessary to begin a work on Kant's political philosophy defensively. Over the past few decades, scholars have revitalized inquiry into Kant's political ideas by publishing new collections of his political essays, new volumes of commentators' papers on significant themes in Kant's political philosophy, new historical collections that set Kant's political theory in the context of late eighteenth-century journalism, several seminal studies by individual scholars on Kant's philosophy, a superb new biography of Kant, and, finally, original works of political thought directly or indirectly inspired by Kant's work.[4] Kant's political writings, through the first two parts of *The Conflict of the Faculties* (1798), are no longer dismissed as the products of senility, as they were in the first half of the twentieth century.[5] Instead, scholars have been learning again to read Kant's political works. The exegetical part of this book is intended as a contribution to this effort to retrieve Kant's works from misreadings that originated with his immediate contemporaries and have continued into the twenty-first century.

TWO COMMON MISREADINGS OF KANT'S POLITICS

Two main types of reading in the literature on Kant's political theory tend to produce less than satisfactory accounts of his work. Either the reader underestimates the importance of Kant's formal, critical philosophy to the more pragmatic political work, or a reader may apply a mistaken version of this philosophy to Kant's politics. In the first case, the unwary reader may approach Kant's political thought without the philosophical apparatus Kant establishes in his *Critiques*. If, for example, as I argue in chapter 4, one misses Kant's complex distinction between regulative ideals and actual political life, then it will be hard to understand the most important element of his legal philosophy, which is the account of provisional right. Kant, like all first-rate political theorists, addresses multiple audiences in his works, and he does try to make his most important arguments available to the uninitiated. For example, there is no mistaking his claim that respect for individual human beings as ends in themselves is a basic requirement of justice. Even so, however plain Kant's fundamental political sympathies may be, any serious account of his political arguments requires the reader to apply his critical method.

I address this underestimation of the systematicity of Kant's philosophy with a developmental account of Kant's political works as bridging the gap left by his critical philosophy between freedom and nature. More particularly, I show that contrary to many commentators' descriptions of his political work, Kant concerns himself less with the strictures of ideal justice than with the institutions that might promote human progress.[6] A politics of transition to republican government, as opposed to the ideal construction of a perfect republic in thought, would be a contribution to the mediation between the norms that express Kantian freedom and the practices that exemplify human nature. Thus I hope to show that Kant's political thought addresses a fundamental concern of his critical philosophy: the gap between freedom and nature.[7]

The second mistake that a reader might make is to apply erroneous conclusions from Kant's critical philosophy to his politics. Though the naive (unphilosophical) reading of the political works described above yields only dogmatic Kantian sympathies rather than grounded political arguments, even a sophisticated reading may err in its application of critical strictures to political life. Probably the most common instance of this type of error is the attribution to Kant's politics of a "rigorism" derived from a narrow reading of his ethics, usually one based on the *Groundwork of the*

Metaphysics of Morals.[8] As I argue throughout the book, a simplistic application of Kant's categorical imperative blinds the reader to crucial elements of his moral philosophy, especially his theory of action as necessarily ends oriented.[9] While adhering to the simple reading of Kant's ethics may allow one to understand Kant's derivation of the elements of the just state, as these are ideals grounded in the moral law, this simple reading will miss Kant's nuanced accounts of how theory relates to practice, of political ethics, of progress, of revolution, and of a number of other topics outside the bare sketch of the perfect state. In short, a rigoristic interpretation of Kant's ethics leads to a static version of his politics. Furthermore, a reader committed to the rigoristic reading of Kant's ethics might conclude that his politics must be stoical rather than progressive, since a would-be moral agent committed to the simple categorical imperative without any commitment to the promotion of moral ends would look inward to the care of his soul rather than outward to the world around him.

Another common mistaken reading of this second type dates back to the first reviews of Kant's critical philosophy, which confused the "epistemic condition" of limited human perception with the metaphysical proposition that there exist two separate worlds, the phenomenal and the noumenal.[10] As Henry Allison writes, this erroneous reading claims that "Kant's transcendental idealism is a metaphysical theory that affirms the unknowability of the 'real' (things in themselves) and relegates knowledge to the purely subjective realm of representations (appearances)."[11] The main problem with such a reading is that Kant's achievement in the first *Critique* is not ontological but epistemological: Kant is concerned with justifying scientific inquiry by setting out the limits within which knowledge is possible. I discuss this problem in greater detail throughout the book, where I revise the understandings of Kant's politics that are based on the common error of taking his epistemology for ontology. To put it very simply: just because Kant claims that human beings cannot grasp the world in its totality does not mean that Kant denies that the world itself is whole.

The conditions of our knowledge of the world matter to Kant's politics. For example, I discuss Kant's claim that while political actors cannot at any given historical moment make accurate judgments about the material consequences of their actions, they always have access to the absolute standards of moral reason. The reading that would follow from mistaking this epistemological claim of Kant's for a claim about the nature of the world suggests that Kant intended to divide the world between free but isolated subjects, on the one hand, and determined objects embedded in nature, on the other.

Bernard Yack reports accurately on this misreading of Kant by his German romantic successors: "From this perspective, the individual can find no reflection of himself, of his special human qualities, in the external world, not even in the actions and interactions of human beings."[12]

Kant's continuous engagement with the problem of freedom and nature, however, did not result in a single definitive solution. Instead, Kant offers his reader a series of attempted resolutions, some of which do seem to posit two worlds rather than two perspectives. Thus, as I discuss in my second chapter, Kant does provide the reader with some textual evidence for the two-worlds point of view, especially in his infamous "nation of devils" argument. I argue that this cannot be Kant's definitive view. A Kant whose human subjects can be considered moral agents only apart from any material activity in the world would also have to posit a kind of radical political irresponsibility. But this is not the case. The division between subjective freedom and objective determination cannot be bridged by any direct observations, since this division is a necessary condition of our human perception (of our knowledge, that is, though not of our existence, necessarily).[13] However, Kant throughout his works makes a series of attempts to address this unavoidable but vexing gap in possible human knowledge, positing for example a number of lesser standards of knowledge beneath theoretical knowledge, in which we might make some rational assumptions about human existence in its totality, rather than presuming that our divided perception of it represents the way life is "in itself." Politically speaking, then, rather than allowing agents to relinquish responsibility for the world simply because they cannot know exactly how they relate to it, Kant proposes some necessary assumptions moral agents ought to make if they are to act in an uncertain world without losing their autonomy. I examine a number of these assumptions in this book, including Kant's claims about teleological history, rational faith, human progress toward enlightenment, and the possibility of pursuit of the highest good.

FOUR WAYS TO FIND KANT'S POLITICS

If it is no longer necessary to defend Kant's political theory as a worthy object of study, it is still necessary to defend a reading of Kant as a nonrigoristic, even worldly student of politics. Kant's political thought offers a dynamic account of the political institutions that might move humanity toward the ideals elucidated by Kant's formal ethical theory. In this book, I do not interpretively elevate one particular text in Kant's work. As is well known, Kant did not write a definitive work of political theory. Instead, I examine his larger effort to build a coherent system around the tension between freedom and nature.

There are, I suppose, four possible responses on the part of the commentator to Kant's failure to write a comprehensive political treatise. First, one might conclude that he wrote no serious political theory. The dismissive view dominated literature on Kant up to the early 1960s. It persists in some circles today, despite its definitive refutation by Onora O'Neill, among many others. This situation is as much Kant's fault as that of his interpreters. Kant does not reflect in writing on the status of his political philosophy, as he does for his ethics and his critical epistemology. Even in *The Metaphysics of Morals,* Kant's most important political work, Kant protests that his doctrine of right remains incomplete. Moreover, he included in his political writings two incompatible points of view: a naturalistic teleology which cannot, I argue, be defended, and the far more defensible theory of freely willed human progress that Patrick Riley calls his "contractarianism."[14] Though, as I argue throughout this book, Kant's work properly understood makes a number of extremely important contributions to political philosophy, it is not surprising that many commentators have simply given up the struggle to find it, given the many obstacles Kant throws in their path.

Admitting, then, that Kant wrote a political philosophy, one might take a second, focused view that it is "really" contained in some one work on another topic. I discuss, for example, in my second chapter Hannah Arendt's famous view that Kant's *Judgment* contains his politics.[15] A subset of this focused view would locate Kant's political theory in his most explicitly political work, namely, the first half of *The Metaphysics of Morals,* the *Rechtslehre,* or "Doctrine of Right" (or "law"). While I consider the *Rechtslehre* to be Kant's most important piece of political writing, I argue that no complete understanding of Kant's political philosophy can be given by a reading of the *Rechtslehre* alone.[16] Kant himself emphasizes the radical incompleteness of the work. Most important for my purposes, the main elements of his definitive, dynamic theory of transition toward more perfect governance are found not in the *Rechtslehre* but in his occasional political essays.

A third, eclectic view would combine elements of Kant's theory of politics from all of his various works, making out of the fragmented writings as coherent a whole as possible. This method is used effectively by a number of excellent commentators on Kant's politics, including for example Alan Rosen. However, the peculiarities of Kant's method make the eclectic reading less successful here than it is when applied to other political thinkers. The status of many of Kant's claims, for example, depends crucially on the context in which they are placed: it matters a great deal whether a particular claim is a step in a formal deduction, an elucidation by example, part of a speculative account of world history, or of a piece of dry satire. As I argue throughout the book, taking Kant's arguments, even those of his lighter essays, out of their historical and philosophical contexts leads to misunderstanding.

Kant aspired to systematicity in his philosophy. His "architectonic" thinking is sometimes confusing, since it tends to move Kant to follow the dictates of form where an argument's function might have provided surer guidance. Nevertheless, Kant's systematicity makes it possible to take a fourth, developmental, view of his political philosophy. Throughout his mature work, from his first *Critique* to his late *Conflict of the Faculties,* Kant wrestles with a single group of philosophical tensions, trying out a series of approaches to the same essential problems. Thus I examine the development of Kant's work on the problem of the transition to more perfect governance, which is a subissue of the fundamental Kantian concern about bridging the gap between freedom and nature.[17]

ONE WAY TO SET KANT'S POLITICS IN CONTEXT

In order to understand Kant's arguments on this transition, I have set his claims in context as I discuss them. On the one hand, I compare Kant's claims with those of his predecessors in social contract theory, particularly those of Hobbes and Locke.[18] On the other, I compare Kant's political ideas with those of his contemporaries in the late eighteenth-century public sphere. Such a perspective illuminates arguments that otherwise would remain obscure. For example, in "What Is Enlightenment?" Kant's arguments about the ability of a church synod to make lasting decisions about dogma for its members make sense only in the context of decades of heated, politically sensitive debate on the subject, and especially on the role of the state in such matters. Additionally, setting Kant's work in context allows the reader to identify Kant's original contributions to political thought. Seen against the backdrop of eighteenth-century Prussian "enlightened absolutist" discourse, for example, Kant's views on the social contract, political obligation, and even the right of resistance appear typical of moderately progressive political thinking of the time. In the *Rechtslehre* and in other works, contextual analysis reveals Kant struggling to make such a moderate republicanism compatible with the insights of his critical moral theory.

Even his odd version of the public/private distinction, which I discuss in chapter 1, was not uncommon in the pamphlet literature and enlighten-ment salons of Kant's time. However, Kant makes significant original con-tributions with his modification of the concept of civil society, his account of provisional right, his vision of the transition toward enlightened gover-nance, and his claim that the mechanism of this transition is the institution of publicity. All these topics stand out from the contextual background against which I interpret Kant's work. One cannot conclude from the fact that Kant participates in particular discourses that his point of view is de-termined by them.

Thus I view political philosophers as simultaneously working within and challenging the boundaries of the political discourses of their times, places, and social positions. As I mentioned above, like all first-rate theorists Kant is capable of writing on multiple levels. In fact, though he exhibits nowhere near the rhetorical talent of his admired predecessor, Jean-Jacques Rousseau, he shares with Rousseau an appreciation of the importance of using the conditions of a work's particular genre in the service of the larger arguments in question. As I show in chapter 3, Kant manipulates the com-positional strictures of the traditional peace treaty in order to suggest to the reader the tension between provisional and conclusive requirements for in-ternational right. Defending his own contextual method, Quentin Skinner has written that it "consists in trying to place [such] historical texts within such contexts as enable us in turn to identify what their authors were *doing* in writing them."[19]

One might say that each generation's scholarly innovators suffer one of two possible fates: the next generation might dismiss their achievements as irrelevant, or they might succeed so well that the next generation cannot see that their achievements are achievements at all. This second fate, I believe, is what awaits the multifarious inheritors of the "linguistic turn," from schol-ars of the "Cambridge School," such as Skinner, to those of the "Geschicht-liche Grundbegriffe" group, such as Reinhart Koselleck, to those outside any definitive "school," such as Hanna Pitkin.[20] The works of Wittgenstein, J. L. Austin, and even Thomas Kuhn drew the attention of these writers to-ward the study of the use (rather than the meaning) of words in political discourse. J. G. A. Pocock advises the intellectual historian to develop "a truly autonomous method, one which offers a means of treating the phe-nomena of political thought strictly as historical *phenomena* and—since history is about things happening—even as historical events: as things hap-pening in a context which defines the kind of events they were." Pocock's version of contextual analysis is a sort of vanguard theory, pitched perhaps a bit too strong to survive its progenitor but at the leading edge of a movement that has established itself. While Pocock is willing to speak of paradigms of discourse that "prescribe what [the political theorist] might say and how he might say it," many others interested in the historical context of political ideas would soften the position from "prescription" to "condition."[21] In other words, context matters for political thinking but does not determine it. Anthony Pagden puts the case nicely in his introduction to a collection of essays in contextual political thought, when he writes that he is concerned "not with the architecture of the linguistic prisons of the past, but with the necessarily limited, but nevertheless intelligible, freedom of those who inhabited them."[22]

For the exegetical parts of this book, the works of the Cambridge School, of Richard Ashcraft, and of the Geschichtliche Grundbegriffe group have provided helpful models of scholarly method.[23] Speaking of his recent Hobbes interpretation, Skinner says that he tries "to indicate what traditions [Hobbes] reacts against, what lines of argument he takes up, what changes he introduces in existing debates."[24] Such a study would be, to use Kantian terminology, a highly useful propaedeutic to an ultimate work analyzing the successes and failures, by both internal and external measures, of an author's political thought. In this book, I illuminate some of Kant's reactions, arguments, and innovations by placing them in their historical and philosophical contexts. By tracing Kant's development of a dynamic theory of political progress against the backgrounds of his own critical philosophy, his social contract predecessors, and his enlightenment contemporaries, I hope to reveal a neglected aspect of Kant's work—worldly, pragmatic, and intensely committed to the everyday pursuit of human freedom.

This new reading of Kant's politics may be interesting in itself, but more important, it should contribute to the study of the dynamic effects of political ideals in the world. Kant's principle of provisional right recommends that existing institutions be judged according to whether they are consistent with the continued possibility of progress, rather than by direct comparison with some set of ideal norms. While some fairly substantial injunctions follow from the principle, including, as I shall show, a commitment to political gradualism and an insistence upon freedoms of thought and expression, the principle of provisional right provides a broad standard for normative political theory that is deeply responsive to historical and geographical particulars. Indeed, attention to such particulars from a Kantian point of view should enable students of politics to conceive of their subject as a unified whole, rather than having to choose between the normative and empirical perspectives. Throughout his many versions of a theory of the effects of commonly held principles on collective life, and most important in his mature theory of the public sphere, Kant directs our attention to the dynamism between our world and our ideals.

1

civil society

The Kantian origins of two of the late twentieth century's most influential political theories, those of John Rawls and Jürgen Habermas, are well understood.[1] Less well understood are the potential contributions of a Kantian political theory to the debates that have evolved out of contemporary liberal and democratic theory. Take the very interesting case of deliberative democratic theory.[2] Deliberative democratic theory argues that politically relevant moral disagreement may sometimes be resolved, at least for political purposes if not definitively, by deliberation under some simple rules, such as reciprocity and a general willingness to work toward agreement. A common criticism of this line of reasoning is that deliberative democrats underestimate the degree to which political disagreements are about real differences of interest rather than moral misunderstandings; this is what Ian Shapiro says about Amy Gutmann and Dennis Thompson's view in their *Democracy and Disagreement*, for example.[3] Gutmann and Thompson might reply that while genuine differences may be revealed in deliberation, participation in the process itself commits the participants to principles that make accommodation more likely. For example, the arguments of moral extremists would be subjected to rational scrutiny along with all other points of view. Such a process would commit all participants at the very least to the principle of noncontradiction, and probably to several other principles (reciprocity, full disclosure, good faith, and so forth). Against this view, Shapiro argues convincingly that it is "hard to imagine a fundamentalist being impressed by [deliberative democratic procedure], particularly when she learns that any empirical claim she makes must be consistent with 'relatively reliable methods of inquiry.' . . . The Gutmann/

Thompson model works only for those fundamentalists who also count themselves fallibilist democrats. That, I fear, is an empty class."[4]

On this point both the deliberative democratic theorists and their critics have something to learn from Kant's dynamic theory of the public sphere, which I discuss in this chapter. Like advocates of deliberative democracy, Kant supports the development of a healthy public sphere where disagreements could be aired and judged on the basis of reasoned argument alone. As I shall show in what follows, Kant agrees that fanatical or even merely wrongheaded or traditional arguments would naturally fall victim to their own shortcomings, once exposed in the public sphere. But unlike Gutmann and Thompson, and in sympathy with Shapiro, Kant never expects this operation to take place all at once, in the head of any particular fanatic. Instead, for Kant the public sphere works slowly, with the effects of any one argument being felt long after any particular advocate identifies them. As I discuss in chapter 5, an ancillary advantage of this Kantian view is that the arguers may submit their judgment entirely to reason by their own lights; thus they are spared potentially agonizing—and, for Kant, corrupting—decisions between what they identify as reasonable and what is unreasonable but attractive in its short-term effects.

Relevant to the debate on deliberative democracy, then, is the Kantian insight that the logic on which deliberative democracy depends does indeed operate in the real world, but on a social, not an individual, and a long-term, not a short-term, scale. As historians of political thought from G. W. F. Hegel to Anthony Pagden have argued, political discourses (if not individual discoursers) over time become constrained to respond to their own inconsistencies.[5] The dynamic on which Gutmann and Thompson place their hopes for progress may well be operable despite Shapiro's and others' well-founded doubts, but at a different level of analysis: that of the public and its political discourses rather than of the individual and his or her conscience. Kant's account of the mechanism of publicity contributes a possible resolution to the standoff between deliberative democracy theorists and their critics, one that preserves the originally liberal insights of the theory while remaining empirically viable.

THE MECHANISM OF PUBLICITY

Kant's concept of publicity as a motor of progress toward an ideal state is among his most important contributions to modern political theory. Though Kant explicitly places some of his political work in the long tradition of imagining and justifying perfect political systems, the more interesting and original aspects of his writing deal not with the ideal state per se but with the transition from the current, imperfect "provisional" state toward political perfection.[6] Scholarly attention to Kant's political philosophy has focused on his theory of the ideal state, at the expense of the far more interesting account of transition via the mechanism of publicity.[7] Kant is rightly honored for his defense of human rights, the rule of law, and the cause of international peace; in short, for his attempt to devise a political system that would protect human freedom at every level of interaction. Nevertheless, what is interesting and original in each of these achievements of Kant's comes not from his doctrine of the ideal state, which is fairly typical of moderate enlightened political thought of the time, but from his theory of the conditions of the gradual approximation of that state in practice.[8]

Kant develops his account of political transition over the course of his career, working and reworking the argument as he writes different texts. Though the details of his theory vary, Kant remains interested in the power of public reason as the driving force behind concrete institutional change. As early as the first *Critique* (1781), Kant writes about the need to protect an enlightened realm of inquiry that would remain free of all but the interests of reason. Throughout his work, Kant proposes a number of different accounts of the progress toward perfect governance that would result from the application of judgment to political practice. These include: the concept of the public sphere in his early essay, "What Is Enlightenment?"; his defense of the moral, intellectual, and political preconditions of self-rule in "Theory and Practice" and elsewhere; his formal principles of publicity in "Perpetual Peace"; the development of the concept of provisional right in the *Rechtslehre;* and his revision of his early concept of the public sphere as the judging public in *The Conflict of the Faculties.*[9] Though the specific solutions to a number of ongoing problems vary, the main lines of Kant's argument remain the same: progress toward the just state results from comparisons made by some human agents between rational ideals and empirical reality. However Kant arranges his various institutional and philosophical proposals, the human judges of right need to be isolated from all but the interests of reason, not only to ensure their freedom to reason from a possibly punishing government but also to prevent the corruption of their reason by the temptations of power itself. Over the long run, Kant consistently argues, the interplay of public judgments should lead both to enlightenment on matters of common interest and to the advent of more enlightened political institutions and practices.

In "An Answer to the Question, What Is Enlightenment?" Kant offers an early version of this theme. Here Kant suggests that the mere interchange of ideas, resulting in the progressive enlightenment of the public at large and of rulers in particular, serves as the engine of positive political change. Though he excludes the possibility of knowledge of freedom's causality in the first *Critique,* and wrestles with compromises that avoid violating strictly rational principles of inquiry in later works, all of Kant's attempts to show the principle of publicity in action require him to prove that ideas of reason, mediated by public judgment, can have concrete effects in the world. His methodology reflects this difficult task. Even in a popular, light essay like "What Is Enlightenment?" Kant tries to blend empirical and a priori principles of inquiry. The actual public sphere of Kant's time provides the empirical model for an institution that might mediate between political ideals and actual governance. Thus, the formal need for an institution like the public sphere is determined by Kant a priori, whereas the material contents of the public sphere are borrowed from the actual public sphere of the late eighteenth-century world of letters.

Kant is simultaneously in dialogue with his predecessors in formal social contract theory, and with his pragmatic contemporaries in the Berlin enlightenment.[10] As I discuss in chapters 3, 4, and 5, with regard to *Perpetual Peace,* the *Rechtslehre,* and *The Conflict of the Faculties,* Kant in his political work habitually addresses multiple audiences with multiple and often disparate arguments. Though this makes for rewarding reading more often than not, sometimes the challenges of keeping, as it were, so many balls in the air overwhelm Kant's best efforts. As I discuss here, "What Is Enlightenment?" is a case in point. Among others, Horst Stuke has complained that the attention paid to "What Is Enlightenment?" is all out of proportion to its merit as an essay. Though Kant's prominence as a philosopher has ensured the essay is now considered the most important contribution to the ongoing late eighteenth-century debate, in its time "What Is Enlightenment?" received little notice. Stuke argues that Kant himself did not consider the essay central to his work, and that it was only "occasional and popular, certainly not systematically and definitively developed."[11] Stuke is certainly right about the history of the reception of Kant's essay. It is also true that the ideas it contains are not very systematically developed in the essay itself. However, "What Is Enlightenment?" does contain an early version of the most important line of thinking in Kant's political philosophy. Even in the incomplete and informal arguments of "What Is Enlightenment?" Kant takes seriously the challenge of promoting progress without undermining what he believed to be the condition of any individual right at all, namely, public order.

Rather than hiding a revolutionary's claims beneath a loyal citizen's protestations, Kant seeks to resolve the contradictions between the two positions.

KANT'S EARLY ACCOUNT OF THE PUBLIC SPHERE

Kant's theory of publicity combines principles of reason with empirical inquiry to answer a problem in modern political theory: How can progress toward rational government be achieved? The theory of the ideal state tells us what the goals of human progress must be, but nothing about how we might reach them. There is a wide gulf between an end recognized by all (the just state) and the means available to an individual to pursue it, since any action to overturn the existing civil order puts the actor in contradiction to the moral law, which enjoins order.[12] "What Is Enlightenment?" is Kant's first major response to the problem of progress, and he offers a characteristically moderate theory of political change. Enlightened writers in the public sphere, who if they are not scholars themselves at least behave like scholars in print, should compare the current state of affairs with the ideals of governance they discover by rational inquiry. Such public discussion will reveal gaps between theory and practice, though Kant argues that such revelation ought never to incite revolutionary change. However, by publicizing the conclusions of reasonable and presumably disinterested observers, the free public sphere should contribute to gradual, state-led reform.

Kant's argument in "What Is Enlightenment?" thus takes up a problem that concerned his predecessors in social contract theory, such as Thomas Hobbes, John Locke, and Jean-Jacques Rousseau. Kant tolerates much less violence in the name of some version of political justice than his predecessors, however. Unlike Locke, for example, Kant cannot allow revolutionary change to close the gap between real and ideal politics. Instead, he attempts to solve the problem of progress by means of another classic problem in social contract theory, the question of who shall be judge of political right.[13] In the absence of perfect divine judgment, and of reliable judgment on the part of politicians, Kant identifies members of the public sphere as those most able to approximate perfect judgment on matters of right. Kant thus advocates gradual reform as the best mode of political progress, and the public sphere as its agent.

"What Is Enlightenment?" is a short, popular essay, and it not surprisingly leaves many serious questions open. The essay was not intended to be a comprehensive political treatise. Rather, "What Is Enlightenment?" is partly a republican polemic, partly a plea for royal enlightenment, and partly speculative social history. In Kant's subsequent political works, he tries to address the shortcomings left by this provocative but incomplete account of the public sphere.

The Enlightenment of a Public

In "What Is Enlightenment?" Kant considers the question that prompts much of his political work: How can humankind make progress toward its perfection? Reason, he argues, provides a universally applicable image of this perfection; unfortunately, we cannot be confident that we have the means to achieve it. Kant begins his essay with a now-famous definition of *Aufklärung:* "*Enlightenment is man's emergence from his self-incurred immaturity. Immaturity* is the inability to use one's own understanding without the guidance of another."[14]

Kant defines *Aufklärung* against a common condition of immaturity or dependence. In an examination of the causes of this unenlightened state, Kant initially points to the individual shortcomings of "laziness and cowardice." Almost immediately, however, he shifts the blame from the individual to society, revealing the origins of these individual barriers to enlightenment in social history. Kant concludes that the problem of enlightenment should be addressed at the level of "a public" (*ein Publikum*), rather than simply by exhorting individuals to think for themselves. Instead of the ahistorical man of his initial definition of enlightenment, Kant becomes concerned with actual men organized as "a public."

Individuals, then, do not break free of their tutelage in socially significant numbers. "But that a public should enlighten itself is more possible; indeed this is almost inevitable, if only it is left its freedom."[15] Kant assumes throughout the essay that the experience of dependence has enduring negative consequences for a person's ability to reason for himself or herself. A long-dependent polity suddenly freed of "personal despotism" or "avaricious or tyrannical oppression" will likely replace its old, unfree modes with new, equally unfree ones. Revolutionary change, therefore, cannot further the cause of enlightenment. A public may make only gradual progress toward that goal. Having ruled out revolution as the motor of public enlightenment, Kant identifies his preferred alternative: the freedom, granted by a ruler to his subjects, to make public use of their reason.

The Public and Private Realms

Like other writers of the late Enlightenment, Kant makes a considerable effort to address worries that increased civil freedoms, especially freedom of expression, will lead to disorder rather than to peaceful reform.[16] Freedom of speech, he argues, should not be absolute: acceptable limits on freedom place boundaries on its "private" use, while unacceptable limits on freedom would limit its "public" use. The public use of reason is exercised "*as a scholar [Gelehrter]* before the entire public of the *world of readers.*"[17]

In demarcating the public realm, Kant excludes every arena of life except that in which members, free of the claims of necessity or of arbitrary differences, express their points of view as equals. Kant's private realm encompasses most of life. It includes not only what we would today understand as private life—the household, private enterprise, religious institutions, and most social organizations—but also much of what we would call public, including especially the state. Kant refers to three types of people in their private roles: military officers, who may not reason with their superiors over every order; tax payers, who must pay even when they do not agree with a levy; and clergymen, who ought to preach the doctrine of their church. Each of these activities is associated with necessity: individuals acting according to motives not completely their own are pursuing what Kant calls "domestic" (*häuslich*) activity. Such cases are relegated to the private sphere, in which an individual's use of reason "may . . . often be very narrowly restricted without this particularly hindering the progress of enlightenment."[18]

Kant's willingness to legitimize government interference in nearly every aspect of a citizen's life reveals that his theory of civic freedom, important as it is, contains only the barest glimmerings of what are now understood as human rights against the state. For example, in the *Rechtslehre,* Kant distinguishes between meetings of private associations and gatherings of private citizens; the state should be allowed to interfere with the former as a possible threat to its rule, though it should refrain from abridging the rights of the latter.[19] Kant would have the individual protected in his capacity as member of the public sphere, but as a subject of the state or even as a productive member of society, the same individual enjoys very few of the rights taken for granted by present-day citizens of liberal democratic states. Kant admits the state's legitimate interest in regulating most matters of common interest, but he seeks to carve out a public sphere free of state regulation in order to protect a realm dedicated to truth from the encroachments of political power. Our ordinary understanding, then, of "private" as a sphere protected from the state, expressed for example in the idea of a "right to privacy," has very little to do with Kant's distinction between private, nonuniversalizable interests that may be regulated by the state, and public, potentially universal interests that the state ought to leave free of interference.

Kant's distinction between public and private has struck a number of commentators as counterintuitive or at odds with ordinary usage. For Kant, one speaks publicly as a scholar to the cosmopolitan reading public only according to one's own lights, independent of any pecuniary, political, or social considerations. One speaks privately in a particular role: not freely, but in the name of some other authority. While acting in a civil or otherwise appointed office, a person makes only private—that is, not free—use of his reason. However, even persons who sometimes speak "privately" in the name of particular institutions retain their "world citizenship," and with it their right to public expression, if only "in writing," and "in the manner of a scholar." Kant's public/private distinction is confusing at first because he excludes the government from the public sphere and ignores the sense of *öffentlich* ("public") as *staatlich* ("of the state," or "official").[20] Such a distinction, however, was not without precedent, even among Kant's fellow contributors to the *Berlinische Monatsschrift* (*BMS*). Moses Mendelssohn characterized Kant's distinction between public and private as "merely a bit strange in its expression." A number of authors from the *BMS* circle made similar distinctions. For example, Ernst Ferdinand Klein distinguishes between "subordination" and "freedom to think aloud" in his anonymous article "On Freedom of Thought and Publication."[21]

Rather than distinguishing between public and private speech on the basis of individual motivation, as Kant does in his ethical works with the distinction between autonomous and heteronomous motives, in "What Is Enlightenment?" he specifies particular realms in which speech is considered public or private. In the public (*öffentlich*) arena for the free use of reason, arguments and evidence in written form are exchanged among participants in public discourse. The same officer, tax payer, and clergyman whom Kant has described in their private capacity as mere parts of the civil machines in which they find themselves are now allowed, in their public capacity, to express themselves freely, even on matters concerning their private roles.[22] Unlike the private use of reason, "*public* use of one's reason must always be free, and it alone can bring about enlightenment among human beings."[23]

Public Institutions for Progress in Religious Doctrine

The question of how such a sphere of public reason would in fact promote general enlightenment arises immediately, especially given Kant's many hints that freedom from self-incurred tutelage is freedom not only to reason but also to rule oneself. In "What Is Enlightenment?" Kant does not provide an abstract account of how the freedom to reason publicly brings about so-

cietal improvements. Instead, after distinguishing between the free, protected, public realm and the necessity-governed, legitimately regulated, private one, he launches into an extended discussion of the roles of the state, the
cleric, and the citizen with regard to official religious doctrines. He makes
clear throughout the essay that what goes for the sphere of religion may
eventually apply to other spheres as well, including other areas of government.[24] By proposing a mechanism for mediating between the views of the
public on religious freedom and the state regulators of religious affairs, Kant
formulates an early version of a modern theory of relations between civil society and the state, in which organized society indirectly and noncoercively
influences government policy, absent any scheme of direct representation.
Most commentators miss this point. It is true that Kant is brave to promote
freedom of expression at all, given the political environment in which he was
writing. But far from simply arguing for freedom of the pen, Kant argues that
such freedom would itself promote progress toward the ideal state.

As Kant introduces his example of the individual clergyman's duty to
preach official doctrine, he is initially able to apply his public/private distinction without qualification. When teaching in the name of the church,
the clergyman must act as a "Geschäftsträger" (roughly, businessman) of the
establishment, since every organization requires "Glieder" (limbs, members), who will act for the organization and not by their own lights. On this
first account, the clergyman need not worry about hypocrisy, because he is
explicitly acting in the name of another. "He will say: our church teaches
this or that; here are the arguments it uses."[25] As an independent scholar,
outside his clerical duties, the clergyman can and ought to make public his
conclusions about the rightness of church orthodoxies and suggest possible
improvements.

This neat division between a civil servant's public and private roles begins to unravel almost immediately, however. First Kant says that the cleric
may in good conscience preach doctrines with which he does not fully
agree, since they may be true in a way he does not understand. But then
Kant adds the requirement that official doctrine may not contradict "der in-
nern Religion"; if it did, the clergyman would have to resign his post.[26] For
the first half of this thought, the clergyman easily negotiates the private/
public boundary by subordinating his own religious thoughts to his role as
speaker in the name of the church. Kant shows us the clergyman modestly
saying to himself that there may be truth hidden in these doctrines that he
has been unable to see. But in the last instance, the clergyman's "inner religion" is the test of whether church doctrine may be preached without en-

dangering his conscience. Using his own reason, the clergyman has access to a source of authority greater than that of the (by implication, temporal, material, worldly) power of the church. Kant does not assume that each individual clergyman will necessarily be correct in his assessment. He does assert, however, that to live with a clear conscience, a member of the clergy may not preach anything that his reason tells him is false.

Kant passes over the difficulties into which he has placed his exemplary clergyman at this point. The claim that the clergyman is ultimately beholden to his own reason is followed by a simple reassertion of Kant's distinction between public and private: "Thus the use that an appointed teacher makes of his reason before his congregation is merely a *private use;* for a congregation, however large a gathering it may be, is still only a domestic [*häuslich*] gathering; and with respect to it he, as a priest, is not and cannot be free, since he is carrying out another's commission [*fremden Auftrag*]." Kant contrasts this private role of the clergyman with the freedom he enjoys as a scholar in public (that is, the reading public): "He enjoys an unrestricted freedom to make use of his own reason and to speak in his own person."[27] Though Kant has been speaking of the clergyman's individual conscience, he makes clear that what matters about clerical consciences is their role as spiritual guardians, or speakers for society. In the first place, Kant states, it would be ludicrous to have unenlightened guardians. But second, even the most enlightened guardians could not rightly establish a permanently authoritative religious doctrine that excludes the possibility of future improvements. This, Kant flatly declares, would "be a crime against human nature, whose original vocation lies precisely in such progress."[28] As I discuss in the conclusion to this chapter, Kantian enlightenment has antipaternalistic implications for contemporary democratic theory. No individual or group, even a legitimate representative group, can make permanent moral claims for another.

To this declaration of a natural right to moral progress, Kant adds a premise from social contract theory's basic idea that legitimate law is grounded in the will of the people. "The touchstone of whatever can be decided upon as law for a people lies in the question: whether a people could impose such a law upon itself."[29] For Kant, the example of the clergyman's relation to the church stands for the relations between individuals and authoritative institutions more generally, and especially for the relation between the subject and the state. His formula for enlightened legislation echoes the formula just given for the conscience-stricken clergyman: preach a doctrine if it is possible that it is the true doctrine, and enact a law if it is possible that it reflects the true will of the people. As I discuss in chapter 4, this is Kant's hypothetical version of the standard social contract test of legitimacy. Kant thus answers Rousseau's challenge to find a form of association in which everyone is simultaneously obedient and free: ideally people would be subject to laws of their own making, but provisionally people should be subject to the laws that are determined to be as close as possible to those they would choose for themselves.

However, the explicit object of Kant's inquiry in "What Is Enlightenment?" is not general governmental reform but how official church doctrine might rightly be instituted. The possibility of a religious free-for-all is not even acknowledged in the essay, since Kant presumes, as did most of his contemporaries, that the state has a legitimate interest in regulating at least external spiritual affairs.[30] Kant proposes more radically enlightened institutional reform for the spiritual arena than for the temporal one. While he proposes concrete institutions for regular consultation with actual members of the public on religious matters, Kant requires only that the people "could have" backed a proposed change in general legislation. In both spheres, the people must be allowed actually to express themselves in public, though they must do so "in the manner of scholars." Only in the case of religious observance, however, does Kant outline an actual procedure for public consultation. This procedure, admittedly, is a feeble one by modern standards. If leading clerics propose a change, members of the public ought to be allowed to discuss it, and once a general sentiment is reached, they ought to be allowed to bring a proposal before the throne.[31] This, however, is as close as Kant comes in the essay to suggesting that publicity might play a representative role, by representing the will of the people to the sovereign.[32] Kant's argument here for protected public discussion of matters of common interest stops short of insisting that such discussion represents the will of the people, a point of view that would have undermined the legitimacy of the sovereign. Rather, in "What Is Enlightenment?" public discussion of matters of common interest serves to develop ideas about improvements, to bring these improvements to the sovereign's attention, and, along the way, to enlighten the members of the public themselves.

Kant does not explicitly propose the creation of institutions for public enlightenment with regard to legislative matters, as he does for spiritual ones. He identifies religious dependence as the most dangerous kind of immaturity, from which it follows that freedom of discussion about matters of conscience matters more than other types of free speech. However, he also mentions more than once that the sovereign would do well to allow public discussion on political topics. The comparison between a free realm for discussion of religion and one for discussion of politics becomes more explicit as the essay progresses. The institutions for carrying on this public discussion, though only illustrated with regard to religion, are clearly meant to facilitate discussion of broader topics.

The Monarch and the Public Sphere

The remainder of the essay is devoted to a series of arguments aimed directly at would-be enlightened rulers. Kant advises them to keep aloof from religious matters, as such interference degrades their majesty. He supports secular rulers' (and not the church's) ultimate authority over established religious practices. Allowing free discussion of these, and even of political matters, will not only not harm the sovereign's civil order, Kant argues, but also actually help both his current rule and his posthumous reputation. For the would-be enlightened ruler, Kant draws a flattering picture of the course of history, with enlightened freedom of public discussion as the result of a glorious ruler's liberation of his people from the primitive bonds of tutelage.

Kant's own protests notwithstanding, in his example of the conscience-stricken clergyman's dual roles, the scholar's (public) reason ultimately trumps the clergyman's official (private) duty. Similarly, Kant's attempts to persuade the ruler to allow enlightenment to flourish fail to disguise his conviction that the ruler's absolute sovereignty must eventually bow to an enlightened people's readiness for self-rule. Just before Kant equates "the age of enlightenment" with "the century of Frederick," for example, he expresses the hope that "people on the whole" will reach a state in which "another's guidance" is no longer needed in religious matters.[33] Each time he stresses that rulers may remove "outward" obstacles to humankind's spiritual enlightenment, and each time he claims that freedom of conscience is harmless to the ruler, Kant reinforces the implication that "inner" religious life is beyond the ruler's power. Rulers' attempts to regulate religious life have only set up blunt, "outer" obstacles to enlightenment. These may hinder a people's rapid progress, but they cannot prevent progress altogether. Another comment on the effectiveness of a ruler's interference in realms Kant claims should be left to public discourse comes in his explanation of why he has focused on religious regulation in an essay on enlightenment: because, he says, tongue-in-cheek, rulers are not interested in regulating the arts and sciences.[34]

Kant is exhorting would-be enlightened rulers to follow a path that, on the one hand, should ensure their present power and glorious reputation but, on the other hand, would over the long term spell their obsolescence. In this and subsequent remarks, including the famous praise for Frederick's policy of "argue as much as you will . . . only obey," Kant seems to be withdrawing the slight suggestion made earlier in the essay that the public sphere might actually represent the people's will, and thus provide an alternative source of legitimate, coercive political authority to the monarchical ruler.[35] Instead, he suggests here that intellectual life, to be fully free, must be walled off from the practice of politics. Such a point of view resonates with the earlier distinction between free public and dependent private reason: public reason functions as such only in an arena designed to protect it from outside influences. In a free public sphere, discussion would be constrained only by the standards governing ideal scholarly debate.[36] Only public life, independent of financial and social considerations, is free to subject itself to the rule of reason alone.[37] This public sphere exists in the world of letters (*Lesewelt*), in which everybody, no matter what his worldly position, functions "as a scholar." Kant insists that the source of authoritative judgment (the public) must remain separate from the corrupting, "private," and particular influence of real coercive power.[38]

Kant has made a case in the essay for the continued political power of an enlightened ruler who would protect a public arena for discussion while monopolizing the use of coercive force to maintain civil order. Paradoxically, he argues, strong rulers will be able to promote enlightenment all the better, since a ruler with a "well-disciplined and numerous army" need not worry about civil disorder. By protecting such a public sphere, however, the enlightened ruler seems to be recognizing it as a source of authoritative judgment. Kant's only explicit illustration of this point, it is true, is his weak-sounding proposal that before religious regulations are promulgated the public should be allowed to discuss them, and to bring the results of such a discussion before the throne. However, even without a politically representative function for the public sphere, the institutions Kant proposes for an enlightened state ensure that the free arena for public discussion is treated not as directly authorizing the sovereign but as the authoritative source of judgment on matters of public concern. The public sphere is the protected realm in which matters of common concern may be discussed by free and equal participants in the manner of scholars. As such, speakers in public can judge each other's arguments only by standards available to all: universal principles of reason. Representatives of the state are necessarily excluded from the public sphere, at least so long as they are acting in their official capacities, Kant argues, because they take as their standard not universal reason but the particular needs of the sovereign.[39]

Kant concludes his essay by responding to the classic worry of late eighteenth-century enlighteners, namely, whether the people can safely be made ready for freedom of thought. He traces a secure path for enlightened progress to take. First, the ruler grants his subjects the freedom to participate in the public sphere "in the manner of a scholar." Then, gradually, in the "space" for "freedom of spirit" provided by restrictions on civil freedom, people learn to think for themselves. They learn, as Kant puts it at first, to overcome their self-incurred immaturity. Only after a presumably lengthy period of mental enlightenment, Kant implies, are the people ready to apply principles of self-rule to political life. Kant reminds the reader at the end of the essay that once the people, thanks to the operation of the public sphere, reach this point of readiness for self-rule, the government will find it "profitable" to allow political freedom. Three comforts are offered to the would-be enlightened monarch. First, he gets to be responsible for the circumstances in which human freedom may develop, which is a great honor. Second, doing the honorable thing will turn out to be in the interest of the state anyway.[40] Finally, the transition of a people to self-rule must be gradual, so the monarch's stability-guaranteeing services are likely to be required for quite a long while.

EMPIRICAL AND A PRIORI SOURCES FOR "WHAT IS ENLIGHTENMENT?"

In attempting to provide a mechanism whereby judgments of political right are brought to bear on actual political life, Kant engages in one of a series of attempts in his work to bridge the realms of freedom and nature. In this case, bridging freedom and nature would mean proving that human freedom is not merely a place holder, something one must assume in order to follow the moral law, but demonstrably active in the physical world. Thus, in his political work Kant struggles to make good the assertion that ideals based in universal reason and expressed via the mediating institution of the public sphere ("freedom") have concrete political effects over the long run ("nature"). The methodology employed by Kant in his essay reflects this challenge: he combines empirical evidence with rational principles to achieve at least the beginnings of a theory of publicity.

Empirical Sources: Enlightened Absolutism

Kant's recommended institutions for the ideal state are hardly original. Like most moderate enlighteners of his day, Kant supports a mixed constitution along the British model, and he advocates republican representative government over despotic nonrepresentative government.[41] Montesquieu's idealized version of the British constitution greatly influenced late eighteenth-century German moderates, who were looking for a way to retain the authority of the absolute monarch, while encouraging reform from above by representing the views of the people to the monarch through an intermediate body.[42] Kant and his contemporaries on the European continent tended to exaggerate the king's role in the balance of power between Great Britain's king and Parliament, a mistake that made the British model more palatable to moderate reformers.[43] Kant described the British monarchy of his time as an absolutist regime promoting "the illusion of a limited monarchy."[44] Even powerful ministers in the Prussian state, including Baron Karl von Stein and Prince Karl August von Hardenburg of the famous reforms of the early nineteenth century, shared this common positive assessment of mixed government.[45]

The problem, then, for a moderate political theorist in Kant's Europe was how to encourage the absolutist state to undergo progressive reform without revolution. Most thinkers of the German Enlightenment were not revolutionaries but supported reform of the existing system by means of gradual improvements.[46] While there was widespread agreement on the necessity of political reform, especially in the area of freedom of the press, even the more free-thinking scholars worried that the progress of the Enlightenment might result in anarchy, or at least in undesirable social upheaval. At the behest of Frederick II, the Berlin Academy of Sciences even chose the question "Is it acceptable to mislead the public?" for its annual essay competition in 1780.[47]

Some thinkers in this tradition later came to be described as defenders of "enlightened absolutism," which is a post hoc, if accurate, term used by historians for a group of eighteenth-century rulers who allowed little political freedom but who instituted some modern reforms. Moderation in his thirst for revolution, however, is not sufficient to place Kant among the defenders of despotism. As I argue below, while Kant agreed with "enlightened absolutists" that revolutionary methods would be counterproductive, he disagreed with them on nearly everything else.

There is an enormous scholarly literature on the historical phenomenon labeled "enlightened absolutism," including, on the one hand, historiographical debates on periodization and on whether the term has any real referent and, on the other hand, and more interestingly for my purposes, on the self-understanding and eventual achievements or failures of its practitioners and theorists. Scholars agree that in the second half of the eighteenth century some absolute rulers in continental Europe encouraged descriptions of their governing styles as "enlightened."[48] Though a number of monarchs may be mentioned under this heading, Frederick II of Prussia and Joseph II of Austria are those most commonly thought of as enlightened absolutists. Beyond these bare statements, historians begin to disagree. However, the following certainly applies to enlightened absolutism as it was practiced by Frederick in Prussia. Frederick styled himself, famously, as the "first servant of the state," rather than as the proprietor of a personal domain. His role, according to this view, is to promote the interests of his people. The view of the monarch as the first servant of the state legitimizes rulership in a new way: rather than ruling by divine right and traditional privilege, enlightened monarchs justified their authority with reference to the good of the people.[49] As countless scholars since Marx and Engels have noticed, enlightened absolutism as a concept thus contained the seeds of its own destruction: it is only a short step from ruling as the people's representative to being replaced by the representatives of the people.

In its heyday in the last decades of the eighteenth century, however, Prussian enlightened absolutism seemed to many to offer a plausible formula for progressive rulership. The most prominent philosopher in Germany before Kant, Christian Wolff, whose many works promoted an earlier, much less critical version of enlightenment than did Kant's, defended a political system of enlightened absolutism in his "Rational Thoughts on the Social Life of Humanity" (1721).[50] In a social contract theory reminiscent of Hobbes, Wolff argued for individual rights as the first principle of politics, but he maintained that enforcement of these rights requires a social contract, the end result of which is the assumption of all power by the state. Dilthey called Wolff's political philosophy the "Musterbuch des allmächtigen Polizeistaates" (roughly, "blueprint for an all-powerful police state").[51] The basic argument for enlightened absolutism relied on a few premises: a social contract outlook justifying total control on the part of the sovereign; a judgment that popular enlightenment had not yet produced large numbers of citizens capable of self-rule; and the concomitant belief that only under the strong hand of an absolute ruler could the necessary reforms be made to a recalcitrant and backward society. The people, the argument goes, must be led to their own well-being. For the enlightener G. F. Lamprecht, the goal of the state is to produce healthier, more enlightened, wealthier, and safer citizens.[52] Against a background of feudal institutions and widespread ignorance and superstition, so the advocates of enlightened absolutism believed, only the strong state is capable of moving the people toward their own long-term interests.

Though his enthusiasm for the regime would cool over time, in this early essay Kant celebrates Frederick as an enlightened ruler, and even identifies the "age of enlightenment" with the "century of Frederick." It is true that the great monarch surrounded himself with leading Enlightenment figures, including most prominently Voltaire, but he also welcomed rogue free-thinkers like Julien Offray de la Mettrie. He considered his Prussian subjects intellectually and linguistically backward and sought to promote progressive culture by allowing them a fair amount of scholarly and literary freedom. In the last instance, however, Frederick was less an enlightened ruler than a despotic patron of Enlightenment culture. The actual ruling style employed by his government was hardly less "feudal" than that of his father, the "soldier king," Frederick William I.[53] While accepting public enlightenment and even public criticism of his own person—he famously stopped his entourage to admire a caricature of himself, and to order it moved higher for better viewing—Frederick attempted to reestablish the power of the hereditary nobility by supporting traditional privileges and favoring nobles with high positions in the state (both in the army and the rest of the bureaucracy, which were hardly separate in Frederick's Prussia). Frederick the Great was ambitious enough to run his state pragmatically, even promoting commoners to high office as necessary, but his preference was for an old-fashioned, rather than modern, style of governance.

Forward-thinking social reforms to be implemented by the absolutist state were in fact frequently proposed by the loyal enlighteners employed and supported by the Prussian monarch. For example, Lamprecht advocated mandatory breast-feeding and a ban on the dyeing of Easter eggs.[54] Such proposals, however, were routinely ignored by a government far more interested in military greatness than in progressive reform. Frederick's bureaucrats learned enlightenment at the university, then toed the line at court. Ironically, Prussia's defeat by Napoleon made possible many more reforms than were passed under the enlightened absolutism of Frederick II.[55]

Neither Kant nor the scholarly advocates of enlightened absolutism supported foreign domination as a means to progressive reform, of course. They agreed on gradual change under orderly conditions. Despite these apparent similarities, however, Kant is not a thinker in the enlightened absolutist tradition. Probably the most important difference is that Kant categorically rejected paternalism as a legitimating principle of rulership, whereas Prussian rulers tended to invoke their paternal interest in the welfare of the populace as a justification for oppressive measures. Kant experienced this argument personally, in the form of an order issued to him by Frederick William II's minister, Johann Christoph Wöllner. Wöllner, in the name of the king, forbade Kant to publish on religious matters, required him to give an account of himself, and ordered him to "apply your authority and your talents to the progressive realization of our paternal [*landesväterliche*] purposes. Failing this, you must expect unpleasant measures for your continuing obstinacy."[56]

Though Kant obeyed this order while the monarch lived, he could never accept paternal authority as just. Paternalistic governance treats the subjects not as human beings able to pursue their own ends but as children in need of protection: "The subjects, like minor children who cannot distinguish between what is truly useful or harmful to them, are constrained to behave only passively, so as to wait only upon the judgment of the head of state as to how they *should be* happy and, as for his also willing their happiness, only upon his kindness—[such a paternalistic government] is the greatest *depotism* thinkable."[57] Furthermore, according to Kant, the justification for rule must be formal, not material (since only formal reasons can be universally given), and thus the happiness of the subjects, however legitimately the ruler pursues this object, can never justify the rule itself. Kant argues against the principle of eudaemonism throughout his political works: the purpose of government is to maximize the freedom of each, not the happiness of each.[58] Kant does not argue that the pursuit of happiness is immoral. It is natural that human beings should seek pleasure. But this empirical fact cannot justify coercion; only a rationally necessary principle could do that. Thus, while Kant agrees with the enlightened absolutists that reform from above is preferable to revolution, and so is in some agreement with them on the means of achieving progress, he cannot agree with their position on the ends of government at all.

Empirical Sources: Debates in the *Berlinische Monatsschrift*

Kant, then, was hardly alone in addressing the problem of reform without revolution. The general inspiration for his essay was practically in the air breathed by a late eighteenth-century Prussian intellectual. Kant found a more direct inspiration for "What Is Enlightenment?" however, in an ongoing debate published in the *Berlinische Monatsschrift* (*BMS*), a journal to which Kant was an occasional contributor. Founded in 1783 by Johann Erich Biester and Friedrich Gedike, the *BMS* became "the most important forum that the German Enlightenment possessed during its last and highest phase."[59] The journal was at the same time intellectually daring and politically pro-establishment, characteristics which led to its longevity (it lasted thirteen years), its popularity, and to its eventual dissolution, after a change of government, in 1796.[60] The contents of the *BMS* included polemics, scholarly articles, poetry (both satirical and more serious), travel reports, proposals for civic improvements, and sermons; such a mix was typical of cutting-edge magazines of the time. The *BMS* was one of a group of new German-language journals that in the late eighteenth century moved beyond the standard format of moral homily, instruction in matters of taste, and literary discussion, toward cultural, social, and even political critique.[61]

The debate that inspired Kant's essay illustrates just the kind of intellectual exchange on politically relevant topics that Kant took as a model for his theory of publicity. In 1783, the *BMS* published a particularly tendentious anonymous piece: "Suggestion, That the Clergy Cease to Trouble Themselves with Performing Marriage Ceremonies."[62] "Suggestion" argues in favor of civil marriage on the grounds that marriage is a contract like all other contracts; while some official support of contracts is necessary, no case can be made for making the marriage contract alone the object of religious rather than civil authority. The author argues further that not only is the religious sanctioning of marriage unnecessary, since enlightened people do not need ceremonies to mark their contracts, but the separation of the marriage contract from other contracts might lead to the denigration of all other civil contracts. The author imagines an ordinary person reasoning thus: "God himself wills that I do not break certain contracts or laws; the others, however, are only made by men, and thus do not mean very much." A reader today might expect such an article to proceed to argue for the separation of church and state. Instead, our radical author argues for the total subsumption of the church into the state. "Let politics and religion, laws and catechisms be one!"[63] The author of "Suggestion" ultimately argues for civil religion in what would later, if briefly, become the French style: the rational union of church and state in the interest of the people's happiness.

"Suggestion" received a number of replies, several of which compared the practices of other countries favorably to those of Prussia.[64] The reply that inspired Kant's essay, however, took the opposite view, invoking foreign customs, such as the alleged decadence of the French, as negative examples while praising ordinary German morality. When the Protestant clergyman Johann Friedrich Zöllner, the author of enlightened moral-advice books and a member of the Berliner Mittwochgesellschaft (Wednesday Society),[65] replies to "Suggestion," he defends the special status of the marriage contract as the basis for its remaining outside state control. Like the author of "Suggestion," Zöllner defends a position different from the one a present-day reader might have predicted, especially from a powerful civil servant and member of the established church hierarchy. Rather than simply defending the current system, Zöllner argues that the intimacy of marriage puts it beyond the state's reach. He treads a very narrow path, not directly critical of the state's role in regulating religion (and not arguing for a separation of church and state) but stressing that the church possesses legitimate spheres of authority independent of the state.[66]

Running through Biester's and Zöllner's arguments about civil marriage is a more fundamental debate of interest to Aufklärer: could the process of Aufklärung itself become dangerous to public morality?[67] Underlying the whole exchange is the common worry that the progress of reason, while good for debunking superstition and eliminating barriers to social and economic change, might go too far and eliminate the bases of social stability.[68] As Zöllner puts it, the useful work of preachers in assisting human happiness and in teaching the young would become endangered by the measures suggested by Biester: they would "destabilize the first principles of morality, bring down the worth of religion, and confuse the heads and hearts of people in the name of Aufklärung."[69] In a subsequent note expressing this anxiety, Zöllner asks the question that inspired Kant's essay: "What is enlightenment? This question, which is nearly as important as: What is truth? ought really to be answered, before one begins enlightening! And I have yet to find it answered anywhere!"[70] Thus the question that directly inspires Kant's essay comes as part of an argument defending social stability against the possibly destabilizing effects of the unfettered pursuit of enlightenment. It is not surprising that Kant's essay is concerned with transition from absolutism without revolutionary violence: this was the most important political problem of his time.

Empirical Sources: The Public Sphere in Kant's Prussia

The need for a mediating institution between universal standards and practical politics was clear already in Kant's Critique of Pure Reason. Yet Kant did not arrive at his image of the public sphere via deductions from the necessary conditions of understanding. The image of the public sphere found in Kant's political essays reflects more than the strictly formal and ahistorical conclusions of his practical philosophy. Rather, Kant's historical account of

the public sphere takes many of its characteristics from the peculiar qualities of the public sphere of which Kant was a part.[71]

Over the course of the eighteenth century, the literary "world of letters"
was transforming itself into a critical public sphere in the modern sense, addressing matters of common interest, including controversial political and
social issues.[72] Kant's writings on publicity are representative of this process. For the early part of the century, the public sphere was dominated by
moral weeklies and literary journals that sought to lead public tastes while
avoiding political entanglements. By the mid-nineteenth century, the advent of mass institutions that sought and formed the new political force of
public opinion made Kant's and his contemporaries' enlightenment ideal of
a sphere representing a single public will based on rational truths seem
quaint indeed. In Kant's Prussia, however, the enlightenment ideal of the
public sphere as a scholarly republic of letters ruled the field.[73]

Rather than inventing the concept of the public sphere as a solution to
purely philosophical problems, Kant approvingly observed and borrowed
from the developing world of letters around him. Kant himself participated
in an ongoing series of controversies published in the *Berlinische Monatsschrift.* This argumentative style that evaluates practical questions of governance on the basis of universalistic ideals available to all rational persons
must have appealed to Kant, who incorporated such a style into his image of
the reasoning public. In addition to the model provided by the actual public sphere of which Kant was both a sympathetic observer and an active
member, he had access to new ideas about the role of publicity that were
published in that arena. As Lucien Hölscher has observed, by this time the
concept of *Publizität* (from the French, *publicité*) brought with it a "new,
mostly positive assessment of freedom of expression, one that had established itself in republican and enlightenment circles since the seventies."
Late seventeenth- and early eighteenth-century celebrations of the musical
and theatergoing publics paved the way for the more egalitarian conception
of the reading public. The participants in the new literary and political public sphere were all fortunate enough to be educated, and thus belonged
mainly to the middle and upper classes. However, the members of the "republic of scholars" defined their group without reference to class distinctions, as open to all persons willing to exercise their own reason in public, in
a new sphere "beyond the political order."[74] Kant was writing in an environment that combined political absolutism with an unprecedented ease of
scholarly and literary publication. University teachers in Frederick's Prussia

were still required to adhere to government-approved textbooks; new books needed the imprimatur of a censor or designated university official. Even so, the last decades of the eighteenth century saw the institutions of the bourgeois public sphere flourish along with their social bases in the educated middle classes.[75]

Kant, then, had ample opportunity to model his image of the public sphere on the rich intellectual exchange going on around him. Part of the appeal of this "world of readers," in fact, was its cosmopolitan nature.[76] Writers addressed each other's arguments according to their persuasiveness, without regard for social distinction, geographic location, or any other particular personal quality. By the time Kant published "What Is Enlightenment?" (1784), he had incorporated a number of the qualities of the actual public sphere into an early version of his concept of the ideal public.

A Priori Sources: Social Contract Theory on the Gap between Provisional and Ideal States

Kant's own historical circumstances, then, encouraged him to investigate the possibility of gradual progress toward politically enlightened rule. But the problem of progress was not simply an interest of the moment; it coincided with perhaps the trickiest issue left to Kant by his social contract theoretical predecessors.

Despite disagreement among social contract theorists about the proper scope of state authority, all of them agree that such authority originates in the will of the people. For social contract theories in general, the state represents the united will of the people, and thus they presume the existence (however minimal) of a common interest. As a theorist in this tradition, Kant is unwilling to accept the state as mere arbiter among competing, ultimately unreconcilable interests. The problem is not to balance the powers of the various estates of society (for example, the nobility and the monarchy). Nor would Kant support a "pluralism" of interests fought out in the state arena, as some recent descriptions of modern democracies would have it.[77] Instead, like Rousseau (and, in his own way, Hobbes), Kant strives to create the conditions under which the state represents a single common interest. As Rousseau expresses it in *On the Social Contract,* the problem facing political theory is this: "'Find the form of association which defends and protects with all common forces the person and goods of each associate, and by means of which each one, while united with all, nevertheless obeys only himself and remains as free as before?' This is the fundamental problem for which the social contract provides the solution."[78] How, on the one hand, can citizens obey only laws of their own making, without those laws being too weak to protect them from each other? On the other hand, if citizens submit to a strong state in the name of mutual protection, how will they ensure that the judgment of the human authority to whom they submit will be just?

Early theories of *societas civilis* try to solve a critical problem of government: Who shall be judge on earth?[79] Social contracts theorists like Hobbes and Locke agree that human nature, while making human beings partly rational and capable of improvement by instruction, also precludes them from being fit judges in their own cases. Irrational passions, such as revenge, and more rational interests, such as greed, inevitably lead individuals astray in judging the rightness of public acts. The search for authoritative political judgment on earth leads Hobbes to propose the artificial person of the sovereign, and Locke to counter with the legislative will of the people (neither writer was willing to abandon the hope of worldly peace for the meager comfort of heavenly justice).[80] Societas civilis, according to the early social contract theorists, solves the problem of authoritative political judgment on earth by investing certain human actors with that responsibility: the Hobbesian sovereign's judgment may be iniquitous, but it is never unjust; Locke's members of a societas civilis entrust all disputes to their representative, though ultimately "the people shall be judge."[81]

Kant, like his predecessors in social contract theory, provides an account of individuals' obligation to enter into the societas civilis; like them, he recognizes that natural human failings will cause both powerful sovereign and obedient subjects to perform their duties less reliably than they ought. The problems faced by Hobbes and Locke as they try to construct a reliable secular substitute for perfect, but unavailable, divine justice were even worse for Kant. Unlike Hobbes, Kant is unwilling to rely on the rational interest of a human sovereign in the well-being of the commonwealth to counterbalance the factors working against that sovereign's judgment (the corruption of power, the temptations of passion, even a simple lack of understanding). Unlike Locke, Kant begins with a moral theory that prohibits citizens from endangering the civil order, just or unjust. Kant will have to find the source of reliable political judgment on earth in the very theoretical innovations that keep him from accepting classical social contract theory.

Kant's own epistemological commitments make what Hobbes calls "inconveniences" into thorny contradictions.[82] In the first place, Kant applies his distinction between phenomena and noumena to the sphere of politics, breaking all possible knowledge of political life into actual (phenomenal) and ideal (noumenal) spheres. Manfred Riedel has translated this distinction into modern terms as a break between facts and norms.[83] Different standards of inquiry apply to possible knowledge of each of these spheres: whereas knowledge of phenomena relies on useful but ultimately uncertain inductive reasoning, knowledge of noumena—of unchanging, "categorically true" things—is reached via deductive reasoning. Accordingly, Kant's ideal *respublica noumenon*[84] serves as a sort of model for the actual *respublica phenomenon*. Such a theory necessitates a mechanism whereby this ideal model (respublica noumenon) would be applied to practical politics.[85]

Hobbes and Locke both offer relatively simple mechanisms for the application of judgment to the political sphere. For Hobbes, once the state is in place, the sovereign retains a monopoly on public judgment. For Locke, in times of serious disjuncture, the right to judge reverts to society. Neither theorist expects that the judgment thus achieved will be perfect, but each hopes to have provided the closest possible human approximation of perfect political judgment. Kant's mechanism for applying ideal political judgments to practical politics is more ambitious and less direct than the mechanisms of his predecessors; he aims for more nearly perfect political judgment but is willing to wait quite a while to achieve it (as I shall explain in what follows).

Further complicating Kant's political thought is a distinction, from his practical philosophy, between inner and outer freedom.[86] Inner freedom has to do with ethics; a person is inwardly free insofar as that person subjects himself or herself to the moral law. Outer freedom, on the other hand, means for Kant much the same thing it did for Hobbes (the absence of impediments to motion), and has to do not with the moral but with the civil law.[87] Kant does not limit his political considerations to those related to outward freedom, though, as I discuss in chapter 4, he concentrates on legalistic considerations in his "Doctrine of Right," the *Rechtslehre*. Instead, Kant seeks to bridge politics and ethics via the pragmatic political *effects* of commonly recognized moral truths.[88] Such a move seems to undermine Kant's own distinction between the phenomenal and noumenal realms, since the empirical effects of ideal causes would presumably be known to human observers. In "What Is Enlightenment?" and elsewhere, Kant attempts to avoid this problem by allowing such knowledge to be gained only indirectly, over the very long term, approaching but never reaching an ideal perspective.

Publicity is the mechanism Kant chooses to connect politics and ethics.

Over the course of several decades of work, Kant develops, rejects, and modifies a number of versions of a theory of publicity that would allow flawed human beings to apply their closest approximations of ideal judgment to practical political life. Kant's views on the mechanism by which people might apply timeless ethical truths to particular political situations change as his theory of publicity develops. However, the old question raised by early theorists of civil society as a societas civilis remains at the center of his inquiry: Who shall be judge of right on earth? In "What Is Enlightenment?" Kant responds to this old question of the social contract theorists with his new conception of organized society in relation to the state; members of the public sphere approximate perfect judgment as best they can. Thus Kant's theory of publicity constitutes an odd, early version of our modern sense of civil society: the public judges state action and thus provides or withholds legitimacy to the state, though of course in Kant's account no material interests may be brought to bear on such judgment, and no coercive consequences follow *directly* from it.

A Priori Sources: The Public Sphere as Solution to the Problem of the Societas Civilis

In the *Rechtslehre,* Kant draws on social contract theory and his own moral philosophy to produce an image of the just state (and system of states) grounded in reason: the perfect societas civilis. As in his major works of critical philosophy, Kant argues in the *Rechtslehre* in the ideal style, drawing conclusions intended to be valid for all "every rational being as such."[89] The formal principles set out in the *Rechtslehre* are based on the moral law, which in turn is supposed to express ordinary moral reason. For example, Kant argues that "morally practical reason pronounces in us its irresistible *veto: there is to be no war.*" He recognizes that the actual world is not in harmony with these moral precepts, but insists on their reality as ideals held in common. Even though Kant's formal political philosophy is ideal (that is, present nowhere on earth except as a model in the minds of rational people), it is nonetheless binding, as it expresses necessary conclusions from "the moral law within us."[90]

The same holds true for more mundane ideals, such as constitutionalism. As Kant puts it in *The Conflict of the Faculties:* "If we think . . . of the commonwealth in terms of concepts of pure reason, it may be called a Platonic *ideal (respublica noumenon),* which is not an empty figment of the imagination, but the eternal norm for all civil constitutions whatsoever."[91] The principles of constitutional government Kant outlined in the *Recht-*

slehre are not products of experience, of historical trial and error, and thus do not vary over time or according to place. As norms, they must be "derived a priori by reason from the ideal of a rightful association."[92] Kant argues that the very universality of the norm of constitutional government promotes its eventual realization, though he realizes that the actual world fails to achieve the standards set by moral reason. Despite their ideal status, therefore, Kant expects the formal principles of the *Rechtslehre* to have practical political effects. The doctrine of right, based on the moral law, is for Kant the fundamental basis of all politics, since it provides the only possibly universal standards of political legitimacy.

The most important standard provided for political life by universal reason is that of the just state (societas civilis). People have an obligation, Kant claims, to enter the societas civilis and to give up their "wild" freedom. This is so because in order to develop his or her capacities, each individual requires that the freedoms of others be restricted: all must submit to a common authority, whose impartial judgment will stand for all parties. Given that human beings are not perfectly rational but are governed by both reason and "pathological" desires, they experience the ideal of the just state as a moral obligation to enter into civil union. (Consider the impossible case of perfectly rational human beings. Such beings would experience the just state not as an obligation but as a law as natural as gravity; no obligation or coercion would be required to get them to obey just laws.)[93] Since individuals recognize the validity of the civil order, but at the same time would except themselves from its restrictions, Kant argues, the "just civil constitution" is one in which "*freedom under external laws* would be combined to the greatest possible extent with irresistible force."[94]

The perfect societas civilis, in which there are no exceptions to the rule of law, cannot be achieved on earth. It exists, for Kant, as an ideal to which actual societies may be compared. Comparisons between commonly recognized ideals and actual political situations have a sort of moral force in their own right. For example, Kant observes that the British government after the Glorious Revolution (1688) suffered from a disjuncture between its publicly acclaimed ideal of constitutional monarchy and the actual state of absolute rule. "This corrupt system, however, must naturally be given no publicity if it is to succeed. It therefore remains under a very transparent veil of secrecy."[95] Here Kant applies his theory of publicity's moral force to a concrete political example: a government can subvert its publicly legitimating ideal only under conditions of secrecy.

Real-world societates civiles are subject to faulty outcomes caused by

flawed human nature, contained in institutions that can only partly miti-
gate those failings (this is Kant's view as well as those of his predecessors).
Locke's solution to the problem of corruption among the people's representatives was to retain the people's right to judge whether the state is legitimate, and to back that right of judgment with the use of force, if necessary.
Thus for Locke the right of revolution was one mechanism for closing the
gap between the just state and the actual state.[96]

This option was not available to Kant. For him, such a right to revolution is incoherent on several grounds. First, it violates our primary duty to
protect our neighbors' rights by submitting to a common authority (the en-
trance to the societas civilis).[97] Second, it violates the concept of sovereignty by withdrawing real authority from the representative and placing it
back in the hands of the people.[98] Finally, and more pragmatically, revolution is unlikely to replace corruption with justice.[99] Kant agrees with his
predecessors in social contract theory that human judges of political right
will never be perfectly just. Instead of responding to this problem by relax-
ing the rights and duties outlined in his ideal conception of the just state,
however, Kant introduces a new institution to mediate between the respublica noumenon and the respublica phenomenon. Drawn from his observations of the actually functioning world of letters in late eighteenth-century
Europe, Kant argues for a public sphere to mediate between political ideals
and governmental reality. He thus attempts to resolve the problem of the
social contract theorists via an innovation of his contemporaries: publicity.

QUESTIONS LEFT AFTER "WHAT IS ENLIGHTENMENT?"

In "What Is Enlightenment?" intellectual freedom has a twofold relationship to political life. First, the enlightened ruler, qua enlightened ruler, treats
the free public sphere as an authoritative source of political judgment. Second, and somewhat paradoxically, this authoritative status is guaranteed by
the public sphere's very separation from the practice of politics. No direct,
potentially coercive, representative role is imagined for the public sphere in
matters of political business. Instead, members of the public sphere are free
both of political interference and of direct political responsibility; these
freedoms, Kant argues, allow them to judge according to (public) standards
of truth rather than (private) needs or political expediency. At the end of
the essay, Kant predicts that, once people grow more accustomed to thinking for themselves, even governments will respond to "the propensity and
calling to *think* freely."[100] This point raises a problem for Kant's view as expressed in "What Is Enlightenment?." If the legitimacy of the public sphere

is guaranteed by its purity (including its separation from the "domestic" affairs of practical politics), then how can Kant expect the people eventually to rule themselves? This he evidently does, flattery to princes and paradoxical implications notwithstanding. Kant's several references to the people's vocation eventually to rule themselves make his view clear.

The questions that Kant leaves unanswered have mainly to do with the relationship between the public sphere and the state: If a person's natural vocation as a reasoner ultimately trumps obligations on that same person as a part of a civil machine (as it did in the case of the clergyman), how can order be legitimately maintained? If the answer to this question has to do with restricting the function of the public sphere to "harmless" expressive speech, then how does Kant expect progress to come from the "free public use of reason"? What does Kant think is the proper relationship between the ruling state and the realm of free public discussion of matters of common interest? Does this change over time? Does publicity, as source of authoritative political judgment, eventually become politically authoritative itself? If so, how does it retain its intellectual authority?

Kant's theory of publicity is not well developed enough in "What Is Enlightenment?" to allow us to draw substantive conclusions even from problems explicitly posed in the essay, such as the clergyman's paradox. However, the unresolved problems of "What Is Enlightenment?" set the agenda for the rest of Kant's political work. The clergyman's paradox, for example, exemplifies the tension between official expectation and reasoned political judgment that will eventually drive Kant's mature theory of political change. Kant wrote "What Is Enlightenment?" as an answer to a question posed by another writer in the *Berlinische Monatsschrift.* In such an occasional essay, however profound and influential, a reader cannot expect to find a complete set of answers to such questions as these. By the time Kant wrote his last major political work, *The Conflict of the Faculties,* he had developed a theory that at least attempted to answer questions like these (see chapter 5). Nevertheless, Kant's early essay introduces an interesting and original account of the transition from absolutism to the just state. First, the essay outlines the problem of locating the worldly source of authoritative political judgment in terms that would be familiar to the early social contract theorists. Second, it hints that the standard solution of the societas civilis will not succeed, mainly because representatives of the state make decisions based not on ethical truth but on particular interests. Finally, Kant proposes a preliminary solution to the old problem via a new conception of the relationship between civil society and the state, in which authoritative political judgment is located in the public sphere. By the time Kant writes *Conflict*, the public sphere will be conceptualized as the mechanism that drives the political enlightenment of humankind.

As the chapter's analysis of "What Is Enlightenment?" has shown, Kant's political theory at this early stage in his writing is relatively undeveloped, leaving a number of important questions unanswered. However, even this preliminary set of ideas points us toward resolutions of the sorts of contemporary problems mentioned in the introduction to this chapter. Kant locates the motor of progress toward a more enlightened politics in the tension between commonly held ideals and pragmatic political reality; he shares this view with John Rawls, Jürgen Habermas, and the proponents of deliberative theory. Of course, Kant did not agree with either Rawls or Habermas about the *source* of commonly held ideals: the overlapping consensus theory Rawls articulates in *Political Liberalism,* for example, is a far cry from the Kantian ethics of *Critique of Practical Reason.* But whether these ideals spring from the common ground held by various "reasonable comprehensive doctrines" or from the "moral law within us" makes little difference to the politically relevant dynamic to which both Kant and the deliberative democrats point: once committed to such principles as reciprocity, proponents of divergent viewpoints have a basis for mutual accommodation, either in face-to-face negotiation (as per the deliberative model), or by means of political discourse over the long term in the public sphere (as per the Kantian view).

Kantian theory does not resolves differences about exactly how the public sphere might operate in various contexts; here there are many schools of thought with very different methods of analysis. For example, where political scientists Margaret Keck and Kathryn Sikkink see a "boomerang effect" from transnational advocacy-group pressure through their (relatively responsive) home governments and onto (relatively) intransigent target governments, students of the history of concepts might look for longer-term developments in the logic of arguments that are possible in particular historical and geographical contexts.[101] However, Kant's theory of publicity contributes not only an initial intuition about the power of public ideas but also an analysis of how their authority might operate politically. Thus, for example, from a Kantian perspective, deliberative democrats are right to stress the function of norms like reciprocity in generating political agreement, but they ought to expect these norms to have their effects at a greater distance, as it were, from the individual constructors of arguments. As an idea gains authority in the public sphere, or as an idea loses credibility there, the constellation of possibly legitimate political arguments changes, changing with it the policy options available. This Kantian modification to one aspect of deliberative theory remedies an oft-noted fault (naïveté about individual commitments to principles like fallibilism) without undermining the essential logic of the argument.

As should be clear by the end of this book, the deliberative democrats have a great deal to contribute to an eventual Kantian political theory, including especially a theory of citizen autonomy. Despite the shortcomings of their model of political change, theorists of deliberative democracy have brought one very important point into clear focus: if a person is to be considered autonomous, he or she must have a voice in deliberations about collective decisions that affect his or her fate. The radical conclusions that follow from this highly plausible condition (including for example at least partial enfranchisement of resident noncitizens) have not yet been given their due.[102]

2

political judgment

The most important book in recent American political philosophy, John Rawls's *A Theory of Justice,* is a reworking of Kantian moral theory for the present day. A renaissance in political philosophy followed the publication of Rawls's book, as it allowed discussion to move beyond stale debates, such as those between utilitarians and deontologists, or between majoritarians and libertarians. Why has there been no similar phenomenon in political theory? True, there have been a number of excellent and important books published on Kant's work itself.[1] Furthermore, some important original efforts in political theory have been indirectly Kantian.[2] But by and large, political theorists have not taken up Kant's political thought as the base from which productive and descriptive theories of contemporary collective life may spring. Much of the blame rests with Kant himself. Political philosophers tend to read Kant's ethical works in isolation from his explicitly empirical and political ones. Rawls cites Kant's *Groundwork of the Metaphysics of Morals,* his first two *Critiques,* and occasionally his theoretical essays, but only rarely does he engage Kant's political theory, as expressed in essays, his third *Critique,* and later works, such as *The Conflict of the Faculties.*

In this chapter, I argue that political philosophers avoid these works for a reason: they contain a fundamental contradiction that Kant, despite his explicit efforts, could not resolve. One strand of Kant's political theory deals with freely willed human action, including his celebrated theory of the public sphere. This element in Kantian political theory can, I argue, provide quite a useful lens for observing the complexities of present-day politics, in many ways superior to our usual liberal sources. But what would have been a natural move for political theorists to Kantian fundamentals is hampered by the other strand of Kant's political work: his teleological theory of quasi-natural progress in human history. Here, then, I analyze the part of Kant's political thinking ignored by modern-day Kantian political philosophers. If Kant's political theory can be freed of its teleological blinders, then perhaps his very interesting account of freely willed human action in practice—his political theory as opposed to his moral philosophy—might help us improve our analyses of contemporary politics.

TWO VIEWS OF THE MECHANISM OF PROGRESS IN KANT

The highest task which nature has set for mankind must therefore be that of establishing a society in which *freedom under external laws* would be combined to the greatest possible extent with irresistible force, in other words, of establishing a perfectly *just civil constitution*. . . . Man . . . is forced to enter this state of restriction by sheer necessity.[3]

Kant published two major essays in the 1784 edition of the *Berlinische Monatsschrift*. As I discuss in chapter 1, in one of these essays, "What Is Enlightenment?" Kant argues that freedom of expression in the public sphere will promote human progress in science, culture, and politics. The other *BMS* essay addresses the topic of progress from a totally different perspective. In "Idea for a Universal History with a Cosmopolitan Perspective," Kant looks at the world through teleological lenses that block out freely willed human action. Taking as given the "teleological theory of nature," that natural capacities are destined to be developed to their ends, Kant spins out a philosophy of human history in which the "unsociable sociability" of natural human beings paradoxically serves the social ends nature sets for them, leading human beings unconsciously and inexorably toward a state of civilized harmony.

This idea was not original with Kant. Bernard Mandeville, Adam Smith, their German-speaking followers, and many others before and since have sought to explain human history according to the quasi-natural dynamic of self-interested individual actors unwittingly promoting collective goals.[4] The teleological theory has some obvious attractions: progress toward the highest good is guaranteed by a source of authority superior to arbitrary human willing, namely, nature itself; the theory provides a heuristic device that reveals political life as law governed and thus susceptible to investigation; the moral conundrum of obligatory pursuit of the apparently impossible highest good is resolved via the distinction between individual being and species being. Such considerations as these must have prompted Kant to include teleology in his early thinking on political matters, despite its incompatibility with the line of thought he would shortly publish in "What Is Enlightenment?" As I explain in chapter 1, in that essay Kant calls for a protected sphere for public discussion of matters of common interest, in order that progress toward enlightened government might be prompted by open comparisons between political ideals and reality. According to this view of the political world, progress comes from freely willed human action—on the part of the public sphere, in judging, and on the part of those in power, in submitting to public judgment. The teleological theory, by contrast, offers guaranteed progress toward the same political goals, but without the conscious effort of human actors. Little wonder, then, that the teleological theory attracts even Kant's adherence, as it enables optimism to flourish in the face of the most pessimism-inducing reality.

TWO PROBLEMS WITH TELEOLOGY

There are two main problems with Kant's recourse to teleology. First, I shall argue, it is incompatible with the rest of Kant's critical system.[5] In his struggle to achieve a "unity of reason," Kant attempts to assimilate a number of disparate lines of thought. However attractive its results, the teleological method cannot satisfy the demands of Kantian critique. Kant's appropriation of teleological theory remains, despite his best efforts, incompatible with both his ethics and his epistemology. Second, I shall argue that even if Kantian teleology were compatible with his philosophical system as a whole, this would not save it from plain implausibility.

Despite its many shortcomings, however, Kant's teleological theory rewards the student's attention. As I argued in the previous chapter, Kant makes a series of attempts in his political philosophy to bridge the realms of freedom and nature. His teleology is one of the most serious of these, and even its failures illuminate Kant's goals and methods. More important for my purposes here, however, is the use that may be made of Kant's theory of politics once it is freed of its incoherent and implausible teleological baggage. Rawls, first in *A Theory of Justice* and later in *Political Liberalism*, constructs a Kantian political theory that aims to secure principles of justice via procedures of reciprocity, abstraction, and hypothetical reasoning, without importing less attractive elements of Kant's theory, such as noumenal metaphysics and teleology. I argue that in addition to Rawls's very important work based on Kantian constructivism, interesting lines of reasoning based on Kant's theories of provisional right, of the preconditions of autonomous citizenry, and of the pragmatics of the public sphere are possible once the teleological straitjacket is removed. Though Kant argues that teleology is necessary to his system of political justice, it in fact contradicts the best elements of his theory of right.

IS *JUDGMENT* A POLITICAL WORK?

To get at the logic of teleological reasoning in Kant, I shall examine his third major work of critical philosophy, *Critique of Judgment*. In this chapter, I look at *Judgment* from the point of view of my project: What does Kant tell us in this work about the transition from imperfect to more perfect governance? In so doing, I criticize what I consider to be the weakest aspect of Kant's philosophy, namely, his teleological theory. Thus, my task precludes me from providing an introduction to *Judgment* worthy of the work. Despite its flaws, *Judgment* contains a brilliant aesthetic theory, the insights of which I find confirmed in nearly all my own appreciative experiences, from the pulp pleasures of Raymond Chandler to the beautifully indeterminate purposiveness of Herman Melville (to stick to works of American literature). As if that were not enough, Kant also considers one of the deepest mysteries of human existence, namely, how we are able to make judgments that might hold universally about things we know only in particular.[6] Here I emphasize this line of thought in connection with the practice of making empirical judgments about political life, but such an approach merely grazes the surface of Kant's thinking on the topic. As Hanna Pitkin points out in *Wittgenstein and Justice,* even given completely different particular experiences of, say, justice, we are able to communicate about it and to make judgments about each other's use of the term.[7] This confounds any theory of truth (such as that of Hobbes) which proposes a simple correspondence between concepts and objects, and for this insight alone, I would argue, *Judgment* is worth reading. Here Kant investigates the human endeavor of making generalizations about the world around us, asking, as usual, a critical *quid juris:* in this case, With what authority can I make judgments?

There is no doubt that Kant intended this work to mediate between the noumenal and phenomenal aspects of the world. He writes, for example, that "judgment makes possible the transition from the domain of the concept of nature to that of the concept of freedom."[8] But as his critical question makes clear, this "transition" is by no means simple. In making judgments human beings bring conditions of their own to the empirical matter presented to them in the world. According to Kant in the first *Critique,* every perception applies rational conditions to the matter provided by sensation; for example, I have to presume that an object exists in space and time, and that it is susceptible to determinations about its quantity, quality, relation, and modality.[9] These conditions of theoretical knowledge Kant discusses in the first *Critique*. In *Judgment,* however, Kant examines conditions we bring to the material world that are not objectively necessary but instead have some lesser, though still essential, status.

Briefly, in making judgments about the world, human beings necessarily make certain presumptions in addition to those already justified in *Critique of Pure Reason*. In making aesthetic judgments, or judgments of taste, Kant argues, human beings presume a common basis that underlies agreement about what is beautiful. As there is no way we could possibly know for a fact that such a basis exists, this presumption is, Kant says, only subjectively necessary. In making teleological judgments, or judgments about natural purposes (Kant is mainly thinking of the natural sciences), human beings presume a preexisting lawfulness on the part of nature, guaranteeing that the appearances available to us as investigators correspond with some underlying systematicity that can be discovered, however slowly, by investigation. Again, however, we have no empirical basis for this presumption of natural lawfulness, and thus teleological judgments, like aesthetic ones, are only subjectively necessary.

In what follows I shall have occasion to examine the status of this Kantian claim of subjective necessity for judgment. Having established that Kant intends *Judgment* as a mediating link between theoretical and practical (moral) reason, however, I would like to discuss the question of why *Critique of Judgment* should be relevant to political theory in the first place. One could, after all, note that the bridging of freedom and nature is a problem larger than the problem of how to organize collective life. In works like the *Rechtslehre* and "What Is Enlightenment?" Kant offers specifically political solutions to this problem, including the theory of the public sphere later taken up by Rawls and Habermas. Indeed, taking "political" in Rawls's broad sense, as including "the basic structure . . . understood as the way in which the major social institutions fit together into one system, and how they assign fundamental rights and duties and shape the division of advantages that arises through social cooperation,"[10] I shall argue that Kant's best solutions to the problem of bridging freedom and nature are all political. However, although political solutions, such as the ideal state, provisional right, and the public sphere may all attempt to bridge the noumenal and phenomenal perspectives, they are not necessarily the only means of so doing. In the third *Critique,* for example, aesthetic and teleological judgments close this gap.

What would "bridging freedom and nature" mean outside politics?[11] For Kant, the big questions are nearly always epistemological: thus, bridging freedom and nature might mean specifying the conditions under which in-vestigators of the empirical world (scientists) are able to find evidence of spontaneity in the physical world (that is, of freedom's causality). Either freedom and nature are strictly alternative perspectives on the same set of empirical occurrences, or there are some things in the world that can only be explained according to freedom (in other words, the second alternative posits empirical evidence that some thing has no antecedent natural cause). I am not the first person to point out that it is not an easy thing to find em-pirical evidence of a lack of a cause. Kant himself assumes that a good scien-tist will always operate under the presumption that absent natural causes may eventually be discovered. The best argument for the presumption of freedom's causality, and the one Kant makes most consistently, is not any particular piece of inexplicable evidence but the subjective necessity felt by investigators faced with an otherwise inscrutable world. "Two things fill the mind with ever new and increasing admiration and reverence, the more of-ten and more steadily one reflects on them: *the starry heavens above me and the moral law within me.*"[12]

The investigator should not expect to find objective evidence of free-dom's causality in nature but may use such a presumption as a rule of thumb in light of this feeling of subjective necessity. In addition, Kant looks for "signs" that, while failing the status of proof, at least indicate the possi-bility of freedom's causality in the world. Politics, or more specifically, evi-dence of the effect of morality in politics, then, provides one of two types of evidence that Kant thinks constitutes not a definitive proof but at least a "sign" that freedom's causality may be operative in the world. In *Judgment,* Kant suggests that the fact of near unanimity on what counts as beautiful is at least a "trace" or "hint" of underlying intelligibility. Here, however, as I shall discuss below, the underlying intelligence is presumed to be nature's, not humankind's.

Only in the political realm does Kant find a hint or sign that human free-dom is operative in the natural world. In *The Conflict of the Faculties* Kant fa-mously claims that Prussian enthusiasm for the French Revolution can be based on nothing but moral principles.[13] In most of his political writing, however, Kant is more circumspect about the material reality of freedom. His introduction to "Idea for a Universal History" is typical: "Whatever con-ception of the freedom of the will one may form in terms of metaphysics, the will's manifestations in the world of phenomena, i.e., human actions, are de-termined in accordance with natural laws, as is every natural event."[14] Nonetheless, the fact that only in the political realm does Kant find even a trace of human freedom's causality would suggest that *Judgment,* the locus of his most sustained consideration of the transition between the two perspectives of freedom and nature, has political relevance.

Are the Teleological and Agency-Centered Theories of Politics Compatible?

A "compatibilist" approach to teleology and freely willed human action would, if successful, save commentators from a painful choice. After all, one could simply decide at the outset whether one is interested in the point of view of the empirical political scientist, in which case one would consider history from a teleological point of view as the unfolding of nature's purposes for man.[15] On the other hand, a commentator could choose the point of view of a philosopher of politics, in which case he or she would take up the account of rational publicity as a motive force in human affairs, considering history from the agency-centered point of view as the product of freely willed action. At first, such a classic Kantian antinomial solution (which I discuss further below) seems very tempting. A number of distinctions made in Kant's political works fall along lines parallel to those between natural science and moral philosophy. For example, the teleological historian examines humankind as a species, interested in the kind of empirical regularity visible only in the aggregate, whereas the rational philosopher looks at individual human decisions, interested in the kind of certainty and style of justification available only in isolated moral decision making considered according to motives and with reference to moral laws.

Do I want to know what regularities I may expect to observe in human political life? the commentator might ask himself or herself. If so, then I should take up the teleological historical perspective, in which I interpret observable data according to necessary assumptions about the purpose of nature for man, without presuming any free decision making on the part of human beings. The meanings of diverse political events are given by Kant along these lines (lines that are taken up by his immediate and not so immediate followers, beginning with the German romantics, through Hegel, Marx, and many others). Revolution may be bloody, war senseless and violent, but revolutions may lead to the institutionalization of enlightened politics, and even a bad war teaches human beings to seek peace. Nature, according to this style of political investigation, is not transparent to the human observer, but it can be presumed nonetheless to guarantee human progress toward the peaceful, republican federalism that principles derived from the moral law define as necessary. Given such teleological assumptions, empirical events become explicable according to their place in the long run of history, even as individual willed action remains a closed book. The universal experience of freedom in the minimal sense of obligation to a moral law is not denied by such a point of view, but neither is it supported. Scientists of politics in this potentially Kantian mode could either relegate reports of free decision making to superstructural, ineffectual noise, or they could consider such reports as empirical facts like other empirical facts. This is similar to what present-day survey researchers do: they report that people live in these types of environment, have those ranges of occupations, and this range of beliefs about political right. Do I instead want to know the degree to which a given political system conforms to the standards of universal justice? If so, then a potentially Kantian philosophical investigator could turn to the evidence provided by moral judgment, which compares current political institutions with unchanging standards of right. On this view, the perspectives of the political scientist and the moral philosopher neither contradict nor support one another. They would be theoretically and methodologically independent.

However, such a "compatibilist" interpretation of Kant's alternative approaches to human progress cannot succeed.[16] Though I shall argue that Kant probably intended the two types of argument to represent mere antinomial contraries (in other words, approaches that are different but compatible), they in fact contradict one another. The dichotomy is false, as I shall demonstrate more fully by chapter 5, because Kant's account of political change incorporates the agency-centered view—of freedom as operative in the world through individual human judgment—into a thoroughly empirical view of the mechanism of the public sphere. Though Kant emphasizes individual moral judgment in his remarks on revolutionary sympathizers, for example, he expects empirically significant pressure for political change to operate at the level of the long-term dynamics of political discourse. Thus, in "What Is Enlightenment?" for example, Kant emphasizes the slow enlightenment of an entire public, rather than the short-term consciousness change of an individual. Kant's double-aspect theory succeeds for epistemology, but it cannot succeed for politics, which occupies a strange and difficult intermediate ground in the Kantian system between freedom and nature.

The Status of *Judgment*

Two kinds of commentators on Kant's political philosophy have placed *Judgment* at the center of their investigation. Those interested in Kant's aesthetics, such as Hannah Arendt, take his theory of the beautiful as a model for politics. Others are more interested in Kant's teleological theory, especially given the long line of philosophers of history who followed Kant; such commentators include Patrick Riley, Yirmiyahu Yovel, George Armstrong Kelly, and William Galston, not to mention many of Kant's contemporary interpreters, such as Garve. Though most of these writers on Kant mistake his epistemological distinction between two aspects or perspectives on the world (noumenal and phenomenal) for an ontological one, they do all rightly recognize that Kant intended *Judgment* as a bridge between the two realms. Furthermore, all of them try to construct a coherent Kantian politics from the fragments Kant in fact wrote. Though I do not agree that *Judgment* is the best place to look for a unified Kantian political theory, as I shall argue below, I am sympathetic to the project of constructing such a theory somehow.

The problem with most attempts to reconstruct a Kantian politics with *Judgment* as a central text is that they fail to take seriously Kant's own view of the status of investigation into the political world. As Kant wrote in what I take to be his most important political work, the *Rechtslehre*, "The concept of right is a pure concept that still looks to practice (application to cases that come up in experience)."[17] Politics, and especially Kant's dynamic account of political transition, is about bridging the realm of freedom, represented here by normative political principles grounded in ethics, and the realm of nature, represented here by the pragmatic arena of actual political institutions. A compatibilist would argue that moral reason as a doctrine of right will tell us all we need to know about political ideals, and what Kant calls practical anthropology will tell us all we need to know about natural and quasi-natural human collectivities.[18] In his best political work, however, Kant is interested not in either isolated sphere but in politics as the dynamic relation between the two arenas. An investigation focused either on the pure realm of ideals of the perfectly just state or on the wholly material realm of empirical politics will miss what Kant has to contribute to political theory. Thus *Judgment* does seem at first to be a promising location in which to search for Kantian political theory, since Kant in this work explores the bridging function of the faculty of judgment. Among recent commentators, no one has grasped this connection more deeply than Hannah Arendt. Unfortunately, both for Arendt's work and for political thought in general, Kant fails in *Judgment* to produce an internally coherent or empirically plausible theory of politics, or even the basis of a coherent or plausible construction of one.

AESTHETIC JUDGMENT IN ARENDT AND KANT

Since Kant did not write his political philosophy, the best way to find out
what he thought about this matter is to turn to his "Critique of Aesthetic
Judgment," where, in discussing the production of art works in their relation
to taste, which judges and decides about them, he confronts an analogous
problem.[19]

Late in her life, Hannah Arendt gave a series of lectures and seminars on
Kant's *Critique of Judgment*, in preparation for her own book on judgment.
Though she died before she was able to write it, the scholar Ronald Beiner
has been able to reconstruct some of the material that would have made up
this third book in Arendt's planned trilogy of works on the human condition. Arendt's lectures on Kant contain thoughtful investigations into judgment, human society, and political life. They are not reliable as Kant exege-
sis, but of course this is not what they were intended to be. I shall not
provide detailed criticism of Arendt's views on Kant, as such an effort would
misunderstand Arendt's intentions in the lectures and she is not generally
accepted as an authority on Kantian philosophy. Arendt herself says that "if
we [in our lecture] went beyond Kant's self-interpretation in our presentation, we still remained within Kant's spirit."[20] However, Arendt's work in
general, and with it her lectures on *Judgment*, have recently been enormously influential in the field of political theory. Thus, in what follows I
shall examine the question of what elements of Kant's theory of aesthetic
judgment made it Arendt's choice for a general Kantian political philosophy. In so doing, my argument will identify four attractive qualities of Kantian aesthetics for political theory: first, Kant's use of political language to
describe aesthetic judgment; second, Kant's claim that judging must be disinterested; third, his account of judgment's universalistic quality (the "sensus communis" argument, which has been much misunderstood); and,
fourth, Kant's theory of aesthetic education.

Political Language in the Definition of the Beautiful

Given the language Kant uses to formulate the *quid juris* of aesthetic judgment, it is not surprising that political theorists have been attracted to it.
"How is a judgment possible in which the subject, merely on the basis of his
own feeling of pleasure in an object, independently of the object's concept,
judges this pleasure as one attaching to the presentation of that same object
in all other subjects, and does so a priori, i.e., without being allowed to wait
for other people's assent?"[21]

Briefly, Kant argues that we make judgments of beauty when our reflection on an object's appearance leads us to make a disinterested claim of liking or disliking with which we expect everyone to agree. This claim of beauty is not based on a concept; that is, it is not determinative. If it were, claims of beauty would follow the structure of ordinary determinative judgment: all roses are beautiful; this is a rose; therefore, this rose is beautiful. But judgments of beauty, Kant argues, are not determinative but reflective, having to do not with the rose itself but with our subjective perception of it. Furthermore, the quality of our experience of the rose that makes us call it beautiful is its "purposiveness without a purpose." I shall discuss purposiveness in more detail in the second half of this chapter. For now, I can say that the purposiveness without a purpose that beautiful things exhibit has to do with the play of my imagination among possible concepts for the rose, none of which ultimately is able to determine my experience of it.

Imagine for example a group of people standing around a painting. "It's beautiful," one person says. "Look at the way the light on one side of the drinking glass is a different shade of green from the light as it emerges from the glass." "Yes, it's beautiful," another agrees, "I love the way those bold outlines make the glass look plain and solid, but the color between them makes it look magical and luminescent." "I see what you both are saying," a third person says, "but what I like about the painting is its subject: it glorifies the ordinary."[22] These three people are engaging in playful positing of concepts about the beautiful object. None of the concepts is quite definitive, but the more the viewers linger in front of the painting, the more possible concepts that apply to it emerge from their imaginations. Now imagine that these three people are actually students of art history, and that they happen to be appreciating this painting while waiting for their professor to appear. Once the professor arrives, she says, "This is a beautiful painting by the great artist Vincent van Gogh. It is beautiful because it calls attention to its own status as painted product by virtue of its dramatic brushwork, while nonetheless encouraging the viewer to consider the object itself, which is lovingly, if self-consciously, represented." All three students write down the professor's words, and the painting, for them, is no longer beautiful. They have found (however illegitimately, since the judgment is based on authority) a single concept that determines the work.

My example may capture the importance of indeterminateness for Kant's concept of the beautiful, but there is one more element of his aesthetic theory that needs elucidation before I consider the theory's attractions for political thought. "*Beautiful*," writes Kant in one of his many versions of a definition of beauty, "is what without a concept is cognized as the object of a *necessary* liking."[23] Not only are judgments of the beautiful indeterminate with regard to concepts, they are absolute with regard to application: everyone *ought* to agree with my judgment. Kant says aesthetic judgment is "subjectively necessary," by which he means that we have no basis for claiming universality from any quality empirically available in the beautiful object itself, but we nonetheless claim universality based on our own experience. This is why, as I discuss below, Kant refers to an aesthetic "sense," rather than a faculty of knowledge of the beautiful, even though judgments of the beautiful must be separate from the ordinary senses and be based only on pure forms of reflection rather than any physical pleasure or displeasure that might accompany the object. He writes that in judgments of beauty "a concern for universal communication is something that everyone expects and demands from everyone else, on the basis, as it were, of an original contract dictated by [our] very humanity."[24]

Kant's political language, even discounting the "as it were" that Kant in this work adds nearly every time he stretches a point, should not mislead the reader into drawing a direct analogy between the processes of aesthetic judgment and the establishment of the social contract. For one thing, the social contract in Kant is not about judgment at all but about an ideal of reason that justifies, by thought experiment, individual obedience to the collective power. Political judgment matters to Kant, but only provisionally. The transition from the imperfect provisional state toward perfect governance is facilitated by public political judgment. Social contract theory, by contrast, is an ideal, a source of the norms that members of the judging public apply. Second, the agreements ratified by political covenant are based on interests, while aesthetic judgments must exclude every kind of interest. Instead of comparing aesthetic judgment and politics here, Kant is trying to explain what he means by the "ought" that accompanies judgments of beauty. When I make an aesthetic judgment, I necessarily believe that everyone else "ought" to agree with me. Something about living together demands that we remain able to reach agreement, even on judgments of beauty about which it is impossible to argue definitively. Still, "the pleasure we take in the beautiful is a pleasure neither of enjoyment, nor of a law-governed activity, nor yet of a reasoning contemplation governed by ideas, but is a pleasure of mere reflection."[25]

Disinterestedness in Aesthetic Judgment

A focus of Arendt's political theorizing is the distinction between thinking and acting: in thinking, one is able to take the long view and subject one's inquiry to standards of truth, while action requires at least the temporary abandonment of both the long view and the standards that go with it. A simple example of this problem is provided by Rousseau: the philosopher at his window, even upon hearing the screams of a person in need, is unable to act (to respond), immobilized by his ability to place himself in an abstract rather than a concrete position.[26] Action, then, seems to require at least the temporary suspension of some of our thinking apparatus. Arendt, speaking loosely of Kant, distinguishes between personal morality (the standard appropriate to action) and judgment.[27] Something about being placed in the midst of action disables accurate judgment, Arendt suggests. Furthermore, one's very ability to act politically seems to depend upon judgment's being disabled. This is indeed a crucial problem for Kant's politics. However, because Arendt does not consider Kant's written political philosophy in any depth, focusing instead on his aesthetics, she misses Kant's definitive attempt to resolve the action/judgment problem in political life, which is to place authoritative judgment in the hands of a politically impotent but culturally influential public sphere. Even so, Arendt's account of Kant's distinction illuminates one of the most interesting elements of Kant's aesthetic theory for politics, namely, his claim that accurate judgment must be disinterested.

In her investigation into Kant's *Critique of Judgment*, Arendt is interested in finding a perspective from which "actor and spectator become united," in order to get beyond the frustrating dialectic between impotent knowledge, on the one hand, and ignorant action, on the other.[28] She looks to Kantian aesthetics for a point of view both authoritative and active. Kant's nuanced if somewhat confusing position on the relationship between moral interest and aesthetic judgment allows Arendt to believe that she has found the perspective she seeks. Though Arendt's reading, as I shall argue, is incorrect on these points, Kant's own ambivalence explains how she could be led to conclude that aesthetic judging can be active.

At first, Kant seems to claim that judgments of beauty must remain devoid of all interest. He separates beauty from charm—though the two are often found together, charm's pleasures are "pathological," whereas the liking associated with beauty is purely reflective. This is one of the reasons Kant can claim that judgments of beauty, while subjective and without a concept (that is, indeterminate), carry with them a kind of necessity, since judgments are based not on pathological, peculiar, incommunicable and arbitrary senses, such as touch or smell, but on the universally communicable play of forms in our imaginations. Kant associates pure judgments of beauty, apart from any agreeableness or concepts of objective purposiveness (such as utility), with free judgment. "Flowers are free natural beauties." "When we judge free beauty (according to mere form) then our judgment of taste is pure."[29]

This disinterestedness is also a condition of the other kind of aesthetic judgment, judgment of sublimity (that is, of our incapacity compared to some object to which sublimity is attributed): "Consider bold, overhanging, and, as it were, threatening rocks, thunderclouds piling up in the sky and moving about accompanied by lightning and thunderclaps, volcanoes with all their destructive power, hurricanes with all the devastation they leave behind, the boundless ocean heaved up, the high waterfall of a mighty river, and so on. Compared to the might of any of these, our ability to resist becomes an insignificant trifle. Yet the sight of them becomes all the more attractive the more fearful it is, provided we are in a safe place."[30] Without the disinterestedness that comes with safe distance from danger, a judgment of the sublime becomes reduced to the merely pathological emotion of fear. As disinterestedness retrieves sublimity from merely emotional fear, so in Kant's politics disinterestedness protects the power of public judgment from the corruption of power. Kant's judges in the public sphere, especially those discussed in *Conflict,* derive their moral authority from a distancing effect not dissimilar to the one provided by safety to the observer of nature's sublimity. Though the analogy is imperfect, it is not surprising that Arendt picked it out.

However, though aesthetic judgments must be wholly disinterested in the sense that only the free play of the imagination among concepts counts in judging whether something is beautiful, Kant also claims that judgments of beauty may *give rise* to what he calls "intellectual interest in beauty." By distinguishing between merely aesthetic judgment and the intellectual interest in the beautiful, Kant allows the power of judgment to become active in the world. He imagines a person appreciating beauty in nature. This appreciation is not based on personal interest. Yet the person is likely to desire that the things he or she is appreciating (beautiful flowers, birds, say) continue to be part of nature. Kant calls such an interest an "intellectual interest in the beautiful." He writes: "We also have an intellectual power of judgment, i.e., an ability for determining a priori with regard to mere forms of practical maxims (insofar as such maxims qualify of themselves for giving universal law) a liking that we make a law for everyone; this judgment [too] is not based on any interest, *yet it gives rise to one.* This pleasure or displeasure in the first judgment is called that of taste; [in] the latter, that of moral feeling."[31]

It is tempting to take Kant's concept of an intellectual interest in the beautiful and use it to apply aesthetic judgment to political judgment. As Kant argues in "What Is Enlightenment?" and in many other places, authoritative political judgment must be devoid of all but the most universal interests.[32] Any "private" or interested speech would corrupt the "public" sphere, whose claims are subject only to the universally communicable standards of reason. But, Kant argues tentatively in "What Is Enlightenment?" and more forcefully elsewhere, though authoritative political judgment must itself be disinterested, it may give rise to legitimate interest on the part of political actors. Consideration of this influence of the public sphere on political action ought never to determine the judgments of those speaking publicly. However, once the judgments are made, the speeches uttered, and the pamphlets written, they may well have concrete political effects. Likewise, it seems, absolutely pure aesthetic judgments may nonetheless give rise, at least intellectually, to moral feeling. Arendt writes, "These uninvolved and non-participating spectators—who, as it were, made the event at home in the history of mankind and thus for all future action—*were* involved with one another. . . . This much we got from Kant's political writings; but in order to understand this position we turned to the *Critique of Judgment,* and there we found that Kant was confronting a similar or analogous situation."[33]

To make her next move, applying Kant's account of "community sense" in aesthetic judgment to politics, Arendt has to find an analogy between aesthetic and political judging. Kant encourages Arendt in this regard by using political metaphors to describe the universality attached to aesthetic judging, as I mentioned above. More important, Kant tries to connect beauty and morality via the "intellectual interest in the beautiful." But as Kant himself admits, the moral feeling engendered by interest in the beautiful is of a kind completely different from the undetermined liking of aesthetic judgment, and it is subject to completely different conditions: "Now the situation is similar with the pleasure in an aesthetic judgment, except that here the pleasure is merely contemplative, and does not bring about an interest in the object, whereas in a moral judgment it is practical. . . . This pleasure is also not practical in any way, neither like the one arising from the pathological basis, agreeableness, nor like the one arising from the intellectual basis, the conceived good. Yet it does have a causality in it, namely, to *keep* [us in] the state of [having] the presentation itself, and [to keep] the cognitive powers engaged [in their occupation] without any further aim. We *linger* in our contemplation of the beautiful, because this contemplation reinforces and reproduces itself."[34]

What is special about aesthetic judgment—purposiveness without a purpose, its concept-free universality—disappears when the intellect takes an interest in it (as it did when the art professor explained the painting). With intellectual interest, we no longer have judgments of beauty, but good old-fashioned reasoning according to concepts.

Kant makes this move away from pure aesthetic judgment toward moral interest as part of the project of *Judgment* as a whole, which is, as I mentioned above, an investigation into the possibility of our human ability to make generalizations about the limited empirical world as we experience it. He would like to be able to argue that aesthetic judgment's claim to universal assent is reasonable, that is, passes the *quid juris* test. Since no direct observation of any such ground of agreement is possible, Kant argues that we can at least look for a "sign" of its reality. The logic Kant uses here is similar to that used in *Conflict,* where Kant looks for a sign that humankind is making progress toward its perfection. This is no accident, but not for the reasons Arendt gives (that is, not because aesthetics and politics operate similarly). As I shall argue below, where Kant discusses the intellectual interest in the beautiful, he is really talking about the reality of purposes, in other words, teleology. In public judgment and in the social ground of aesthetic judgment, Kant finds "traces" of empirical evidence of freedom's causality. We judge the beauty of nature as purposiveness without a purpose, but our reason has an interest in there being some natural basis (some actual purpose) giving rise to the beautiful. Of course we cannot find one, as it would not be observable. But nature might at least show

a trace or give a hint that it contains some basis or other for us to assume in its products a lawful harmony with that liking of ours which is independent of all interest (a liking we recognize a priori as a law for everyone, though we cannot base this law on proofs). Hence reason must take an interest in any manifestation in nature of a harmony that resembles the mentioned [kind of] harmony; and hence the mind cannot meditate about the beauty of *nature* without at the same time finding its interest aroused. But in terms of its kinship this interest is moral, and whoever takes such an interest in the beautiful in nature can do so only to the extent that he has beforehand already solidly established an interest in the morally good.[35]

The interest, therefore, that we take in natural beauty has to do with our human reason's natural search for the ultimate cause of objective ends, for the giver of the lawlikeness that purposive beauty exhibits, even as this quality remains undetermined for us. Such a search for ultimate causes is moral, not aesthetic. Kant's account of aesthetic disinterestedness is relevant to politics only insofar as Kant discusses judgment in general, rather than aesthetic judgments in particular. For, as I have shown, as soon as judgments of beauty begin to do more than merely make us "linger in our contemplation of the beautiful," they become determinate rather than reflective, and moral rather than aesthetic. As Kant says, "An objective principle of taste is impossible."[36] However, disinterestedness is not the only quality of aesthetic judgment that attracts Arendt's attention.

Community Sense in Aesthetic Judgment

We saw that an "enlarged mentality" is the *sine qua non* of right judgment; one's community sense makes it possible to enlarge one's mentality . . . communicability is again the touchstone.[37]

In his discussion of common sense and the *sensus communis,* Kant again makes it easy for Arendt to conflate aesthetic and political judgment, by failing to emphasize reflectivity, the main criterion for aesthetic judgments. Kant is interested in the presumption of a common human sense as a necessary condition of aesthetic judgment. The argument runs as follows: aesthetic judgment is subjectively necessary and makes a claim to which everyone ought to assent; this cannot be based on a determinative concept, or the judgment would not be aesthetic; thus, it must be based on some other source of unanimity, which Kant identifies, as I shall discuss, as the sensus communis. However, he is much more interested in the underlying ground of this presupposition itself, which he will find in teleological nature. It is no accident that Kant's *Judgment* begins with beauty and ends with two proofs of the existence of God.[38] Kant's critical scruples lead him to lace his teleological arguments with "as it were's" and other disclaimers, reminding the reader of the conditional nature of these kinds of claim. The presupposition of a common basis of aesthetic judgment in the sensus communis is one such claim, while the proposition that ordinary human beings share some source of value called common sense is another. To see what is at stake in this distinction between two phrases, I shall examine Kant's famous paragraph 40 at some length.

Kant has already argued that aesthetic judgment's subjective necessity is conditional, not categorical, and that the condition on which it rests is the idea of a common sense. We cannot know whether such a thing exists (as he says, we don't collect votes on how people feel). Instead, we present the presupposition of such a sense as necessary. Kant's argument here is different from the sorts of necessary suppositions he proposed in the first and second *Critiques,* which identified necessary *concepts* for theory and morals. Here, instead, we presuppose not concepts but a *sense,* in other words, a common source of *feeling* resulting in a nondeterminate way from the presentation of certain objects that exhibit a "purposiveness without a purpose."[39]

Kant begins with a distinction between the ordinary meaning of the phrase *common sense* and the use he would like to make of "sensus communis."[40] Ordinary "common sense," or more properly "common human understanding," which Kant says is the "very least that we are entitled to expect from anyone who lays claim to the name of human being" is not really a sense at all but an ability to make use of our "higher cognitive powers" to pronounce universal rules.[41] We say people have a sense of truth or justice, but this is only what we say. We mean that even the most ordinary human being has the cognitive ability to recognize truth, justice, decency, and so forth, by concepts. This is the basis on which judges in the public sphere make their determinations. In judging the gap between political ideals and reality, Kant's members of the judging public apply standards derived from common moral principles to actual institutions of government. Such judgment does not require "enlarged thinking." It only requires applying to the present day universally accessible standards of right based on moral truth, which is really a process of abstraction from one's circumstances (rising out of the day's prejudices toward enlightened thinking), rather than a process of universalization. For Kant, universalization is the mode of thinking that helps human beings to determine what morality demands in the first place. Political judgment, by contrast, merely applies these principles of practical reason to actual collective life. Common sense, as ordinary sociability, requires no special act of imagination.

Kant's description of the sensus communis is quite different: "We must [here] take *sensus communis* to mean the idea of a sense *shared* [by all of us], i.e., a power to judge that in reflecting takes account (a priori), in our thought, of everyone else's way of presenting [something], in order *as it were* to compare our own judgment with human reason in general . . . we compare our judgment not so much with the actual as rather with the merely possible judgments of others, and [thus] put ourselves in the position of everyone else, merely by abstracting from the limitations that [may] happen to attach to our own judging."[42] Kant then compares this aesthetic sensus communis with the common sense (in the sense of common human understanding) that is ordinarily at work in political judgment. He does want to reveal the similarities between the two sources of judgment, yet

Kant consistently stresses a fundamental difference, namely, that common sense is based on concepts. Of common sense, Kant says: "The following maxims may serve to elucidate its principles: (1) to think for oneself; (2) to think from the standpoint of everyone else; and (3) to think always consistently. The first is the maxim of an *unprejudiced,* the second of a *broadened* [which Arendt translates as "enlarged"], the third of a *consistent* way of thinking." Kant stresses that these three maxims apply to absolutely everyone, "no matter how slight may be the range and the degree of a person's natural endowments."[43] In his discussion of the common sense and thus of the basic mental apparatus of everybody, judgment is included ("enlarged thought") as well as understanding and reasoning. But sensus communis, the maxim of enlarged thought, is only part of common sense as ordinarily understood. Aesthetic judges exclude determinative judgment from their judging, while practicers of ordinary common sense (such as the judges in the public sphere) are required first to think for themselves, and only secondarily to think from the point of view of everyone. Enlarged thought is not a criterion for political truth according to Kant. It is merely the basis for the presupposition of universality expressed in a judgment.

Kant began his section 40 looking for the basis for the subjective necessity of judgments of taste. He finds it in the sensus communis, the underlying source of our assumption that others will, like ourselves, be able to play imaginatively in applying concepts in an undeterminative way to certain objects we call beautiful. The sensus communis, then, is indeed a source of a kind of unity, yet it is strictly speaking not a sense at all but a cognitive ability, albeit an undeterminative one. Kant writes: "Resuming now the thread from which I just digressed, I maintain that taste can be called a *sensus communis* more legitimately than can sound understanding [he has made this distinction primarily to show that common standards based on concepts are not sensed, but known], and that the aesthetic power of judgment deserves to be called a shared sense more than does the intellectual one."[44]

Incidentally, this is why Bernard Yack errs when he complains (in his superb *Longing for Total Revolution*) that Kant unrealistically expects individuals to perform this act of abstraction, as I shall discuss in chapter 4. Kant is not optimistic about our actual ability to step into another person's perspective: "The universal voice is only an idea. . . . Whether someone who believes he is making a judgment of taste is in fact judging in conformity with that idea may be uncertain; but by using the term beauty he indicates that he is at least referring his judging to that idea, and hence that he intends it to be a judgment of taste."[45] Furthermore, Kant makes clear here that the enlarged perspective, *pace* Arendt and Yack, is a normative standard by which to judge actual, always still particularistic judgment.

Aesthetic Education

Despite the shortcomings in Arendt's interpretation of Kant's philosophy, Arendt is able to identify quite an interesting line of thought in Kant, namely, that the judgment we require of political actors faces some of the same theoretical constraints as the judgment we require of critics of art. One strong point in Arendt's favor is Kant's repeated insistence that taste can be cultivated in society over time. He makes this argument in a vein quite similar to his claims for political cultivation of society through enlightenment: the advantages of cultivation go both ways, in that individuals are made fit for society via aesthetic/political education, and society is improved by cultivated individuals. As society progresses, aesthetic judgments become more purified of charm, that is, more perfectly communicable— from decorations of ourselves, to forms of objects, to the point at which "the pleasure that each person has in such an object is inconsiderable and of no significant interest of its own, still its value is increased almost infinitely by the idea of its universal communicability." Taste is, writes Kant, a "strange ability," but it is a natural ability that is susceptible to cultural improvement.[46]

Arendt, like most commentators on Kant's political philosophy, focuses on Kant's picture of the ideal state rather than on his pragmatic politics of real life between the state of nature and the perfect republic. In this provisional state, which includes all really existing states, social harmony is a goal, not a condition of any original contract (as Arendt suggests). Kant asks, "Is taste an original and natural ability, or is taste only the idea of an ability yet to be acquired and [therefore] artificial, so that a judgment of taste with its requirement for universal assent is in fact only a demand of reason to produce such agreement in the way we sense? In the latter case the *ought*, i.e., the objective necessity that everyone's feeling flow along with the particular feeling of each person, would signify only that there is a possibility of reaching such agreement."[47] Arendt rightly calls attention to the role of education in aesthetic and political progress for Kant, but she misunderstands its importance. The feeling of objective necessity that accompanies aesthetic judgments cannot stand in for some absent source of authoritative political judgment—aesthetics cannot be the substitute for traditional or divine judgment sought by contractarians and other modern legitimizers of the coercive state. The production of authoritative judgment is a *process,* the possibility of which is signaled by this feeling of necessity accompanying aesthetic judgments.

Why would Arendt ignore Kant's distinction between determinable concepts and necessarily indeterminate judgments of taste? Arendt gave her lectures on Kant as part of the preliminary work for the third book in her planned trilogy on the human condition. Arendt's premises about that human condition were those of a twentieth-century philosopher, especially insofar as she participated in the past half-century's search for a justification of democratic principles that does not rest on some culturally arbitrary set of premises. Arendt may have thought that in Kant's aesthetic theory, with its criterion of indeterminacy and its outcome of universal communicability, she had the beginning of an answer to this question. Kant, however, is not worried about the cultural particularity of his republican premises. For Kant, moral principles are determinate, though the human beings interpreting them are never perfect but only on the way to an ideal. The fundamental difference separating Arendtian and Kantian political thought, then, is the difference between Kant's view that humankind is on the way to determinacy and Arendt's view that indeterminacy is a permanent fact of collective life. Both recognize the requirement for social harmony despite these sources of disunity. But this difference regarding determinacy explains why Kant, unlike Arendt, could never consider aesthetics a model for politics.

TELEOLOGY AND FREELY WILLED HUMAN ACTION

In Kant's politics there seem to be two incompatible answers to the question of how humankind can hope to achieve this goal of social harmony. On the one hand, Kant gives a mechanistic, teleological-historical account of the transition of humankind from barbarism through contemporary civilization and on to ever more perfect republican federalism. This strand in Kant's thought, which reads like an amalgam of Mandeville, Hobbes, Montesquieu, and Smith, appears in many of his occasional essays, as well as in *Judgment* (though only indirectly there). On the other hand, Kant provides several versions of an account of freely willed human action as a causal force in history. This second story carries with it one big advantage and one big disadvantage from the point of view of the Kantian system as a whole. The advantage of Kant's theory of publicity as the motive force of progress in political life is that it links the realms of politics and morality via the judgments of historical human beings interpreting timeless political principles of right. The disadvantage of this theory is part of its advantage, namely, that to provide such a connection between these realms, Kant is forced to presume (and in *Conflict* even to claim to have observed) the empirical causality of freedom. This is a risky procedure, in that any such presumption seems to toss the would-be Kantian analyst of politics right back with the metaphysicians of the schools. The first *Critique* established strict limits on possible claims of knowledge. The key to the success or failure of this effort of Kant's to bridge politics and ethics without violating his own epistemological conditions will lie in whether the standard Kantian solution to antinomies succeeds in this complex case.

As is well known, in his first *Critique* Kant takes up the question of whether one is justified in attributing reality to the concept of free will. He presents an antinomy between two points of view: the first states that every phenomenon may be explained according to natural mechanisms; the second states that some phenomena cannot be explained according to natural mechanisms, and therefore are attributable to the nonnatural mechanism of freedom. Kant cannot establish the reality of freedom in the resolution of this antinomy. Instead, he argues that mechanistic and nonmechanistic (Kant would say "technical") explanations are compatible, since the explanatory strategy chosen depends upon one's point of view. The completeness of the mechanistic explanation for observable phenomena does not in principle rule out correct nonmechanistic explanations of these same events from a nontheoretical (that is, practical) perspective. Moreover, Kant also argues that natural mechanism, however completely it may be applied to all parts of the observable world, also falls short if applied to the world as an empirical whole: causality can in principle always provide a preceding condition for natural things, except for the existence of all natural things itself. He uses this argument to bolster his contention that the presumption of a spontaneous will is necessary for human investigation of nature.

If the two possible approaches to political progress, teleological history and freely willed human action, can be reconciled along the same lines outlined in Kant's third antinomy, then Kant's system is secure. Kant probably intended the two types of argument—teleological and agency centered—to represent mere antinomial contraries. But as I anticipated above, though compatibilism may succeed in epistemology, it cannot succeed for politics, which occupies a strange and difficult intermediate ground in the Kantian system, between freedom and nature. In fact, for Kant, politics is where freedom and nature collide: it is about the concrete effects of freely willed human action. Though tempting as an interpretive tool and even as a spiritual comfort, teleological arguments can have no place in such a theory.[48]

Riley on Teleology in Kant

I have been contending that the teleological logic in Kant's political thought is incompatible with Kant's arguments based on the presumption of freely willed human action.[49] Patrick Riley has also argued that Kant's political philosophy contains two competing, at least partly incompatible threads; he calls them teleology and contractarianism.[50] Pure contractarianism, Riley argues, is vulnerable to the Hegelian "empty formalism" critique.[51] But Kant's politics are not empty, he continues, because Kant posits "objective ends" for human action. For example, moral principles tell us that persons must be treated as ends in themselves, not as means to any other end. Riley argues that Hegel's charge of empty formalism can only be met by stressing Kant's teleology at the expense of his universalism.[52]

Though Riley is certainly right to identify a trade-off between the strands of teleological and contractarian reasoning in Kant's political theory as Kant in fact wrote it, it seems to me that a Kantian argument on the basis of the moral theory alone, without the addition of any strong teleology, can refute Hegel's charge. Kant does need an account of the substantive ends of moral and political life if he is to avoid Hegel's charge of empty formalism. If Kantian morality were the formal, rigoristic set of principles to be applied to the challenges of the moment that some have claimed it is, then surely we could discard it as empty.[53] On this reading of Kantian morality, a person could simply apply the universality test to decisions as they arise naturally, taking no responsibility at all for the world at large. But, of course, Kant is not a stoic or an empty formalist. As has been well argued by recent students of his moral philosophy, Kantian ethical principles posit necessary ends of human action.[54] Action *as such* is end directed. Even as Kant insists that the moral worth of an action comes from its originating will rather than any (necessarily arbitrary) results it might have, he recognizes that this original will aims at *something*. A good will aims at a good end (though it may never reach it). The refutation of the Hegelian empty formalism critique lies therefore in Kant's moral theory itself, not in any separate teleological story.

The question for Riley thus becomes: Is Kantian moral theory itself necessarily teleological in a sense that is incompatible with contractarianism? Here Kant offers us a useful if subtle distinction between teleology as "natural purposes" and teleology as "purposes of nature."[55] Only the latter is "strong" teleology, in that to presume the existence of "purposes of na-ture" is to presume at least an original intelligent causality in the world giv-ing ultimate goals to the things in nature, including human beings. Along with intelligent original purposiveness goes a historical account of the quasi-natural and ultimately inevitable progress of humanity toward the goals set by nature. This is the teleological story mentioned earlier, which Kant tells in "Idea for a Universal History" and elsewhere: the story of the achievement of the just republic via the unwitting actions of pawns in God's long game. Hardly anyone working in moral philosophy would attempt to make such a claim today, except on faith. In the weaker sense, however, tele-ology as "natural purposes" is just the formalization of the investigator's rule of thumb that nature makes nothing superfluous. It is thus a working presumption of lawfulness in nature. According to this weak teleology of natural purposes, I can presume for every thing (and also for every action) an intrinsic purpose. Kant's moral theory does not entail the strong teleo-logical account of purposes of nature. I can assign purposes to my acts with-out reference to any original purpose of creation as a whole. Moreover, a weak teleology of natural purposes guaranteeing in a minimal way the in-vestigator's enabling presumption of underlying lawfulness in nature is compatible with Kant's substantive moral theory of end-positing agents.

Riley argues that Kant needs teleology if his system of politics is to avoid the charge of empty formalism. But strong teleology, far from saving Kant's political thought, actually undermines it. There can be no doubt that in many of his political writings, especially in "Idea for a Universal History," Kant adheres to the strong teleological view. But a focus on the real politics of progress, rather than the outlines of the ideal state, demonstrates the in-adequacy of Kant's strong teleological story. If objective ends are the only source of value for human action, then the means taken to achieve them are irrelevant. As Riley says, in reference to the strong teleological story of quasi-natural human progress toward the ideal state, "Unless the moral ends are real, there is no reason to hope that the self-loving citizens of a re-public will choose the right thing for the wrong reason."[56] But the Kantian doctrine of ends, as I have just argued, is part of his explanation of moral motivation on the part of ethical actors, and it relies on no strong teleology at all. Ends can be intrinsic to an object or an action; the moral presumption of objective ends does not entail an original ends-setter, nor does it entail a guaranteed achievement of those ends.[57] The ends cannot justify the means for Kant; we have ends just because moral action is qua action goal oriented.

But these ends, Kant continually repeats, are mere ideals governing the real actions taken under their normative aegis. Just as Kant, in the *Rechtslehre*, cannot accept Hobbesian social contract theory with its "pathologically" legitimated goal of security but has to move beyond that mere state of order toward an autonomous civil society, so he cannot accept any doctrine that treats human beings merely as means to an end, even an end as great as the highest good on earth.[58] Commentators and Kant himself have recognized this problem—that the existence of objective ends seems to diminish the dignity of the individual human actor as an end in himself.[59] Unfortunately, Kant himself plays down his best response to the problem, which is the priority he accords to the transition toward the just state over the ideals of any image of perfection. Real human beings acting as freely as possible in pragmatic and imperfect conditions are the "bent wood" with which Kant at his best is fundamentally concerned.

Two incompatible kinds of observation are possible with regard to this transition toward the just state. Either one attributes concrete effects to freely willed human action or, on the other hand, nature can be said to move humankind toward its ends by quasi-natural means (that is, without the conscious participation of human actors). Discussing this dilemma, Riley complains that another scholar, Howard Warrender, "seems to think that Kantian politics requires the right kind of willing."[60] It is true, as Riley argues against Warrender, that for Kant the legal order functions without regard for the moral quality of the individual wills within it. Riley is also right that "for Kant, politics and morals share ends but not incentives."[61] However, the overwhelming fact determining the course of human politics is the practical reality of the moral law.[62] Mere legal order is possible according to natural incentives, as Hobbes argues, and as Kant recognizes with his "nation of devils" argument.[63] Such an argument is compatible with the strong teleological story according to which nature moves humankind toward ideal goals by quasi-natural means. However, for Kant, humankind cannot rest at mere legal order and will never reach the political perfection moral reason requires of us by natural means. Instead, human beings are in a constant state of transition from imperfect (though potentially legal and fairly secure) order toward more perfect and more perfectly free order. "[Putting an end to progress in enlightenment] would be a crime against human nature," writes Kant, "whose original vocation lies precisely in such progress."[64] Mere legal order, as Riley correctly points out against Warrender, requires no special moral willing, according to Kant. But progress in political life, which Kant argues in a weak teleological vein is humankind's "original vocation," does require the application of freedom to practice. Freely willed human action, such as the public judgment in favor of French revolutionary ideals expressed by Prussians at some personal risk, is the motive force behind substantial political progress.

Teleological History

In the preceding discussion, I introduced my claim that though Kant himself sometimes argues for the strong teleological theory, this theory is neither internally coherent, nor compatible with the rest of the Kantian ethical and political theory, nor even externally plausible. I would now like to argue that Kantian teleological history, especially as Kant explains it in sections 83 and 84 of *Judgment*, is incompatible with the rest of his political theory.

Kant's account of teleology applies most readily to the natural sciences, that is, to investigators into nature who are forced to use inductive reasoning. As Henry Allison has explained, the natural scientist must presume some minimal law-governedness on the part of the objects he or she investigates, if only to guarantee that the external characteristics one observes correspond with some internal characteristics.[65] How much law-governedness is the scientist justified in presuming? asks Kant in a typically critical *quaestio juris.* Kant concludes that both the weak and the strong versions of teleology, while not provable, are nonetheless necessary presuppositions of any investigation into nature. He writes, "It goes without saying that this principle [for judging nature teleologically] holds only for reflective but not for determinative judgment, that it is regulative and not constitutive. It only serves us as a guide that allows us to consider natural things in terms of a new law-governed order by referring them to an already given basis [a purpose] as that which determines them. Thus we expand natural science [*Naturkunde*] in terms of a different principle, that of final causes, yet without detracting from the principle of mechanism in the causality of nature."[66] What is a relatively old-fashioned but still interesting consideration of induction in the natural sciences when applied to Kant's classic example of a blade of grass (Does it exist according to a plan of its own? Is it explicable in terms of its ability to feed the cattle that human beings, as the only final purposes on earth, use to eat?), becomes a fairly pernicious theory of history when applied to human beings. In sections 83 and 84, Kant spins out the perspective on human progress that follows from the view of life that includes both weak (intrinsic purposiveness) and strong (final causes) teleology. As he has already made clear, any empirical history of humankind must disregard individual willing, as necessarily nonobservable. But the perspective of teleological history allows the historian to inquire, if not about actual human wills, about eternal will on the part of nature, expressed as purposiveness. The historian cannot know this purpose with any certainty. However, the historian may, Kant says, proceed by subtraction to get at nature's aim for man.

Kant makes the familiar arguments against happiness as a legitimate principle of progress. He eliminates any discovery of nature's "final" cause for man and thus concentrates on the one immediately preceding any final cause, nature's "ultimate" aim, which must be man himself. Even this argument might have been compatible with Kant's agency-centered theory of publicity, as the concept of man as an end in himself is based on the same moral principles that ground it. However, Kant chooses instead to define nature's ultimate goal for humankind as the "cultivation" of the species over time. Dividing culture into the "positive" culture of skill and the "negative" culture of discipline (that is, freedom from the despotism of desire), Kant goes on to argue that positive culture depends empirically on the material subjugation of most of the population. This is presumably the case so that the rest may be free to develop their inner capacities, which apparently do not include, at least not in the near term, legitimate self-government.

Kant in section 83 rehearses a common set of eighteenth-century ideas about cultural progress. History is cyclical, exhibiting cycles of rise and decline as civilizations alternate between youth and corruption.[67] War and commercialism are each pressed into historical service as paradoxical promoters of peace and disinterest: "Despite the terrible tribulations that war inflicts on the human race, and the perhaps even greater tribulations that oppress us in time of peace because then we are constantly preparing for war, still war is one more incentive for us to develop to the utmost all the talents that serve culture (while the hope for a permanent happiness of the people continues to recede)."[68]

The problem with Kant's teleological view of history, which is here especially distasteful, but which he repeats with essentially the same logic in the more popular historical essays, is that it is fundamentally incompatible with his political theory. Kant's problem for progress in politics is usually formulated as follows: moral reason tells us the goal of collective self-government, but little about how to achieve it. We can use such natural incentives as those Hobbes describes to achieve a minimally secure legal order, but not to progress beyond that to the just state. Thus the problem, given Kant's arguments against revolutionary change, is to find a mechanism of gradual political reform that will move humankind toward ever more enlightened, peaceful, republican government. Both elements of Kant's political theory, the Hobbesian social contract theory and the reforms to move beyond it, are clearly voluntarist in nature.[69] Teleological accounts of human history preclude meaningful voluntary action. Commentators have considered Kant's teleology part of his political theory because the two theories posit the same goal for human progress: the establishment of social harmony in the just state. But although the ultimate purpose of nature, according to the teleological story, is human enlightenment, the mechanism is not political but natural.

In section 83, Kant outlines a teleological theory that is incompatible with his political theory. In section 84, he provides detailed analysis of that theory, which shows it to be not only incompatible with his system as a whole but also plainly implausible. In section 84, he views the strong and weak versions of teleology as inseparable. In order to consider objects in nature as purposes, Kant argues, one needs to accept that there are supersensible "purposes of nature." "But morality and a causality in terms of purposes that is subordinated to it is absolutely impossible through natural causes. For the moral principle that determines us to action is supersensible."[70] This is not the place for theological debate on the necessity of the existence of a higher power. However, clearly natural scientists have managed to undertake fruitful research projects without any such assumption. Furthermore, empirical observation in the form of public opinion research confirms the existence of moral systems that we at least say determine our actions. Disagreement about whether morality in fact determines our actions still exists, of course, as does disagreement on whether there is a difference in kind between moral claims and natural ones. But one need not conclude that morality must be based on something supernatural just because it is not directly observable.

Though Kant clearly argues that teleological judgment is necessary to guarantee the possibility of achieving in the natural world the goals set for us ideally, I would have to disagree with his own assessment of his system. "Ought implies can" is a rule fully derivable from practical reason, from the nature of action as goal oriented, without any assistance from the concept of judgment. Kant says this rule (ought implies can) depends on the presumption of a purposiveness of nature.[71] I would say rather that the rule functions regulatively based solely on practical reason and requires no further proof of its reality than the standard Kantian hypothetical argument: if

I am to be a rationally acting being, then I must pursue goals determined by reason. But Kant here clearly feels that corroboration from nature, at least as nature appears to us, is needed.[72]

Despite this strong support for the necessity of teleological judgment, drawn not only from Kant's explicit statements but also from the structure of his book, Kant does undermine his own teleological argument with a number of caveats aimed at limiting the status of conclusions drawn under the concept of purposiveness of nature. Already in the critique of aesthetic judgment Kant calls attention to the weakness of his teleological presuppositions. In the comment to the deduction of taste, he adds that though we can understand the possibility of making judgments of taste, we cannot similarly understand the possibility that nature presents itself to us as purposive as a whole, since this would be a determinative judgment according to nature's concept.[73] Furthermore: "There is clearly a big difference between saying that certain things of nature, or even all of nature, could be produced only by a cause that follows intentions in determining itself to action, and saying that *the peculiar character of my cognitive powers* is such that the only way I can judge [how] those things are possible and produced is by conceiving . . . a cause that acts according to intentions."[74] Here, it seems to me, is the place where Kant's *Judgment* is contradicted by his own critical principles. Thinking a thing in terms of necessary lawfulness, even a lawfulness that is beyond our possible comprehension, is not necessarily thinking a thing in terms of its production by a being with intentions. Lawfulness is one thing, natural purposiveness another, and being a purpose of nature still a third. Why should we have to presume an author? Only to explain the origin of the whole, if that.

At best, as Kant sometimes admits, the concept of a purposiveness of nature may serve as a "heuristic" for investigating particular laws of nature, including perhaps those that apply to human beings considered collectively.[75] What remains most useful for political theory from Kant's *Critique of Judgment* is the distinction that he maintains (and that Arendt attempts to undermine) between the two perspectives available to human beings viewing their own political history: the perspective of the judging spectator and the perspective of the moral actor. The next chapter continues to examine these issues, with a look at, among other things, Kant's use of teleological argument in his famous "nation of devils" example.

3

progress toward peace

In this chapter I argue that Kant achieves more than is usually acknowl-edged in his famous work *Perpetual Peace*. Not only is the work an outline of a just system of right for an interdependent world, not only does it set out Kant's famous principles of publicity, it is also the work in which Kant first demonstrates the principle of provisional right in practice. Though he had not published a formal defense of provisional right itself (this would come two years later, in his *Rechtslehre*, which I discuss in my next chapter), Kant was already using the concept in connection with the particularly political problem of applying universal norms to day-to-day politics. For example, in a note to *Perpetual Peace* Kant writes that during the "transition from the state of nature to the civil condition" acquisition of states by means of prac-tices that are unjust from an ideal point of view (such as inheritance) ought to be respected if done in good faith, even though "this authorization to continue in possession would not occur if such an alleged acquisition were to take place in the civil condition; for then, as soon as its nonconformity with rights were discovered, it would have to cease, as a wrong."[1] Provisional right calls for judgment according to the maxim of preserving the possibil-ity of progress toward the just state; Kant uses this standard in *Perpetual Peace* to distinguish between two kinds of injustice listed in his "preliminary articles": those that must be corrected immediately and those that may rightly be allowed to persist for a while even though they are unjust.

Many readers will be surprised that Kant specifies particular practices contrary to the rule of right that may nevertheless be allowed. This surprise comes from applying Kant's ethical system directly to the practice of poli-tics, a mistake Kant himself rarely made. Instead, Kant argued that in the

messy realm of political action, in which the results of policies are fundamentally unpredictable and the price of short-term justice may be the loss
of the possibility of lasting peace, provisional rather than conclusive right
provides the appropriate standard.

As I discuss in the following chapters and in the conclusion, a Kantian
theory of provisional right should help political theorists focus away from
stale and overanalyzed objects of inquiry, such as juridical debates over absolute principles, and toward the kinds of politics that affect the quality of
citizenship experienced by most people in the world today. Not that the
courts, especially the nascent system of international adjudication, are
unimportant, but political theorists have ignored the rest of political life to
their detriment. A focus on provisional rather than conclusive right makes
it possible to analyze institutions that do not make absolute pronounce-
ments on what counts as just. For example, in most people's experience of
citizenship what matters is their degree of access to the legal system rather
than any one of the system's particular claims. A Kantian politics of provisional right looks at the norms of process rather than anticipating any particularly just outcome for a given policy question. As I discuss in the conclusion to this book, given that no policy prescription, regime, or political
institution may be deemed conclusive under this theory, the Kantian theorist would look instead to the preconditions of just processes of decision
making. Kant provides a brilliant example of this kind of political reasoning
in *Perpetual Peace*.

Of Kant's political works, then, *Perpetual Peace* is both the most influential and the most underappreciated. From the standpoint of philosophical coherence, however, it is not one of his best. At the root of the problem
with *Perpetual Peace* is that Kant is trying to do a number of different things
at once: write a serious political treatise on international legal order, satirize
the pretensions of absolutist governing cliques, and simultaneously attempt
to convince those same partisans of the old regime to submit to the rule of
reason.

Nonetheless, to follow Kant in the essay as he struggles with his most
important political themes is instructive and sometimes inspiring. One of
Kant's last works, *Perpetual Peace* shows him wrestling with the big political
questions and reveals the choices he would have to make to resolve them. In
the essay Kant contradicts himself, proposes standards that he later drops,
and at several points refuses to follow his own logic toward uncomfortable
conclusions. Despite these many failings, *Perpetual Peace* achieves at least
three things: its principles have influenced generations of politicians and

others committed to setting up international institutions; its arguments, particularly its arguments about the principles of publicity, inspired important twentieth-century political theorists, such as Rawls and Habermas; finally, and most important for this book, despite its shortcomings *Perpetual Peace* is Kant's most far-reaching exploration of the problem of the pragmatic application of ideal principles to imperfect political reality.

Most readings of *Perpetual Peace* focus on a few topics: whether Kant makes a covert argument for world government, whether his general theory can be saved from a narrow view of national sovereignty, whether philosophers should play a prominent role in public life, and whether Kant's proposals are relevant to today's world. A focus on Kant's most substantial political argument, that politics must be about the gradual transition from imperfect toward more perfect government (and thus that right is in practice always provisional), allows me to address these questions in a spirit more appropriate to Kant's own project than previous considerations of it have been.[2] Taking the first question, for example, commentators can be divided into two camps, those who argue that Kant did support world government, complete with universal coercion, and those who argue that Kant in fact supported only a limited, voluntary federation of sovereign national states.[3] Attention to Kant's theory of provisional right helps resolve the problem: Kant consistently refers to world government as a necessary ideal of practical reason, but he raises pragmatic barriers for the implementation of the ideal in practice.

BACKGROUND TO THE TEXT

Attention to the context in which Kant wrote *Perpetual Peace* can illuminate our understanding of it by showing where Kant echoes elements of ongoing debates among members of the Berlin Enlightenment and, more important, by revealing the places where Kant diverges from the discourse of his contemporaries. With *Perpetual Peace,* Kant placed himself within two major lines of thought: first, the series of projects for perpetual peace and, second, the debate on whether ordinary morality applies to sovereign rulers.

Kant's main predecessor is Abbé Saint-Pierre, who in 1713 published the first parts of his *Projet pour rendre la paix perpetuelle en Europe.* In this work, the abbé envisioned a European union of Christian nations governed by a strong federal power at its center.[4] Though the plan never moved from the literary salon to the ministerial drawing table, it received a great deal of attention, even from foreigners like Kant. Kant's "philosophical project," while rejecting most of the abbé's concrete suggestions, retains his goal of perpetual peace and, importantly, Saint-Pierre's formal conceit of imitation of a traditional peace treaty.

Rousseau, who in his early days attempted to complete an edition of the abbé's unpublished papers (an unwieldy task that Rousseau brought to a close with an abbreviated collection and commentary), criticizes his predecessor and submits his own proposal on the same topic for the consideration of the public.[5] Rousseau appreciates the ambitions of the abbé's *Projet* but complains that it neglects the political reality in which any plan for peace must be implemented. Ambitious seekers after power, rather than disinterested moral paragons, are enthroned throughout Europe, and wars, he argues, will continue to serve their interests. Furthermore, Rousseau complains, the abbé focuses too exclusively on considerations of international politics, while domestic political conditions—such as the sovereignty of war-mongering tyrants rather than peace-loving republicans—are ignored. For Rousseau, then, another problem with Saint-Pierre's proposal for peace is that such a treaty would require the central European authority to protect existing signatory regimes, since any new regime might refuse to obey. Rousseau points out that such rules would lead to the paradoxical result that the institution in charge of promoting peace would be responsible for the entrenched power of the tyrants responsible for European wars in the first place.[6]

Kant's Response to Garve in *Theory and Practice*

Rousseau criticized the *Projet* from the left, but his complaint that the dream of perpetual peace ignores political reality was echoed in Kant's time by the right wing of the Berlin Enlightenment. Kant's contemporaries Christian Garve and Friedrich Gentz were among those who argued that philosophical projects in general, and Kant's philosophy in particular, are irrelevant to the strong man's business of rulership.[7] Though the critiques of Kant's practicability were usually based on misreadings (though often durable misreadings) of his philosophy, they also contain a more generally defensible view that political ideals and reality inevitably conflict. Like the British conservative Edmund Burke, the conservative members of the Prussian Enlightenment employ a modern realist sensibility to reach the conclusion that traditional authority is the best ground for politics.

Garve is the most prominent of Kant's critics along these lines. As early as the publication of the first *Critique*, Garve argues against Kant's supposed idealism.[8] Like many supporters of "enlightened absolutism," Garve was an admirer of an idealized version of the British monarchy, along with much in British letters. He translated into German Adam Smith's *Wealth of Nations*, Burke's *Observations of the Sublime and the Beautiful*, and Ferguson's *Principles of Moral Philosophy*. Garve aspired to be the German Hume in politics and social thought, if not in epistemology.[9] Garve's disquisition on the relation of morality to politics defended the realpolitik of Frederick II, arguing that monarchs must adhere to rules different from those that apply to ordinary citizens.[10]

Kant directed one of the three sections of his essay, "On the Common Saying, That May Be Correct in Theory, but It Is of No Use in Practice," against this contention of Garve's. Were Kant the rigid moralist he is often taken to be, he might have argued that the moral law applies to all limited rational beings, rulers and ruled alike. Instead, however, Kant adopts the perspective of the ruler to show that even apart from the moral law applied personally, ordinary ethical laws come to matter for rulers, since these commonly held beliefs constrain the environment in which rulers operate.[11] In his reply to Kant's essay, Garve makes excellent arguments against a stock image of Kantian idealism but scores no points against Kant as he ought to be understood. In a plausible move given a generous reading, Garve argues that some rights, including the right to revolution, depend on empirical circumstances for their legitimacy. Mainly, and with very little basis, however, Garve accuses Kant of dogmatically applying a priori moral precepts to pragmatic problems of political life. Garve's misdirected criticism has endured to the present day. In his time, such contemporaries as Friedrich Gentz concurred with Garve's determination that Kantian philosophy could not apply to the real world, while frequently admitting Kant's arguments so long as they remain strictly ideal. But Kant himself makes no such error.[12]

Kant wrote the essay against Garve only a few years before he composed *Perpetual Peace*. The debate around the status of Kantian critical philosophy would have been fresh in his mind, as news of an outrage against international right had just reached his ears. The Treaty of Basel (1795) had recently been concluded between Prussia and revolutionary France. With this treaty, Prussia secured France's tacit agreement not to interfere with the third and final partition of Poland among Prussia, Austria, and Russia. Kant had by this time long been privately critical of Frederick II's foreign policy (the qualified enthusiasm for the regime Kant expressed in "What Is Enlightenment?" having been worn away by a decade of cynical, self-aggrandizing activity on the part of the Prussian state). As Kant writes in *Perpetual Peace*, most current peace treaties (the Treaty of Basel is clearly implied in several instances, see further below) are such in name only. Rather than guaranteeing peace, they merely institute a mutually beneficial cessation of hostilities. Thus, while Kant was defending his critical philosophy against misreadings in the world of letters, in particular defending its potential application to pragmatic politics, the pragmatic arena of international relations provided him with an additional reason to polemicize against crude realism in political life.

The Form of the Text

As is usual in his popular essays, Kant takes up the traditional forms of the genre in which he is operating but modifies them to reflect his system of critical philosophy. Attention to the form of the essay, and especially to the places Kant deviates from the expectations set up by its formal structure, can help untangle the often confusing and apparently conflicting lines of thought presented in *Perpetual Peace*. Like his predecessor Abbé St. Pierre, Kant imitates the formal structure of a peace treaty. Thus he divides the main body of the essay into "preliminary" and "definitive" articles, just as a traditional peace treaty would be divided. Preliminary articles normally outline the conditions necessary for peace, while a treaty's definitive articles prescribe specific institutions.

Kant begins with six preliminary articles, each of which makes a comparison between an international political ideal, based in reason, and the reality of international relations in Kant's time. In the second preliminary article, for example, Kant writes that "no independently existing state . . . shall be acquired by another state through inheritance, exchange, purchase, or donation"; in the fifth he writes that "no state shall forcibly interfere in the constitution and government of another state" and adds that, except in cases of total civil war resulting in anarchy, foreign governments may not intervene to divide a country.[13] None of Kant's contemporary readers would have failed to recognize the implicit criticism of the most recent (1795) and final partitioning of Poland among three foreign countries (Russia, Prussia, and Austria), with the acquiescence of a fourth (France). Each preliminary article takes the form "no *x* shall *y*," defining the elements of the current real world that must be changed before a lasting peace can ensue.

The six preliminary articles, therefore, stand in this essay for the judging function that Kant always includes in his pragmatic political work. In order to make the transition from the imperfect present toward an ideal future, human actors must have access to the most reliable political judgment available, judgment that mediates between ideals determined by practical reason and the reality of the provisional state. Here Kant himself plays that role, offering a philosopher's determinations of what is wrong with the current international system.[14] As I discuss toward the end of this chapter, Kant in *Perpetual Peace* is concerned with the appropriate role for philosophers in promoting progress toward peaceful, republican governance. Already in the first paragraph of the essay Kant identifies himself as a philosopher with a right to promulgate his scholarly ideas ("fire off all his skittle balls") without punishment by the state.[15] In *Perpetual Peace*, then, the judging role usually played in Kant's mature theory by the public sphere is instead played by the philosopher, represented by the author himself.[16]

In traditional peace treaties, preliminary articles are followed by "definitive" ones which define the specific institutions that will govern the peace between the parties to the treaty. Accordingly, in *Perpetual Peace* definitive articles offer institutional specifics. Thus here we have Kant's concrete proposals for enacting the changes recommended by a philosopher's political judgment in the previous section of preliminary articles. However, just as Kant's preliminary articles set out not mere static conditions but dynamic comparisons between an ideal world and pragmatic reality, Kant's definitive articles define institutions not for maintaining a peace agreed upon at a truce but for what Kant calls the establishment of a condition of peace. Traditional peace treaties, Kant argues, merely institute a cessation of hostilities mutually beneficial to the parties involved. Real peace would mean the establishment of institutions to prevent states from resorting to war at all, just as the state itself is an institution that prevents citizens from resorting to violence.[17]

Kant's definitive articles for such a lasting, genuine peace call for institutions to facilitate the transition from the state of nature to the civil condition on three levels—individual, state, and cosmopolitan [*Weltbürgerrecht*, literally "world-citizen-right"]. First he calls for republican constitutions, then for a federation of all states, and finally for universal cosmopolitan right. Each level of change is aimed at promoting the transition toward ideal political life. The first, of course, moves human beings out of the state of nature and toward republican self-governance: "The civil constitution in every state shall be republican." The second level of change, a federation of the world's states, is intended to allow states to resolve their differences legally rather than violently, in a manner analogous to the establishment of the rule of law in the first case: "The right of nations shall be based on a *federalism* of free states."[18]

However, in the third case, of cosmopolitan right—that is, the right of individuals considered as citizens of the world rather than citizens of a state—Kant breaks with the form established in the previous two articles. Instead of defining an institution needed to implement cosmopolitan right, Kant merely sets out the limits within which such right is to be understood: "Cosmopolitan right shall be limited to conditions of universal *hospitality*."[19] As I shall discuss below, in the second definitive article, Kant has already provided a weaker set of institutions than the formal structure of his essay would suggest, replacing an expected internationally coercive sovereign power with a relatively powerless federation. Even more surprisingly, in the third definitive article, Kant presents no institution at all. Instead, he discusses what the right of hospitality means in practice, namely, that individuals, wherever and in whatever political condition they are found, must be accorded some basic respect. Stateless barbarians, for example, may not be deprived of their land, either by trickery or by sham legal means; thus Kant criticizes European colonizers for "count[ing] the inhabitants [of the Americas, Africa, and elsewhere] as nothing."[20]

The general aim of the definitive articles is to extend human freedom under the rule of law to all three of the possible types of political relations: citizen-to-citizen relations are governed by the state; state-to-state relations are at least regulated by the federation; but relations of citizens of the world (that is, of individuals considered apart from any state membership) to foreign states and their representatives are given no governing institution at all. Instead, Kant simply insists that cosmopolitan right is a necessary supplement [*Ergänzung*] to the other kinds of political rights. This claim is then followed by two supplements [*Zusätze*], the first providing a teleological history of humankind's progress toward peace, and the second (added a year later) insisting on the right of philosophers to criticize political conditions.[21]

What can one conclude from Kant's deviation here from the expectations set up by the form of the essay? In the first place, in both the preliminary and the definitive articles, Kant is carefully distinguishing between rational political ideals and their gradual implementation in practice. He notes at the end of the section of preliminary articles that only three of them demand immediate implementation, recognizing that provisional right allows for the gradual approximation of practice to ideals. These ideals are suggested by the *form* of the second section on definitive articles, but the *content* of this section limits itself to pragmatically acceptable reforms from the point of view of an eighteenth-century Prussian.[22] As Kant says in the second definitive article, there is a gap between the institutions demanded by reason and those acceptable to actual governments.[23] Thus the apparent deviations in content from the expectations set up by the form of the essay are for the most part accounted for by the disparity between ideals and reality.

Such a distinction, however, cannot explain the *increase* in Kant's deviation from expectations as the essay progresses: by the end of this chapter, I shall be able to demonstrate why cosmopolitan right is so much harder for Kant to express in institutional form than individual and state right. For now, let me note that Kant's first supplement seems to be an attempt to substitute the guarantee of progress provided by the purposiveness of nature for the institutional guarantee of cosmopolitan right that Kant believes is pragmatically unacceptable. As I argue here and in chapter 2, Kant's attempt to replace practically necessary human action toward political improvement with the natural consequences of empirical conditions is the least successful part of his political thought.

The first section of *Perpetual Peace*, containing the preliminary articles, compares the current state of international affairs with ideals provided by practical reason; the second section of the essay, the definitive articles, offers a mechanism for progress toward those ideals in the form of freedom-guaranteeing political institutions. Thus the main body of *Perpetual Peace* represents an exception in Kant's mature political thought. Usually for Kant comparisons between real and ideal are themselves a mechanism for gradual progress, as the judgments offered in the public sphere slowly affect the rules by which collective life is governed. Though he deviates from his usual system in the first two sections of *Perpetual Peace*, by the appendices Kant is once again offering publicity as the mechanism of progress toward the institution of political right. This tension between the two accounts of the mechanism of progress reflects, I believe, a formal rather than a substantial problem in the essay. As in his other political works (most notably the *Rechtslehre*), there is a tension between the traditional forms appropriated by Kant (a peace treaty, here, or a standard treatment of social contract theory, in the *Rechtslehre*) and the philosophical system with which he grounds his serious arguments. Imitation of the traditional divisions of the peace treaty encourages Kant to locate judgment in the preliminary articles and mechanism in the definitive ones. Normally, however, these two functions would not be separate, and indeed they are not in the more philosophically grounded appendices.

I shall discuss this problem, and the remaining formal aspects of Kant's essay, along with their material, in the rest of this chapter. These include Kant's late addition of the "secret article," which constitutes his second supplement, an argument for the right of philosophers to exercise their public reason. This section is important not only for the light it sheds on the contexts of Kant's own trouble with publishing his views under conditions of censorship but also for its especially clear statement on the corrupting influence of power on truth seeking. Finally, Kant includes two substantial appendices, whose form derives not from the form of a traditional peace treaty but directly from Kant's philosophical writings.

PRELIMINARY ARTICLES: CRITIQUE OF EXISTING INSTITUTIONS

Kant qualifies the judgments of the current international situation he offers with a number of apparently modest caveats given at the outset of section 1, the preliminary articles. As a philosopher, Kant's judgments reflect the "sweet dream" of perpetual peace; they are mere "ineffectual ideas" that pose "no danger to a state." Kant compares his philosophical expressions of judgment on politics to "skittle balls."[24] These comparisons are valid so long as Kant continues to argue from the point of view of the statesman, whose interests are determined by his wish to maintain state power. But from the point of view of someone interested in the truth about politics, the pragmatic ineffectuality of Kant's philosophical viewpoint raises rather than lowers the value of his insights.[25] As he says in the second supplement, "Possession of power unavoidably corrupts the free judgment of reason."[26] Though he offers the choice in a playful tone in the first sentence, by the end of *Perpetual Peace* Kant will have made clear that the choice between the peace of the graveyard and the peace of thriving international harmony is the choice between the point of view of the statesman and the point of view of the philosopher.[27]

The judgments offered by the philosopher in section 1 compare the so-called peace of 1795 to the rational concept of a genuine peace. In three of the articles (1, 5, and 6), the current state of affairs is judged totally unacceptable; the abuses of Kant's day in these cases ought to end "*at once.*"[28] In the other three articles (2, 3, and 4), aspects of current politics found wanting by comparison with rational ideals ought to be corrected, but delay in the implementation of such corrections is permissible.[29] Even as he makes absolute judgments about moral-political necessity, by (for example) prohibiting standing armies and the funding of international adventure by a national debt (articles 3 and 4), the philosopher recognizes that all right in practice must be provisional, in that it is applied to imperfect polities on the way to better governance.[30] As Kant argues in the *Rechtslehre*, provisional right supersedes a lawless state of nature but does not yet approach the standards set by reason. Thus, under the rule of provisional right, some practices in international politics constitute unacceptable contradictions to the idea of the rule of law itself, while other practices merely hinder progress but do not contradict lawfulness per se. The moral laws that prohibit this second type of practice are permissive (*leges latae*), as opposed to strict (*leges strictae*). Kant writes that these permissive laws authorize the sovereign, "not to make exceptions to the rule of right, but to postpone putting these laws into effect, without however losing sight of the end." Kant insists that this permission exists only to prevent a "premature" enactment of justice, which might "counteract its very purpose."[31] This is the basis on which Kant distinguishes between the totally unacceptable practices prohibited in 1, 5, and 6 and the temporarily acceptable ones of 2, 3, and 4.

Preliminary Article 1: No Duplicitous Treaties[32]

Article 1 argues that a peace treaty that does not eliminate the causes of war is no real peace treaty but only "a mere truce, a suspension of hostilities."[33] He criticizes the legal casuistry by which rulers and their ministers extract justifications for war from previous treaties, a practice that would be fresh in the minds of Europeans in the eighteenth century. Even Frederick II, who at least in Kant's early work comes in for some praise as a relatively enlightened ruler, appalled Kant with his behavior in the international arena. After deciding for power-political reasons to invade Silesia, for example, Frederick requested post hoc legal justification from his ministers. Frederick later congratulated one initially dubious minister for producing "the work of an excellent charlatan!"[34] Kant bitterly notes that warmongering despots can "with indifference leave the justification of the war, for the sake of propriety, to the diplomatic corps, which is always ready to provide it."[35] Such peace treaties cannot be given a provisional reprieve, since reason exposes them as contradictions in themselves. By insisting that the only possible peace treaty is one that does away with the causes of war, the philosopher makes a much stronger claim than it appears at first. If the concept of peace is to have any meaning (is not to contradict itself), it must be employed in establishing the conditions of permanent peace, which, as the reader soon learns, include the institutions guaranteeing the rights of subjects, states, and world citizens. Kant writes at the end of section 2 that all three relations must be on a legal basis "for the sake of any public rights of human beings and so for perpetual peace; only under this condition can we flatter ourselves that we are constantly approaching perpetual peace."[36]

Preliminary Article 2: States Ought Not Be Treated as Personal Patrimony

By contrast, Kant does not call for the immediate cessation of the policies criticized in preliminary articles 2, 3, and 4. Though none of these practices—treating states as personal patrimony, maintenance of standing armies, and use of national debt to fund wars—can be part of an ideal condition of international peace, none of them directly contradicts the rational ideal of peace itself (as do the objects of articles 1, 5, and 6). The acquisition of one state by another, say through royal marriage, contradicts "the idea of the original contract, apart from which no right over a people can be thought," Kant argues in the second preliminary article.[37] The task of bringing a state's constitution into line with the idea of an original contract, which would in this case exclude the state's being given as so much property to some other power, is a necessary task called for by practical reason. No really existing state, however, conforms to the strictures of the ideal state; all actual states are provisional ones in the process, however gradual and marked with setbacks, of moving toward republican self-governance. While treating states as patrimony, then, contradicts the ideal of an original contract, it is not in direct contradiction with the ideal of peace among states. Kant frequently argues that the move to republican governance in itself will reduce wars of aggression, since the same people who suffer from war will be unlikely to start one.[38] Provisionally, however, in an international context made up of many different types of states, the "inheritance, exchange, purchase or donation" of a state might in the short run actually prevent war. In such cases, therefore, Kant allows that immediately "implementing the law prematurely [might] counteract its very purpose."[39]

Preliminary Articles 3 and 4: No Standing Armies or Debt-Financed Wars

In addition to permitting the continued treatment of some polities as patrimony, Kant regards standing armies and debt-funded war treasuries as provisionally acceptable institutions. These third and fourth preliminary articles are harder to explain than the second one, since both practices are presented by Kant as leading directly to the risk of war. In the case of standing armies, Kant does make an ancillary argument that "the use of human beings as mere machines and tools in the hands of another (a state) . . . cannot well be reconciled with the right of humanity in our own person." This argument might relegate standing armies to the same category as patrimonial states, in that the ideal contradicted is not peace per se but some other rational ideal (human dignity). However, Kant also argues that the very existence of a standing army leads, by a logic familiar to present-day political scientists, to war: "For they incessantly threaten other states with war by readiness to appear always prepared for war; they spur states on to outdo one another in the number of armed men, which knows no limit; and inasmuch as peace, by the costs related to it, finally becomes even more oppressive than a short war, a standing army is itself the cause of an offensive war, waged by a state in order to be relieved of the burden."[40] Similarly, Kant criticizes the new financial mechanisms for national debt pioneered by the English and used in France and elsewhere, which allowed states to use wealth from outside as well as within a state to prosecute a war. Such financial instruments are directly detrimental to the cause of peace. Kant's argument here is simple: despite the basic inclination to go to war on the part of nonrepublican rulers of states, they are nonetheless restrained by the limits of their own resources. Removing this limitation—by providing "a treasury for carrying on war that exceeds the treasuries of all other states taken together"—promotes war.[41]

How, then, can Kant call the prohibitions of preliminary articles 3 and 4 permissive, since they seem to address practices directly in contradiction with the cause of peace? The answer lies in Kant's consistent concern that progress be gradual rather than revolutionary.[42] Kant makes his main arguments against revolution not in *Perpetual Peace* but in the *Rechtslehre*. In *Perpetual Peace*, he summarizes the case for provisional right in a note, as follows:

> These [conditions under which a ruler may postpone bringing his state into compliance with the rule of practical reason] are permissive laws of reason that allow a situation of public right afflicted with injustice to continue until everything has either of itself become ripe for a complete overthrow or has been made almost ripe by peaceful means; for some *rightful* constitution or other, even if it is only to a small degree in conformity with right, is better than none at all, which latter fate (anarchy) a *premature* reform would meet with. Thus political wisdom, in the condition in which things are at present, will make reforms in keeping with the ideal of public right its duty; but it will use revolutions, where nature of itself has brought them about, not to gloss over an even

greater oppression, but as a call of nature to bring about by fundamental reforms a lawful constitution based on principles of freedom, the only kind that endures.[43]

Any abrupt cessation of the practices prohibited by 3 and 4 might have counterproductive effects in practice, destabilizing states and possibly leading to violence, rather than promoting the eventual advent of peaceful international relations. Kant's willingness to grant provisional permission to some unjust practices of states (in articles 2, 3, and 4) is easier to understand in light of those prohibitions from which he offers no such reprieve (in 1, 5, and 6).

Preliminary Article 6: No Misuse of Human Agents[44]

Preliminary article 6 prohibits the misuse of human agents of the state in ways that undermine the possibility of eventual progress toward ideal political life: "No state at war with another shall allow itself such acts of hostility as would have to make mutual trust impossible during a future peace; acts of this kind are employing *assassins* . . . or *poisoners* . . . *breach of surrender, incitement to treason* . . . within the enemy state, and so forth."[45] The argument given here is similar to the one given in preliminary article 1, in that the practices prohibited would, if allowed, undermine the very possibility of peace. In both cases, Kant says deferentially that such acts would demean the dignity of the ruler. But his more substantial argument is that the practices in question are contradicted not only by the ideal of perpetual peace but by the basic standards of the rule of law, even of order itself. For example, even the most cynical ruler could agree with Kant's arguments against duplicity from preliminary article 1, whether in peace treaties or in the practice of war itself: while the short-term gain from duplicity may be real, over the long term, duplicity by a ruler undermines the very basis for his rule. Thus duplicitous practices are contrary not only to the ideal of peace but also to the interests of rulers of provisional states. Kant stresses this point by making the argument of preliminary article 6 in terms of the transition from the state of nature to the civil condition: "For some trust in the enemy's way of thinking must still remain even in the midst of war, since otherwise no peace could be concluded and the hostilities would turn into a war of extermination (*bellum internecinum*); war is, after all, only the regrettable expedient for asserting one's right by force in a state of nature (where there is no court that could judge with rightful force)." The misuse of human agents is a contradiction in itself, in that the long-term results of the practice undermine the goals for which it is used (in this case, the integrity of the state, in both the moral and especially in the physical sense). "[These practices] would also be carried over into a condition of peace, so that its purpose would be altogether destroyed."[46]

Preliminary Article 5: No Forcible Interference in Another State's Affairs

Preliminary article 5 prohibits forcible interference by a state in the constitution and government of another state: Kant thus provides strong support for the concept of state sovereignty. At first such a prohibition seems odd, given the hope Kant expresses in section 2 that an international community of republican states will grow from a few that reach that stage early. However, what Kant here prohibits is interference by violence rather than by example and positive encouragement (say, by friendly trade terms). Even violent interference is not completely ruled out, since Kant would allow a state to intervene on behalf of one party in cases of total anarchy. Finally, preliminary article 5 prohibits interference by states, not by individuals or by supranational organizations, though he gives very little support to either of these alternatives in the rest of the essay.

Much has been written on Kant's concept of sovereignty, most of it critical of his strong defense of an old-fashioned sense of state sovereignty.[47] Additionally, many recent commentators have noted that new international organizations, from multinational commercial enterprises to war crimes tribunals with global mandates, have undermined the viability of Kant's concept.[48] What matters here, however, is not whether Kant's concept of sovereignty is viable (I discuss this issue later in the chapter) but why Kant thought it so important to peace that he not only declared any violation of this principle contrary to the rational idea of peace but also insisted that it must stop immediately.

Kant writes that forcible interference in another state's government or constitution "would make the autonomy of all states insecure."[49] One possible criticism of Kant's argument in the fifth preliminary article is that it is circular: to say that sovereignty must be respected because otherwise states' autonomy would be insecure is almost to say that without sovereignty we would have no sovereignty. A more sympathetic reading, however, would note that Kant is prohibiting violations of sovereignty by *any given* state, because such a single violation would render *all* state sovereignty questionable. This argument has more substance. It resembles the formula of the universal law for the categorical imperative: "Act only in accordance with that maxim through which you can at the same time will that it become a universal law."[50] Still, it is hard to see, based on the arguments offered here, why Kant holds that violation of state sovereignty merits the strict rather than the permissive type of prohibition. He writes that violations of preliminary articles 1, 5, and 6 are so serious that they must stop immediately. Practices banned in these articles are not mere relicts of an unenlightened age, like proprietary states, standing armies, and borrowing for war, but outright contradictions to the principles of right. Furthermore, as Kant argues in preliminary articles 1 and 6, these violations of the principle of right not only contradict the ideal of peace, they also contradict the narrow interests of the ruler of a state, in that they undermine the basis of a state's security. Though he does not explicitly make the argument here, Kant must be saying that any ruler who violates the principle of sovereignty unwittingly undermines his own authority. The maxim under which the ruler of one state allows himself to interfere in the government or constitution of a foreign state would, if universalized, undermine the very notion of sovereign states in the first place and, with that notion, the ability of a ruler to govern.

As I discuss later in this chapter, Kant's defense of the notion of sovereignty was not based on blind acceptance of the status quo. This has not been well understood. Howard Williams, for example, writes that a "reformer and republican more passionate than Kant might, indeed, recommend intervention in the name of progress."[51] Kant does not subordinate his republicanism to a rigid view of sovereignty taken over from his contemporaries. Instead, he argues, in terms of his version of social contract theory, that the only ground for legitimate violence, including potentially revolutionary intervention, is the protection of individual rights by a common authority. Kant took individual autonomy to be the ultimate legitimating value in the name of which state authority, and the coercion that enforces it, may be justified. If there is a problem with appropriating Kant's defense of sovereignty for the current world, it is that national states seem to be losing what ability they have had to defend individual autonomy. Thus a Kantian political theorist need not criticize Kant's priorities or his supposed lack of passion but ought rather to revise the Kantian account of the institutional resources able to defend autonomous individuals. Kant argues that the basis of all political right, the idea of an original contract, requires that individuals submit to the authority of a sovereign state. The party injured by a violation of preliminary article 6, then, would be not the post-Westphalian status quo in international relations but the potential freedom and security of individual citizens.

What matters for my purposes here is that in all three cases of immediately prohibited political practices (*leges strictae*), Kant identifies a contradiction in the practice itself. These three practices, prohibited in preliminary articles 1, 5, and 6, all contradict the very concept of legal order and thus interfere with the possibility of progress under the rule of provisional right. As Kant will argue in the *Rechtslehre*, such practices as those provisionally allowed in articles 2, 3, and 4 (*leges latae*) do stand in contradiction to political ideals derived from the moral law, but so long as they do not also prevent the establishment of some unjust but orderly regime, they do not prevent a people from making progress toward a better state.

To recap my argument: with the preliminary articles in section 1, Kant compares prevailing political practices with ideals of political right. In distinguishing between absolutely forbidden and temporarily permissible violations of international right, Kant provides an early demonstration of the concept of provisional right in practice. The demonstration itself constitutes an act of judgment of the sort Kant usually argues constitutes in itself a motor of progress. In *Perpetual Peace*, however, Kant first provides some institutional suggestions for the promotion of political enlightenment, and only in the appendices does he revert to his usual position that public judgment is itself the way to the just state.

DEFINITIVE ARTICLES: INSTITUTIONS FOR ESTABLISHING THE CONDITION OF PEACE

In section 2 of *Perpetual Peace*, Kant defines the institutions necessary to facilitate the transition from the state of nature to the civil condition. Numerous commentators have complained that the text vacillates between, on the one hand, strong recommendations for all three levels of government and, on the other hand, plans much less ambitious for international relations and cosmopolitan law than for the establishment of national republics.[52] Though Kant did not publish the formal grounds for his distinction until two years later, in the *Rechtslehre*, he makes use of the contrast between provisional and conclusive right in *Perpetual Peace* to offer a dynamic theory of the transition to better governance. Kant's text does *not* in fact vacillate between two mutually exclusive alternatives (world government or loose federation, for example). Instead, he provides a fairly consistent if insufficiently explained theory of rationally grounded political ideals and the mechanisms real political actors may use to approximate them.

Kant introduces the theme of transition from an unjust condition toward a just one in the first paragraph of section 2. Peace, he argues, is not the mere absence of overt hostility but a condition that must be established over time. The analogy to the social contract is explicit. Just as individuals in the state of nature must submit to a universal coercer in order to enjoy any rights at all, so must states find an institution to govern relations among them if they are to control their own destinies. (Though he does not make the argument here, this is why sovereignty is a necessary idea for states: in an insecure environment, states would have a meaningless kind of license, meaningless because their putatively free actions would in fact be determined by the need to secure themselves from their neighbors. Thus, to exercise any real sovereignty, that is, any real self-rule, states must embed themselves in a context of international security.) In a note, Kant summarizes the philosophical grounds for the claims he will make about ideals of political right. This includes the familiar "globus terraqueus" argument that since agents necessarily interact with one another, they must regulate these interactions if they are to enjoy any rights at all.[53] He lists three levels of political right (individual, state, and cosmopolitan) and the three ideal institutions that would, in a perfect world, guarantee these rights (states, international law, and a "universal state of mankind"). Finally, Kant summarizes his classic point that the political ideals he supports are not merely chosen at random but follow necessarily from principles of practical reason, in this case, the idea of peace as such.[54] Elsewhere he defends the necessity of the idea of peace as the highest political good.[55]

Why would Kant relegate such important arguments to a footnote? He does so because the formal strictures under which he is operating in section 2 do not allow for a philosophical deduction of ideal international institutions. Instead, the definitive principles of section 2 offer pragmatic solutions to the problem of guaranteeing not instant peace but the possibility of eventual peacefulness. The definitive principles set down provisional institutions for the establishment, over time, of the conditions of peaceful international relations.

First Definitive Article: Republican, Not Despotical, Constitutions

The first definitive article says that the "civil constitution [*Verfassung*] in every state shall be republican."[56] This might have been a good deal clearer had Kant sacrificed succinctness for clarity in his three definitive articles. As he explains a couple of pages later, the "civil constitution" refers to the source of legislative authority ("form of government," either despotic or republican) in a state, not to the "form of sovereignty" actually operating (which may be autocratic, aristocratic, or democratic, he says, using the classic terminology when what he means are the modern types of monarchy, mixed government, or plebiscitory democracy): "So that a republican constitution will not be confused with a democratic constitution (as usually happens), the following must be noted. The forms of a state (*civitas*) can be divided either according to the different persons who have supremacy in a state or according to the *way* a people *is governed* by its head of state, whoever this may be; the first is called, strictly speaking, the form of *sovereignty* (*forma imperii*). . . . The second is the form of government (*forma regiminis*) . . . and with regard to this [second distinction], the form of a state is either republican or despotic."[57]

The first definitive article really means that authority in a state must be republican rather than despotic, and thus that the legislative authority must come from the people, however they are represented, rather than from the same source as the executive power. Indeed, for Kant, as for Montesquieu, combination of executive and legislative authority defines despotism.[58] In theory, then, a constitutional monarchy may be republican in character (in its "form of government") if the public will is represented even just virtually in its laws. A clearer statement of the first definitive article would have expressed the provisional character of the right it promulgates, and it might thus have read: "The civil constitution, if not the form of sovereign authority, in every state shall be republican."

Kant's often confusing distinction between the form of sovereignty (autocratic, aristocratic, or democratic) and the form of government (either republican or despotic) allows him to excuse provisionally monarchical governments that are republican in spirit.[59] "Frederick II, for example, at least *said* that he was only the highest servant of the state."[60] To pursue the goal of establishing the conditions of peace, a state must represent the general will in its legislation. Representative republicanism would be just according to ideal standards of right based in the original contract. Moreover, representative republican states are much less likely to go to war at all.[61] Republicanism, then, is called for not only by the moral law as practical principle but also by the goal of international peace (which is a moral *end*, as opposed to a principle). As Kant writes,

> In addition to the purity of its origin—its having arisen from the pure source of the concept of right—the republican constitution does offer the prospect of the result wished for, namely perpetual peace. . . . When the consent of the citizens of a state is required in order to decide whether there shall be war or not . . . nothing is more natural than that they will be very hesitant to begin such a bad game . . . on the other

hand, under a constitution in which subjects are not citizens of the state, which is therefore not republican, [deciding upon war] is the easiest thing in the world . . . [the head of state] can decide upon war, as upon a kind of pleasure party.[62]

An accurate reading of Kant's first definitive article for perpetual peace, then, reveals a proposal for provisionally acceptable institutions for relations between individuals and the state. In order to promote the possibility of eventual peace, the decision to go to war must be in the hands of the representatives of the people. Any other form of government is a despotism incompatible with progress. Kant does not advocate the immediate transition of all states to fully representative republican rule, even though this would be the only system (of state sovereignty) that conforms completely to principles of practical reason. To do so would undermine the goal of the rule of reason—peace—by using revolutionary means to achieve it. Instead, Kant calls for states that are compatible with gradual improvements; these are republican in character, in that the legislative will of the people is represented, even if they do not directly control the executive power of the state. "The kind of government, however, is of incomparably greater concern to the people than is the form of state (though a good deal also depends on how adequate the latter is to the former's end)."[63]

The first definitive article calls not for the immediate institution of republican rule but for the representation of the people's will in decisions in international relations, especially whether to go to war. In other words, in the first definitive article Kant calls for representative as opposed to despotic government, be the form of the state what it may. Though pragmatic hindrances to the immediate institution of the ideal republic certainly provide a strong reason for Kant to make provisional, rather than ideal, suggestions, these empirical considerations are not Kant's main reason for suggesting a gradual rather than a quick transition. Instead, Kant argues that the immediate transition to republican rule would contradict its own ultimate goals, substituting revolution and violence for the rule of law and peace.[64] Thus there are theoretical as well as empirical reasons for Kant to advocate provisionally rather than conclusively just institutions for the promotion of perpetual peace.

Second Definitive Article: The Right of Nations (State Sovereignty)

This insight is particularly helpful in untangling Kant's famous second definitive article: "The right of nations shall be based on a *federalism* of free states."[65] As is well known, Kant calls attention to the analogy between the state of nature among individuals and the state of nature among nations. Just as lawless freedom among individuals ought to be exchanged for the rule of law under a universal coercer, so the state of war among states ought to be replaced with an international order under which differences may be resolved by legal rather than violent means. "In accordance with reason there is only one way that states in relation to one another can leave the lawless condition, which involves nothing but war; it is that, like individual human beings, they give up their savage (lawless) freedom, accommodate themselves to public coercive laws, and form an (always growing) *state of nations* (*civitas gentium*) that would finally encompass all the nations of the earth."[66] The idea of a global state thus follows naturally from Kant's analogy between the domestic and international state of nature. However, as in the first definitive article, Kant does *not* advocate the immediate institution of an idea of reason, which in this case would be world government. Instead, he supports the creation of a "pacific league" of nations, which, without subjecting any nation to coercive laws, would promote peace by an ever-expanding network of peaceful alliances. This "federalism of free states," he argues, will promote the ideal end of peace without violating the rights (that is, the sovereignty) of existing nations.

The problem for Kant in the second definitive article is to discover a means of promoting the "freedom of states," which like the freedom of individuals seems to require the coercion of the rule of law if it is not to degenerate into meaningless license, without violating the "right of nations." Kant is quick to point out that the right of nations cannot be what his contemporaries think it is, namely, the right to go to war. Kant is on difficult ground here. Provisionally speaking, the locus of the decision to go to war determines for Kant whether a state counts as republican (the people's will is at least represented in such decisions) or despotic (the decision is made independently of the people). The responsibility for the use of coercive violence in the name of the state is coterminous with state sovereignty. However, even though the determination of sovereign power matters a great deal in the provisional international system inhabited by all real states, sovereignty cannot be called a *conclusive* right on such a provisional basis. Right as such presumes lawful order. Just as in the state of nature among human beings, there is no right to kill, only a lack of justice in general, so in the state of nature among nations, a so-called right to go to war would only be a "unilateral maxim through force."[67] Nevertheless, at least in practice (that is, in the state of nature among states), Kant recognizes a "right of nations" that is incompatible with submission to a world government.

Kant mentions the "right of nations" in three places in the second definitive article. First, he argues that a world government ("state of nations") is a contradiction under the right of nations, because if all nations were to submit to coercion under a single sovereign, they would become a single nation, and the premise of a right of plural nations contradicts that. Such an argument is hard to credit. In the case of individuals, under the idea of an original contract they give up their lawless freedom to become a people, who submit to a single sovereign. Kant's contradiction at the level of international law seems to rest on mere semantics. If individuals can belong to a people while remaining human beings endowed with rights, what is to prevent nations from belonging to a community of nations? Kant's next two points are more substantial.

Second, Kant argues that "in accordance with the right of nations," the imperative to leave the state of nature cannot apply to states, "since, as states, they already have a rightful constitution internally and hence have outgrown the constraint of others to bring them under a more extended law-governed constitution in accordance with concepts of right."[68] This is a strange claim on the face of it, especially given Kant's willingness throughout *Perpetual Peace* to argue on the basis of the analogy between the state of nature among individuals and the state of nature among nations. However, attention to the ground of the legitimate use of force in Kant's political philosophy makes his claim more plausible. As I explain in the next chapter, Kant makes a contractarian argument that individuals ought to submit to a universal coercer to adjudicate their disputes. Any use of force, then, is justified ultimately by the need of individuals for a rule-governed sphere of action. Even in an international state of nature, and even without ideal domestic governance, provisional states will be able to provide minimally stable environments in which their subjects may act. The need to prepare for and to fight wars will certainly hinder subjects from pursuing their individual projects of self-development, and less-than-ideal governance means that the laws they obey will not always correspond with the general will. Nonetheless, the basic obligation that grounds legitimate coercive violence in the first place, that is, the obligation of individuals to submit to a common authority for adjudication of their disputes, has indeed been fulfilled. Though he does not spell out the argument as I have done here, this is why Kant can argue that "as states, they already have a rightful constitution internally and hence have outgrown the constraint of others to bring them under a more extended law-governed constitution in accordance with concepts of right."[69] If the only ground for legitimate coercion is the protection of individual autonomy through the rule of law, then once provisional states have been established, one could argue, no further coercion can be justified in the name of order (though persuasion ought to be used to promote progress).

Finally, Kant repeats that moral reason calls for the establishment of a world government that would bring an end to war for all time. However, he adds, "In accordance with their idea of the right of nations, they [the states] do not at all want this, thus rejecting *in hypothesi* what is correct *in thesi.*"[70] Kant means that even as states' acceptance of the right of nations means that they accept the idea of the rule of reason, and thus ultimately ought to commit themselves to the end ("thesis") establishment of a secure peace, their provisional version of international right bars the means ("hypothesis"), world government, since it would interfere with state sovereignty. Even the most cynical rulers are unwilling to give up the idea of legitimation per se, while they violate right in practice.[71]

Clearly this "right of nations" to sovereign determination of their own affairs contradicts what Kant says is an imperative of moral reason: "Yet reason, from the throne of the highest morally legislative power, delivers an absolute condemnation of war."[72] Why does Kant recognize a right of nations at all? His three arguments on the right of nations all show that the concept of world government contradicts the idea of a right of nations. None of them, moreover, supports the right of nations itself from the point of view of reason.

Again, recognition of the difference between provisional and conclusive right can explain a troubling claim of Kant's, though in this case perhaps not redeem it. As Kant argues in the *Rechtslehre,* generally recognized rights acquired before the advent of the civil condition, such as the right to property used over time but never legitimately acquired, must be provisionally respected in the interest of public order. So long as the right is acquired in good faith, overturning it because it does not accord with perfect standards of justice would itself contradict these standards, since general instability would hinder the gradual reform needed to bring political life closer to its idea. In the *Rechtslehre,* Kant uses this argument to defend property rights in general, even though from the ideal perspective all property acquired outside the civil condition is illegitimate. Among the arguments marshaled by Kant in defense of property is the claim that the revolutionary dissolution of all property rights at the advent of a civil constitution would be counterproductive, destabilizing society when security and order are needed to establish lawful freedom.[73]

Now, in *Perpetual Peace,* Kant is making a similar argument for the right of nations. From the perspective of reason, world government is a necessary institution, and there is no rational right of nations. However, in the long period of provisional governance before a civil constitution may be implemented on an international scale, people have managed to construct a system of right that at least has reference to universal principles of right, even if it is manifestly imperfect. This provisional system includes the so-called right of nations. The provisional right of nations refers to the concept of state sovereignty, which though it can be understood broadly as a people's right to determine the actions of their state independent of foreign interference, is perhaps best measured by and most widely understood to mean independence in the decision to go to war. Kant himself uses this measure to distinguish between absolutist and genuinely representative regimes: whatever a country's outward institutions, if a single ruler can take the country to war, then the regime is absolute.[74] Though the right of nations is not an idea of reason, it does express some working principles that conform to rational judgment. For example, the aspiration of a people to determine their political fate independent of foreign interference is a provisionally legitimate version of Kantian autonomy: obedience to laws of one's own making. The difference between the provisional right of nations and an ideal version of international right is that the provisional right of nations, set as it is in an imperfect world characterized by ever-shifting international threats, embeds self-determination realistically in the context of war. Though the provisional right of nations falls far short of rational legitimacy, it at least preserves the possibility of progress toward more perfect governance.

Even though it interferes with the establishment of a world government that would guarantee the conditions of a permanent peace, then, the right of nations must be accorded provisional respect. Undermining the right of nations would, in the short run, be counterproductive, since what current world order there is bases itself on that provisional principle. Furthermore, under the idea of the right of nations, a "surrogate of the civil social union, namely the free federalism that reason must connect necessarily with the concept of the right of nations if this is to retain any meaning at all," can be constructed.[75] A pacific league of free states, while unable to provide the security that a coercive world government could, would at least ensure the continued possibility of progress toward peace.

However, even though, like individuals outside the civil condition, states without a world government will not enjoy perfect security, unlike individual human beings, states, especially republican ones, may be reasonably expected to act rationally. Kant cites the malevolence of human nature to explain the need both for civil constitutions to ensure domestic order and for republican governance to restrain the ambition of despotic rulers for war. In a pacific league of independent republican states, the causes of war would be doubly hindered: first, states would have institutional if not coercive means to resolve their differences and, second, the basis on which states would make the sovereign decision to go to war would take into account the full horror of the act, since the people's will would be represented at the national level: "The citizens of a state . . . would have to decide to take upon themselves all the hardships of war (such as themselves doing the fighting and paying the costs of war from their own belongings, painfully making good the devastation it leaves behind, and finally—to make the cup of troubles overflow—a burden of debt that embitters peace itself, and that can never be paid off because of new wars always impending)."[76]

A federalism of free states is not the ideal institution for preventing war.[77] However, unlike reason's ideal, it is practicable under the rule of provisional right. Given that the idea of international right is expressed at least partly in reality by the right of nations, Kant says that "(if all is not to be lost) in place of the positive idea *of a world republic* only the *negative* surrogate of a *league* that averts war, endures, and always expands can hold back the stream of hostile inclination that shies away from right, though with constant danger of breaking out."[78]

Third Definitive Article: Limited Cosmopolitan Right

Kant's third definitive article contains the shortest discussion of the three, and it falls shortest of the mark set by practical (moral) reason. On the topic of cosmopolitan right, or the right of individuals considered as citizens of the world, it would follow logically from the form of Kant's essay that cosmopolitan right entails the protection of human rights from violation by any moral person, either by other individuals in relations outside a single state's authority or by other states themselves. If reason calls for individuals to secure themselves from each other by submitting to a common authority (state), and for states to secure themselves from each other by submitting to a common authority (state of nations), then should not relations among world citizens and states be governed, too? Even as he lowers expectations in his second definitive article by calling for the pragmatic makeshift of a pacific league, Kant provides a description of the ideal institution called for by reason, a world government or state of nations. In the third definitive article, however, Kant shies away from any discussion at all of an ideal rational institution at the cosmopolitan level. Instead, he proposes a bare-minimum version of the human rights that must be universally respected if humankind is to retain hope of progress toward peace.

"Cosmopolitan right shall be limited to conditions of universal *hospitality*."[79] The argument here focuses on the preconditions of potentially law-governed relations between individuals outside state authority (such as those at sea) and between individual noncitizens and foreign states. In order to retain the possibility of civil relations at this level of interaction, Kant claims, individuals must be able to expect to communicate with foreigners, and even to visit their land, without being killed. Without the general expectation that the rule of hospitality will be respected, cosmopolitan relations will continue to be inimical to future peace. Kant lists piracy, enslavement, colonial oppression, and subversion of a foreign people as the typical crimes against cosmopolitan right committed by his contemporaries.[80] He criticizes both European and non-European violators but reserves particular scorn for the connection between Protestantism and the slave trade: "[The powers behind the Sugar Islands trade] make much ado of their piety and, while they drink wrongfulness like water, want to be known as the elect [*Auserwählte*] in orthodoxy."[81]

The gap between rational political order on the cosmopolitan level and the political possibilities visible to Kant must have been too wide for him even to suggest bridging it, as he did in the first and second definitive articles for the state and international levels.[82] Kant seems to have believed that the only imaginable institutional protection for people without even an internationally recognized state to protect them would have to be founded in a strong world government. In a provisional situation where even the rational interests of member states cannot entice them to sacrifice sovereignty for security, how much less likely must it have appeared that states would bow to international law in the name of human rights? Even though Kant could not foresee the (admittedly fledgling) international institutions of the present day, however, he did, astonishingly, accurately suggest the basis on which cosmopolitan right would some day come to enjoy at least a small amount of protection. Kant writes, "Since the (narrower or wider) community of the nations of the earth has now gone so far that a violation of right on *one* place of the earth is felt in *all*, the idea of cosmopolitan right is no fantastic and exaggerated way of representing right; it is, instead, a supplement to the unwritten code of the right of a state and the right of nations necessary for the sake of any public rights of human beings and so for perpetual peace; only under this condition can we flatter ourselves that we are constantly approaching perpetual peace."[83]

Present-day protection of cosmopolitan rights combines weak international coercive institutions like the International Criminal Court with the occasionally powerful force of international civil society, including both the public sphere in general and nongovernmental pressure groups like Amnesty International in particular.[84] Much has been written comparing Kant's *Perpetual Peace* with the current state of international human rights protection.[85] What I would like to point out is different: Kant recognized that in the absence of ideal international institutions (that is, under provisional right), publicity would have to substitute for coercion.[86] He makes this argument in an appendix to the essay.

TELEOLOGICAL HISTORY IN THE FIRST SUPPLEMENT

Before Kant begins the appendices to *Perpetual Peace,* with their philosophical account of the role of publicity in progress toward ideal civil relations, he adds a supplement that undermines this very effort. (Kant also adds a second supplement, on the right of philosophers to criticize the state, but only in the second edition of the essay [1796].) In the first supplement, Kant argues that the purposiveness of nature guarantees that peace on all three institutional levels will come about, "whether we will it or not."[87] As I said in chapter 2, Kant's use of teleological reasoning undermines the main current of his political thought, in which he argues for gradual transition to more perfect governance on the basis of practical (moral) necessity. In section 2's three definitive articles, Kant has demonstrated the inadequacy of real human institutions to the task of guaranteeing perpetual peace. He now offers the teleological account here as a sort of substitute for the ideal institutions that actual human beings are unable to construct. However, such a substitute is neither coherent nor necessary to Kant's system.[88]

As I discuss in the next section, the teleological explanation of the first supplement is incoherent because it cannot distinguish between the two kinds of peace Kant describes at the outset of the essay: the peace of international harmony and the peace of the vast graveyard of humanity. The teleological explanation is not only incoherent, however, but also unnecessary. One argument for the necessity of an explanation according to the purposiveness of nature might be that ordinary human beings, even if they recognize the rightness of the moral law, are motivated instead by natural rather than ideal impulses. This argument would stress that individual human conduct can be explained as action based on rational interest in personal self-preservation. The hidden hand of nature moves human beings without their knowledge toward providential goals, motivating them naturally by their interests, even as they progress, taken as a whole, toward ideal institutions. Now, given that the actor in question is a human being and not a divine one, and thus that the actor requires some motivation for action beyond simple recognition of moral truths, the question is whether Kant requires the teleological explanation to account for human action. He does not. In his ethical works, Kant ascribes moral motivation to a kind of feeling that he calls "respect" for the moral law. In his political thought, Kant offers a collective version of this same account of motivation for human action in the form of publicity: people, Kant argues, will be moved by public comparisons between political reality and the precepts of political right they already, if only tacitly, recognize. Kant never denies that rational self-interest is a powerful motivation for action. If he did, he would not have to wrestle with the problem of the corruption of the public sphere by power, as he does throughout his political works. But in judgment of questions of public interest, Kant argues, the application of ideals to political life is not reserved to higher powers. Instead, ordinary people (or, sometimes in his work, scholars) take on this role that would otherwise be reserved for providential reason.

Practical judgment thus provides not only recognition of ethical law but also moral motivation. For individual ethics, moral motivation comes from awe before the moral law; in politics, moral motivation is prompted by public judgment.[89] Thus Kant does have a theory of ends-oriented action that depends on human judgment rather than the hidden hand of nature. Furthermore, other elements in Kant's political thinking that are much less questionable from the point of view of their status as knowledge serve as well or even better as guarantors of human progress toward peace. In the teleological argument of the first supplement, Kant describes self-interested inclination as the hidden mechanism of nature that eventually brings about international order. In the appendices and elsewhere, however, Kant's account of publicity provides a superior version of the mechanism of progress.

Natural Order but Not Natural Justice

Kant argues in the first supplement that nature, without relying on conscious human agency, guarantees that humankind will eventually reach a

stable regime of peace on the state, international, and cosmopolitan levels.[90] "[N]ature comes to the aid of the general will grounded in reason,
revered but impotent in practice, and does so precisely through those self-
seeking inclinations."[91] He provides a standard, Hobbesian account of social contract theory, arguing famously that "even for a nation of devils" the
problem of establishing the rule of law is soluble.[92] Indeed, if establishing
the rule of law in the sense of universal coercion were all that justice required, Kant's teleology would be a great deal more plausible.[93] But he
needs nature not only to create a stable order; the principles of right must be
established on earth, and this requires not only stability but also freedom
under laws of the people's making.

Kant exposes the limits of his argument with his formulation of the political problem the social contract is supposed to solve: "'Given a multitude
of rational beings all of whom need universal laws for their preservation but
each of whom is inclined covertly to exempt himself from them, so to order
this multitude and establish their constitution that, although in their private dispositions they strive against one another, these yet so check one another that in their public conduct the result is the same as if they had no
such evil dispositions.'"[94] This is not a formula for establishing justice in the
Kantian sense of obeying laws of one's own making; rather, it is a formula
for ending civil war, reminiscent of Hobbes in its moral neutrality and of
Locke in its attention to the problem of free riders. Most of Kant's social
contract thinking is much more attuned to Rousseau, whose famous formulation of the problem of social contract theory stands in sharp contrast
to the one offered here.[95] Even conceding for the moment the point that nature, by an invisible hand, might lead human beings to unite in order to secure each of their private interests, Kant makes no case that nature might
lead human beings toward institutions that might embody any public goal
beyond mere security. Teleology might be able to account for the exit from
anarchy, but not for the entry into the civil condition as Kant understands it
(for my overview of this complex topic, see chapter 4). Kant cannot achieve
a state that respects human dignity without the operation, at least provisionally, of the public sphere. The interests of a state are very often opposed
to the principles of right (even, Kant suggests elsewhere, if the ruler and
people are perfectly well disposed, since even then they will put short-term
welfare above long-term right). Without the goad of public judgment,
states may achieve order, but they will not approach juridical perfection.

Kant does provide two more pieces of empirical evidence for his claim
in the first supplement that, even in the absence of human agency, perpetual

peace and the regime that guarantees it are inevitable. Like the nineteenth-century British political theorist John Stuart Mill, among others, Kant hopes that the "spirit of commerce" will convince erstwhile enemy states to suspend hostilities in the name of profit. Political scientists have found evidence both for and against this proposition.[96] Kant himself argues that modern financial institutions enable war making to an unprecedented degree, interfering with a formerly natural end to war, namely, fiscal exhaustion. This argument from the preliminary articles is not, strictly speaking, incompatible with the hope that commercial ties will promote peace. Nevertheless, given the equivocal character of the evidence for and against the proposition that "the *power of money*" might naturally substitute for intentional peace making, it cannot form part of a strong teleological argument here.[97]

Kant also considers the empirical fact of the division of humankind into linguistic and cultural nations in light of the argument that nature "wills" perpetual peace. Though cultural difference seems at first to be a cause of war, Kant argues, it is in fact a bulwark against universal despotism. The argument runs as follows: every state seeks to expand its power globally; eventually some states become strong enough to do so; but the diversity of culture and the tendency of expanded territory to cause "laws progressively to lose their vigor" combine to prevent such "soulless despotism" from prevailing over the long run.[98] Strangely, Kant has provided his own best counterargument. The quasi-natural progression of coercion-guaranteed order he describes at first does indeed seem to lead to a renewal of the Pax Romana on a global scale. Such a peace is, as Kant puts it, "the graveyard of freedom," even as it guarantees order. The natural bulwarks against such an outcome, cultural and linguistic diversity, seem frail indeed beside the inexorable progress of order fueled by self-aggrandizing human inclination. Far from eliminating the possibility, Kant in his teleology, at least in *Perpetual Peace*, has reinforced the idea that without human agency, no international justice beyond mere order can come about. Paradoxically, Kant's strong teleological arguments in the first supplement support an account of freely willed human agency as a necessary element in political progress.

Practical Necessity Beats Natural Necessity

Throughout his moral philosophy, Kant argues from practical necessity. In other words, the reality of the moral law has consequences for human beings. The truth of these principles cannot be proven theoretically, since the moral law is an ideal and not accessible to our limited faculties for gathering knowledge. Instead, Kant speaks of "practically necessary" principles, whose basic logic is hypothetical: if we are to understand ourselves as free beings, then we must recognize practical principles. This is not to say that Kant believes the mere admission of human freedom *causes* every one to behave morally. Instead, since human beings are "limited rational beings," we require not only practical principles but also moral motivation. It is possible, in other words, for us to act contrary to the moral law. But, Kant argues, it is not possible for us coherently to deny that the moral law applies to us.

There is no reason to jettison this standard of knowledge at this point in Kant's work. Practical necessity provides sufficient justification for moral action, and even, as I discuss later in the book, for the presumption of progress on the part of humankind.[99] Why add an epistemologically dubious and systematically unnecessary account of teleological history to an otherwise coherent essay, especially since this account contradicts critical arguments made elsewhere in the text? In fact, Kant does seem to hesitate in the first supplement to attribute much theoretical weight to his teleological argument. Kant's formula for the coherence of both the account of moral willing and of teleological nature reminds the reader of his arguments in the *Critique of Judgment:* we cannot directly apprehend the purposiveness of nature, but for practical purposes "(e.g., with respect to the concept of the duty of *perpetual peace* and putting that mechanism of nature to use for it) [it] is dogmatic and well founded as to its reality."[100] At the end of the first supplement, Kant reminds us that his account of nature's guarantee is not sufficient for predicting the future (not a theoretical principle), but "still enough for practical purposes." Had Kant taken his own caveats or his readers' commitment to enlightenment more seriously, he might well have omitted the first supplement.

THE NECESSITY OF PUBLICITY IN THE APPENDICES
TO *PERPETUAL PEACE*

Kant divides his argument in the appendices between a critique of materialist reductionism in politics and a proposal for a new formal principle of politics based on publicity. The titles of the two appendices alert the reader to the structure of the argument that is to follow. The first one, "On the Disagreement between Morals and Politics with a View to Perpetual Peace," is a standard Kantian critique of dialectical illusion based on taking the material aspect of life for its only aspect (that is, ignoring the importance of formal principles). The second appendix, "On the Agreement of Politics with

Morals in Accord with the Transcendental Concept of Public Right," takes the form of a practical deduction, in this case a deduction of the principles of publicity. Free in these appendices from the rhetorical conceit of imitating a peace treaty, Kant rehearses and deepens his philosophical account of possible political progress and its relation to political ideals.

In this essay, Kant uses the term *politics* to refer to "the art of making use of the [mechanism of nature] for governing human beings," and he contrasts "politics" with "right," which is the application of moral reason to politics. In this book, I use the term *politics* more broadly, referring to the organization of collective life, thus including both empirical and moral principles. The term *realpolitik* conveys to the modern ear what Kant meant by "politics" in this essay.[101] Both appendices reinforce the warning Kant offers throughout the text: promoting the materialist reductionism of realpolitik over the principles of practical reason in politics will lead humankind to the second of the two kinds of possible peace: not the peace of international harmony but that of the graveyard.

Kant's Critique of Realpolitik in the First Appendix

In the first appendix Kant is concerned to expose an illusion to which many of his colleagues, even some of the most enlightened ones, are subject: the illusion that, at least in political life, talk of ideals is mere superstructural cover for the real politics of material interests.[102] Pioneered in the first *Critique,* Kant's technique for exposing dialectical illusion identifies problems in thinking that arise naturally from the logic of imperfect human reasoning. As reasoners, for example, we try to explain particular empirical events, such as a falling leaf, by subsuming them under general principles, such as the law of gravity. Though this element of our reasoning apparatus (the ability to derive general laws from particular instances) is responsible for many good things, such as human progress in the sciences, it is also at the root of some errors human beings tend to make when they overestimate the power of their reason. In this case, I might pursue the cause of my falling leaf further than limited human reason can take me by attempting to extend my explanation beyond the physically observable world and into transcendent noumenal "causes." Even the claim that there are no nonobservable principles at work in the world (materialism) is an illegitimate step beyond the limits of the knowable.[103]

Kant aims to expose just such a dialectical illusion on the part of the "practitioner (for whom morals is mere theory)."[104] He seeks to apply empirical principles to politics without respect for principles of right, and even claims that such empirical politics can achieve the practically (morally) necessary goal of perpetual peace. The practitioner still governs his political actions with principles, yet these will be principles not of "political wisdom" but of political "prudence, that is, a theory of maxims for choosing the most suitable means to one's purposes."[105] In keeping with his material reductionist credo, the practitioner draws such principles exclusively from the realm of experience. Kant lists some of the better-known empirical political maxims, such as "act first, justify it later" and "divide and conquer." Kant then offers a number of criticisms of this point of view. First, no one can deny that the concept of right, empirically speaking, has currency in the world. If this were not the case, Kant notes, why would no ruler be willing to deny principles of right in public? As Kant argues here and in other places, "they dare not openly base politics merely on machinations of prudence and so disown all allegiance to the concept of a public right."[106] Elsewhere Kant argues that the fact of public judgment based on common concepts of right has a pragmatic effect in the world, namely, to promote enlightened political progress.[107] Here, however, the empirical fact of mass allegiance to the concept of right is not sufficient to disprove the material reductionist position. Thus Kant offers clearer, more damaging criticisms.

For Kant, the key flaw in the material reductionist worldview is its inability to reach unequivocal results. The practitioner arrives at principles of political prudence by abstracting general laws from the history of the world's governments. Even with all the evidence in the world, however, this process will not yield definitive results. Kant's outline of the necessarily equivocal questions that plague the material reductionist reads like a call for proposals from an eighteenth-century Social Science Research Council: "Whether a people can better be kept obedient and also prosperous for a long period of time by severity or by the bait of vanity, whether by the supreme power of one individual or by several leaders united, perhaps even by an aristocracy of merit only or by the power of the people within it, is uncertain. History provides examples of the opposite [resulting] from all kinds of government (with the single exception of the truly republican government, which, however, can occur only to a moral politician)."[108] More fundamentally for Kant, the knowledge that comes from empirical observation can never be certain, as new evidence could always confound an old generalization. Rational concepts, by contrast, even as their scope is quite severely limited, carry certainty with them. Put simply, we know what moral reason commands, while we cannot know with any certainty whether some particular prudential maxims would lead us to any desired goal.[109]

Material reductionism, however, would not be worth Kant's trouble if its epistemological difficulties were enough to render it harmless. In fact, Kant argues, the attitude of material reductionism itself hinders progress toward peace. In *The Conflict of the Faculties*, Kant criticizes those "Jewish prophets" who ensured that their prophesies of national dissolution were accurate by contributing to the predicted events themselves.[110] Similarly, in *Perpetual Peace* Kant objects against material reductionism that "such a pernicious theory itself produces the trouble it predicts, throwing human beings into one class with other living machines, which need only be aware that they are not free in order to become, in their own judgment, the most miserable beings in the world." Speaking of "moralizing politicians" who bend morality to suit political interests, Kant adds that "by glossing over political principles contrary to right on the pretext that human nature is not *capable* of what is good . . . [they make] improvement *impossible* and perpetuate, as far as they can, violations of right."[111]

Thus far Kant has argued that material reductionism must operate in bad faith, cannot achieve the epistemological certainty it would require to make accurate prudential judgments, and hinders its own purposes insofar as its principles become known. Probably Kant's most serious charge against material reductionism, however, is that it misunderstands the pragmatic operations of politics itself, and so must misjudge the maxims necessary to achieve its ends. The material reductionist thinks that he faces two choices in political action: political prudence, on the one hand, and pure political right, on the other. In fact, however, all politics is subject to the claims of both prudence and justice, as Kant's concept of provisional right makes clear. The requirements of practical reason set out necessary ends for politics (these are the concepts of right that Kant argues no real politician may publicly deny, however little respect they are accorded in actuality). Yet the practice of politics has less to do with the operations of the ideal state than with institutions that could bring actual governance gradually into compliance with the commands of the moral law. From the point of view of provisional right, then, the "moral politician" must consider maxims of prudence that will promote the ideals set down by reason. As Kant has repeatedly shown, revolutionary change, even in the name of justice, will undermine its own goals by a too-abrupt institution of ideals. Thus "it would be absurd to require that those defects be altered at once and violently; but it can be required of the one in power that he at least take to heart the maxim that such an alteration is necessary, in order to keep constantly approaching the end (of the best constitution in accordance with laws of right)."[112] For Kant the choice is not between realism and idealism but between a false material reductionism and the world as it really is: subject to the rule of provisional right in the absence of an ideal state.

Similarly, Kant criticizes the practitioner for complaining that the origins of all really existing states are not those of the just social contract that every one recognizes as ideal but those of the unjust assertion of power to unify a collection of individuals. Granting the empirical claim of the practitioner, as any student of history must do, Kant refuses to draw his nihilistic conclusions. Of course "in actual experience there will be great deviations from that idea (of theory)," Kant says. But political right is not therefore meaningless. Moral principles are a fact of political life, inevitably appearing as the standard by which governments are judged no matter what the regime in power. Far from being powerless, "the moral principle in the human being never dies out, and reason, which is capable pragmatically of carrying out rightful ideas in accordance with that principle, grows steadily with advancing culture." Political progress toward lasting order on all three institutional levels—a goal that is shared by the material reductionist and the moral politician—can only be achieved by gradual changes in real political institutions that bring them closer to compliance with the laws of reason.[113] This, as Kant's readers already know, is a product of the operation of publicity as a mediator between political ideals and real institutions.[114]

The Principles of Publicity in the Second Appendix

In the rest of Kant's mature political work, publicity operates to promote ideal governance via public comparisons between commonly held principles of right and commonly experienced political reality. Though the actors designated by Kant vary (the literary public sphere, the scholarly elite, professional philosophers, or spectators in the public sphere), their role does not: they judge political institutions on the basis of standards provided by reason, and issue these judgments publicly, but do not exercise direct political power. Kant uses these judges in the public sphere to provide as authoritative an account as possible of what changes are called for by right.

Kant's arguments for publicity in *Perpetual Peace* are aimed at encouraging provisional rulers to improve. From their point of view, Kant argues, rulers may profit from the judgment of philosophers. Kant's contemporary, Christian Garve, had argued that rulers qua rulers cannot act as moral beings. Here, and in *Theory and Practice*, Kant shows rulers that they can.

In *Perpetual Peace*, Kant's use of the idea of publicity is split between two very different functions. On the one hand, the agents of publicity in *Perpetual Peace* are the philosophers, though Kant does allow the representatives of the people a serious if limited role with the exercise of veto power over the decision to go to war. In most of his mature political writing, Kant *derives* the principles of right from the moral law and the ideal of original contract, using publicity to *apply* these principles of right to reality. In *Perpetual Peace*, philosophers play that role. However, in this essay Kant also *derives* two new principles of public right *from the idea of publicity itself*: the negative and positive formulas of publicity.

No satisfactory account of Kant's formal principles of publicity exists, despite the fact that Kant's concept of publicity itself has been a popular topic in recent years. This lacuna in the Kant literature is less surprising once one sees that the formal principles themselves are unnecessary to his general argument. In fact, Kant drops them as a measure of political right after proposing them in *Perpetual Peace*. Even a writer as thorough and as interested in transition as Claudia Langer is unable to make much of Kant's formal principles of publicity. That they cannot perform the judging function Kant proposes for them is clear from the divergence in the literature on what they would allow and deny. For example, Arendt argues that to make the principles coherent one must assume that Kant argues not against revolution in general, only against coup d'état. The best uses of Kant's principles of publicity have either developed the insight that conditions of public discourse might provide intersubjectively defensible standards of right (Rawls, Habermas), or they have applied the principles to a synthetic (rather than exegetical) Kantian political theory (Rosen).

Why would Kant add new principles of publicity to a system that seems already complete? Kant's attention to multiple audiences for his arguments provides an answer. The principles of publicity are aimed not at philosophical interlocutors, or even at the general public, but at provisional rulers. Their form is the same as that of Kant's deduction of the categorical imperative in his second *Critique*. With the formal principles of publicity, Kant creates a sort of categorical imperative for provisional rulers.[115] As is usual with Kant when he practices in the advice-for-princes genre, what seems at first highly favorable to the rulers' interests turns out to render them obsolete in the long run.

Kant begins with a "negative" principle: "All actions relating to the rights of others are wrong if their maxim is incompatible with publicity."[116] He grounds the principle with a standard version of a practical deduction, by abstracting from everything empirical in a political relation, after which,

Kant claims, one is left with the "form of publicity." Without going into too much detail here, it should be noted that these formulations (the negative and affirmative principles of publicity) have inspired a number of interesting and important works on formal justice, most prominently that of Rawls and Habermas but also more recently the theory of publicity in Gutmann and Thompson's work on deliberative democracy.[117] Kant's idea that the criterion of justice is its communicability has proved to be a durable source of inspiration for contemporary seekers after a standard by which to judge (and thus to unite) us all. However, here I should like to discuss the formal principles of publicity as they relate to Kant's account of the transition to republican rule, rather than to any theory of the just state itself.

In such a context, Kant's principles of publicity make sense only from the point of view of the ruler. As Kant has argued in "Theory and Practice" and elsewhere, progress toward political enlightenment need not occur under democratic governance, but it does seem to require freedom of thought and discussion. Taking up where he left off in "What Is Enlightenment?" Kant argues that the ruler who guarantees a free public sphere is acting not only in the best interests of justice but in his own best interests as well. Lest a ruler be dissuaded at the outset by such an unusual argument (after all, governments have long been accustomed to seeing secrecy as a useful means to some of their ends), Kant's very first example of the negative principle of publicity in practice is designed to comfort a wary ruler.

> *With regard to the right of a state* . . . a question arises here that many consider difficult to answer and that the transcendental principle of publicity quite easily resolves. . . . The wrongfulness of rebellion is therefore clear from this: that the maxim of rebellion, if one *publicly acknowledged it as* one's maxim, would make one's own purpose impossible. One would therefore have to keep it secret. But this would not be necessary on the part of the head of state. He can freely declare that he will punish any rebellion with the death of the ringleaders . . . since . . . he need not be concerned that he will thwart his own purpose by acknowledging his maxim.[118]

As I discuss in chapter 1 and at greater length in chapter 4, Kant deploys a number of arguments against the right to rebellion. He does not require the formal principles of publicity to make his case against revolutionary, as opposed to gradual, political transformation. Kant's claim that revolution requires secrecy is empirically plausible, but hardly definitive. If the principles of publicity are to do the heavy lifting of determining absolute principles of justice, then surely some argument stronger than the assumption that the exposure of a conspiracy always condemns its purpose to failure is needed. Furthermore, in none of his other writings on rebellion does Kant mention the formal principles of publicity. He drops the principles almost as soon as they are proposed (whereas with other political ideas, such as the concept of the public sphere, Kant works and reworks them). Why, then, include the formal principles of publicity at all?

However fruitful Kant's principles of publicity may have proved for his successors, for Kant himself they represented not a major theoretical innovation but an argument, aimed at contemporary rulers, to preserve the public sphere for their own and their subjects' interests. Kant's introductory language is suggestive here: the formula is "very easy to use," and it yields results that we can "cognize at once."[119] Kant's attempt to show the ruler that publicity is good for him begins with a demonstration that rebellion violates its principles; such an argument must have been appealing, if not to the rulers themselves, then to the intellectual supporters of enlightened absolutism found in their ministries. The rest of Kant's treatment of the negative principle of publicity supports my reading that Kant aimed his argument squarely at those in power. Following the structure established in the rest of the essay, Kant moves from the right of the state, through international right, and then to cosmopolitan right. After using the negative principle of publicity to deny a right of rebellion, Kant moves to the level of international right. There he attacks the same practice he has criticized earlier, one associated with despotism as opposed to republican rule: holding secret reservations when making an international treaty.[120] Kant has already argued that private individuals are necessarily untrustworthy internationally as representatives of state interests, since they will always preserve their self-interest whatever their previous commitments. With this and two more examples, Kant argues for state sovereignty, but against private interests represented at the highest level. Finally, with regard to cosmopolitan right, Kant says, "I pass over it in silence here; for because of its analogy with the right of nations, its maxims are easy to state and to evaluate."[121] It is hard to ignore the shade of Machiavelli at this point in Kant's argument. He is providing advice to princes, and he is engaging in that classic Machiavellian rhetorical device, pretermission, regarding facts that a ruler might find uncomfortable. As is clear from Kant's earlier discussion of cosmopolitan right, it is likely indeed to discomfort current rulers, since the logic of cosmopolitan right ultimately undermines state sovereignty.

Kant also declines to provide examples of his affirmative principle of publicity. While the negative principle, Kant argues, can test whether a given maxim is incompatible with political right, it cannot tell a ruler whether such a maxim is in fact just. With very little argument and no concrete examples, Kant proposes his affirmative principle: "All maxims which *need* publicity (in order not to fail in their end) harmonize with right and politics combined."[122] Having convinced, he hopes, at least the ministers of would-be enlightened despots with his favorable treatment of their rule under the negative formal principle of publicity, Kant sharply distinguishes between legitimate moral politics and "spurious politics." The ruler who takes Kant's bait and identifies with the moral politician rather than the practitioner is in for a tough lesson. For along with the denial of the right to revolution and the justification of state sovereignty comes the acknowledgment of the priority of right over any political expediency. Just before Kant discusses his affirmative principle, he criticizes in a note Garve's defense of what we now call realpolitik (in which Garve argues, as I report at the beginning of this chapter, that rulers need not adhere to ordinary morality). Added to what has been argued thus far, this move of Kant's should make clear that in this section, Kant is concerned not with justice writ large but with the possibility of moral rulership.

In *Perpetual Peace* Kant writes not once but twice that politics must bend its knee before right. His second use of the phrase is quoted much less often than the first, because without the context of his address to the ruler, it is hard to understand. First, arguing directly against Garve, Kant says that rulers have not only a duty of beneficence toward their subjects but also a superior duty to respect human rights. Rulers must not only act in the interests of their subjects' welfare (the ethical duty of beneficence). They must first respect their rights (the unconditional duty of justice). Kant writes, directly to the ruler:

> Whoever wants to give himself up to the sweet feeling of beneficence must first be completely assured that he has not transgressed this unconditional duty. Politics readily agrees with morals in the first sense (as ethics), in order to surrender the rights of human beings to their superiors [in other words, rulers are eager to cite their duty to promote the public welfare as a reason to demand obedience]; but with morals in the second meaning (as doctrine of right), before which it would have to bend its knee, it finds it advisable not to get involved in any pact at all, preferring to deny it any reality and to construe all duties as benevolence only; but this ruse of a furtive politics would still be easily

thwarted by philosophy, publicizing those maxims it uses, if only politics would venture to let philosophers publicize their own maxims.[123]

Kant has provided two easy formulas for the would-be enlightened ruler. The first, negative principle of publicity provides moral reasoning attractive to such a ruler, convincing him, Kant hopes, that the operation of justice is not only right but also in the ruler's interest. Once the ruler accepts the negative formulation, however, it is hard to deny the affirmative one, whose results over the long run would be considerably less attractive. Rather than spelling out the consequences of the affirmative principle of publicity, Kant makes a number of rhetorical moves intended to keep the would-be enlightened ruler in his camp. Once he has affirmed the rational justification for his rule, what leader would want to abandon the camp of proud, ethical publicity, joining instead the secretive band of casuistical Jesuits, whose furtive politics subverts the right? Accepting Kant's invitation for rational legitimacy, however, comes with a high price for the ruler. Just as Kant hinted in "What Is Enlightenment?" while promoting publicity as bolstering the enlightened absolutist in the short run, over the long run it spells his obsolescence.

As Kant does not explain the consequences of the affirmative principle of publicity, the reader is required to do so. What might it mean to adhere to such a rule, issuing only those policies whose success requires publicity? What is most important, such a rule implies that any legislation must represent the will of the people.[124] For Kant, *pace* Hegel, publicity does not equal democratic public opinion; Kant expects that a sort of filtering of interests will occur via the institutions of publicity. Ultimately, however, the principle of publicity requires at least the *form* of republican government. The moral law applied to rulers as the affirmative principle of publicity grants them an exalted role as agents of their own obsolescence.

As I argued at the outset of this chapter, Kant's *Perpetual Peace* performs a number of different, often mutually incompatible, tasks. Here the reader finds Kant's most definitive statements on international right, on citizenship, and on cosmopolitanism. Here too Kant sets out his formal principles of publicity and provides discursive essays on the role of the philosopher in society and on teleology. As in the early essay "What Is Enlightenment?" Kant is also addressing the would-be enlightened ruler of a should-be progressive state, providing advice for the two transitions: to a legacy of greatness, for the ruler, and toward more enlightened governance, for the subjects and their heirs. But most important for the argument I am making in this book, and for any reading of Kant as a political theorist, in *Perpetual Peace* Kant demonstrates that the principle of provisional right may be applied pragmatically to distinguish between provisionally acceptable and absolutely unacceptable violations of the rule of right.

However radical the implications of Kant's principles of publicity for the absolute rulers of his day, Kant was not so radical as to propose that political legitimacy be drawn directly from democratic public opinion. Republican government for Kant is defined in opposition to despotism: in a republican form of government, the will of the people is sovereign. As I argued earlier in this chapter, for Kant at least the form of republicanism is available provisionally even to monarchies, provided their rulers do not possess the absolute power to declare war on their subjects' behalf. Rather than argue for direct public judgment of these matters, Kant requires would-be enlightened rulers to support a public sphere in which public judgment can be heard. In *Perpetual Peace,* this public forum is occupied by philosophers.

In the second edition of the essay, in 1796, Kant added the "Secret Article for Perpetual Peace," in which he insists that it is in the state's interest to protect a right to public speech for philosophers. Though, he says, a ruler may not admit with dignity that he needs philosophers to advise him on the public will, he ought tacitly to do so. That Kant does not equate the legitimate public judgment of philosophers with the public opinion of a democratic majority is made very clear here, since he claims that "kings or royal peoples (ruling themselves by laws of equality)" are equally in need of the philosophers' services.[125] Sovereign power must be exercised in the name of the people. However, as I discuss in chapter 5, this power's exercise must be separate from the determination of the will that legitimates it in the first place. As Kant writes here: "That kings should philosophize or philosophers become kings is not to be expected, but it is also not to be wished for, since possession of power unavoidably corrupts the free judgment of reason."[126]

Perpetual Peace, then, has a variety of messages for a variety of audiences. For those interested in the form of a perfectly just international society as dictated by Kantian principles of reason (and, given the popularity of Kant's critical philosophy, there was indeed a significant readership of this type), Kant offers the standards of the preliminary articles. For international lawyers interested in the status of different standards of state conduct, Kant distinguishes between provisional and conclusive rights of states, on the model of permissive law and absolute law. For the political theorist interested as much in the mechanism of change as in the standards by which change is judged, Kant provides an application of the concept of provisional right with his dynamic account of the transition from an international state of nature to increasingly law-governed international relations. For would-be enlightened absolutists and their even more enlightened ministers, Kant argues against material reductionism in politics and provides them with a rule of thumb (the principles of publicity) by which to judge their actions. And, finally, for enlightened citizens hoping for human progress, who clearly make up Kant's most important audience, Kant clarifies the standards by which the citizen already, if confusedly, judges the political institutions of the day, and he encourages action and hope both through his account of necessary progress and through the underlying message of the affirmative principle of publicity, which is that just legislation must be based on the will of the people.

4

provisional right

The concept of provisional right applies to institutions that imperfectly mirror their own normative principles; since all existing political institutions do this, pragmatic politics must follow a rule of provisional rather than conclusive right. A general formulation for provisional right in Kantian language is: "Always leave open the possibility . . . of entering a rightful condition."[1]

Present-day political theorists have, of late, discovered that they can move beyond stale debates by means of the concept of provisional right. For example, theorists of deliberative democracy have incorporated insights from communitarian thought (such as the embeddedness of actors in particular social contexts) into their essentially liberal systems of deliberative politics. Two of the leading exponents of deliberative theory, Amy Gutmann and Dennis Thompson, argue that a view of political principles as "morally provisional" allows us to avoid static debates among "first-order" theories like communitarianism and liberalism by focusing on a "second-order" theory for assessing the procedural justice of any deliberation.[2] To take a different example of the recent interest in provisional right, Jane Mansbridge argues that an essential element of any democratic polity must be the maintenance of a variety of sources of opposition. Rather than attending strictly to problems of "political obligation and civil disobedience," democratic theory ought to recognize the "ongoing imperfection of democratic decision." She grounds this view on the premise that the principles that regulate democratic procedures must always remain "provisional."[3]

Despite these and other recent innovative uses of the concept of provisional right by political theorists, however, very little has been written about what it means to focus on provisional rather than conclusive elements of right. Present-day thinkers like Gutmann, Thompson, and Mansbridge readily recognize the advantages of provisional rather than conclusive theorizing of political life. However, this specifically Kantian concept of provisional right has not been given its due by intellectual historians, nor have political philosophers sought to understand it. As I discussed in chapter 3, Kant was already using the concept of provisional right in *Perpetual Peace,* to determine which violations of international right were immediate threats to the possibility of world peace, and which might be provisionally tolerated.[4] As I shall demonstrate in this chapter, the *Rechtslehre* contains Kant's most sustained treatment of this important topic. I argue in this chapter and in the conclusion to this book that a Kantian theory of provisional right offers useful innovations in a number of areas of contemporary relevance, such as citizenship theory.

PROVISIONAL RIGHT AS A CONTRIBUTION TO CONTRACT THEORY

Perhaps the most overlooked part of Kant's political thought is his writing on the transition of the world's states to peaceful, republican governance.[5] We tend to associate Kant with foundationalism and rigorous first principles, not with civil society and provisional right. In his political writing, Kant combines universal norms with natural facts, historical analyses, and even hopeful prognostication. He achieves a plausible if not provable theory of how humankind can expect to move from the unjust present toward an ideal future.

Kant is pragmatic and moderate in his goals for the medium term. As is well known, Kant saw himself as a reformer rather than a revolutionary. What is less well known is that Kant's support of reform over revolution in no way reflects a general conservatism on Kant's part.[6] Kant criticizes revolutionary activity not for its goals but for its methods—and even here the attack is at least partly based on the pragmatic shortcomings of revolutionary politics, rather than on pure matters of principle (see below).[7] While differing on method, Kant and a typical eighteenth-century revolutionary would have agreed on a number of things, including the desirability of an end to absolutism and the institution of republican government. In his political essays, which were written for a broad audience, and also in the formal legal theory of the first half of *The Metaphysics of Morals* (*Rechtslehre*), Kant addresses the problem of transition to republican governance.

This is not to say that Kant abandons his "transcendental idealism" when he takes up political topics. Kant's pragmatic focus on how actual people can come to enjoy political freedom springs from fundamental concerns about the meanings of human agency and autonomy. Both of these concepts are explored in Kant's formal ethical works. But political life, as Kant notes in his preface to the *Rechtslehre*, resists purely ideal analysis.[8] Kant is not satisfied merely to sketch the outlines of the ideal political realm that follows from a priori ethical principles; instead, he struggles in several works to provide an account of how humankind might progress toward the ideals that, Kant argues, all of us share by virtue of our nature as limited rational beings. A mere image of the perfect state, however ideal, can make no claims on actual human beings in the empirical, historical world without some sort of fundamental connection to them.

"Publicity," or free and public deliberation on matters of common interest, is the mechanism Kant chooses to connect politics and ethics.[9] Over the course of several decades of work, Kant develops, rejects, and modifies a number of versions of a theory of publicity that would account for progress toward the ideal state without condemning that state to utter lawlessness.[10]

While Kant's concept of the public sphere provides a historical agent of progress toward republican governance, his concept of provisional right provides the standard of justice applicable during the transition. Provisional right exists, Kant argues in the *Rechtslehre*, in the intermediate stage between the absence of civil order (the state of nature) and the advent of the ideal republic (the civil condition).[11] Since all actual societies on earth occupy such an intermediate position, provisional right is the rule that applies to them. Simply put, Kant's notion of provisional right requires that the norms of the ideal republican state be respected so far as possible without violating current civil order: this boils down to acting in such a way that one does not render the eventual realization of the ideal state impossible. Those on the way to the ideal republic find themselves in the provisional state between the perceived realms of freedom and nature, in this case represented by the ideal and actual political states.[12]

Of course, Kant knows very well that ideal republics as described in the *Rechtslehre* (and also in *Perpetual Peace* and elsewhere) do not exist in the world. The transition from the state of nature to the rule of law in the civil condition is for Kant an extremely long one.[13] But travelers on that road do not have to endure a Hobbesian nightmare of lawless insecurity until the dawn of the ideal republic. En route, the rule of provisional right applies.

PROVISIONAL RIGHT IN KANT'S *RECHTSLEHRE*

The *Rechtslehre* as a work in Kant's system has a peculiar status. On the one hand, it is Kant's only formal political work, and thus belongs with Kant's critical philosophy, since it contains primarily a priori arguments. On the other hand, the nature of its political subject matter required Kant to base some of his arguments on matters of fact rather than pure a priori reasoning.[14] Although the claims about justice and virtue put forth in the *Rechtslehre* are intended to have a priori status, the necessarily particular nature of political life precluded Kant from achieving a genuinely universal theory of right. Instead, some very general claims (such as the claim that private property is possible) would be given the status of practical postulates—things which cannot be known with absolute certainty, but which are conditionally true. Other, more empirical arguments would be, Kant said, "relegated to the remarks," which, over the course of the *Rechtslehre,* come to dominate the argument.

Principles and Examples

Kant struggles with the status of his inquiry throughout the text, constructing an only partly successful firewall, as it were, between particular facts and universal reasons. He begins with an announcement that a priori arguments will be printed in the main text, while examples, made necessary by the particular subject matter, will be left in the "remarks."[15] This distinction is largely given up by the end of the *Rechtslehre.*[16] However, at a number of relevant points in his argument, Kant fairly successfully defends a general distinction between arguments based on facts and those based on reason. For example, his early contrast between ordinary jurisprudence and the doctrine of right (the former being the science of what is in fact laid down as right by existing jurists, while the latter is the sum of claims about external freedom that can be defended on the basis of the moral law and its corollaries) makes sense, and it is maintained consistently throughout the work.[17]

More important, Kant is never willing to ground an argument for an element of the formal doctrine of right on empirical fact, even though this refusal makes it quite difficult for him to argue for some points of social contract theory that his less idealistic predecessors defended with ease. Hobbes could base the need for the exit from the state of nature on a couple of empirical claims about rational self-interest; Locke defended his right to property upon an interpretation of God's will for his creatures. To make very similar claims, Kant builds a general argument on precepts from his moral theory, such as the inviolability of human autonomy and the definition of agency. Even so, he is forced to include at least one fact in his case, the empirical condition that human agents must interact with one another, given the limited surface of the world, the "spherical shape of the place they live in, a *globus terraqueus*."[18]

By the time Kant wrote his response to an early review by Friedrich Bouterwek, he had honed this distinction down to a manageable simplicity: the doctrine of right contains only universal, a priori rules, but such rules may set necessary conditions for matters of fact. Explaining a complaint by Bouterwek, Kant writes, "But what seems to shock the reviewer's reason is not only this principle [that existing authority must be obeyed], which makes an actual deed (taking control) the condition and the basis for a right, but also that the *mere idea* of sovereignty over a people constrains me, as belonging to that people, to obey."[19] For reasons given below, Kant argues that reason alone provisionally justifies the coercive power of any state that can keep public order. Roughly speaking, Kant deduces this principle from a priori rights of individuals to constrain one another to respect property. To act in obedience to this principle requires an agent to make an empirical observation about which authority is actually maintaining order; the results of this investigation are also empirically conditioned, in that whoever is currently in power rules on the basis of some original historical event during which power was acquired. Thus an "actual deed (taking control)" determines which authority is to be obeyed in a particular case. But the empirical fact only allows an agent to construct a maxim for practical use in the real world; the principle on which the maxim is based remains universal, regardless of accidents of time or place. Thus, while Kant experiences some difficulty maintaining the strict division between empirically grounded conjectures and universal principles he envisioned at the outset of the work, he nevertheless manages to produce a coherent and consistent account of the relationship between the two types of inquiry about political life. Kant's concept of provisional right deals with exactly this problem of applying universal principles based on ideals of justice to a world that will never achieve them. This is why the concept of provisional right is Kant's attempt in the realm of law to achieve a connection, in Habermas's words, between facts and norms, analogous to the public sphere in politics or teleology in human history.

Strict Right

Kant makes a similarly important and difficult distinction in the *Rechtslehre* between external and internal freedom, expressed most frequently as the difference between right (*Recht*) and virtue (*Tugend*). "Strict right" for Kant is devoid of any moral considerations; justice, in other words, has only to do with external relations, never with motives. Questions of *Recht* have to do with concrete, empirically observable actions by an agent that affect at least one other agent.

> The concept of right, insofar as it is related to an obligation corresponding to it (i.e. the moral concept of right), has to do, first, only with the external and indeed practical relation of one person to another, insofar as their actions, as deeds, can have (direct or indirect) influence on each other . . . in this reciprocal relation of choice no account at all is taken of the matter of choice, that is, of the end each has in mind with the object he wants; it is not asked, for example, whether someone who buys goods from me for his own commercial use will gain by the transaction or not. All that is in question is the form . . . and whether the action of one can be united with the freedom of the other in accordance with a universal law.[20]

If the theory of right excludes moral considerations by definition, then what can Kant mean by a "moral concept of right"? After all, Kant defines strict (that is, narrowly construed) right as "that which is not mingled with anything ethical."[21] These apparently contradictory statements rest on Kant's insistence that there is a difference between the general justification of a principle and the particular incentive that should motivate moral reasoners to adhere to it. Kant scholars call this the *Triebfeder* problem, or the problem of moral motivation (a *Triebfeder* is literally the driving spring inside an old-fashioned watch; figuratively it means "motivating force"). If, as Kant argues, no material incentives are acceptable for morally worthy action, and if, as Kant also argues, human beings require incentives to moral action (divine beings, on the other hand, would automatically follow the moral law), then how is morally worthy action possible at all? Kant answers this question by claiming that respect for the moral law in general provides a sufficient incentive for human beings to follow it. For example, in *Critique of Practical Reason* Kant writes that "the incentives of the human will (and of the will of every created rational being) can never be anything other than the moral law." Regarding legal, as opposed to moral, action, however, Kant argues that material incentives, such as the threat of punishment, are the appropriate motivation for human actions.[22]

One can distinguish, then, between Kant's two spheres of legal right (*Recht*) and virtue (*Tugend*) on the basis of incentives alone: legality cannot require moral incentives, though these may be present incidentally. Only external incentives, such as the threat of sanction, count as *rechtlich* motivation. Legal right has to do with external, empirically observable (and thus adjudicable) actions between persons, while virtue applies to internal, morally motivated choices for which no external sanction is possible. Kant uses the example of a creditor pressing his debtor for repayment: "Thus when it is said that a creditor has a right to require his debtor to pay his debt, this does not mean that he can remind the debtor that his reason itself puts him under obligation to perform this; it means, instead, that coercion which constrains everyone to pay his debts can coexist with the freedom of everyone, including that of debtors, in accordance with a universal external law."[23] The "moral" in the "moral concept of right," then, has to do not with agents' particular motivations but with the general justification of the standards governing their interactions.

For example, as interacting moral agents we have a general duty to promote justice. Another way to put this is that each limited rational being who may come into contact with another limited rational being (that is, all of us) ought to uphold the rule of law. This duty to enter and support civil society is a standard point of departure for social contract theory.[24] Hobbes, for example, draws the same conclusion, but he justifies it according to the rational self-interest each person has in seeking peace with his neighbors. Unlike Hobbes, however, Kant distinguishes between the *principium diiudicationis* and the *principium executionis:* in other words, between the general principle and the particular incentive to follow it ("a principle of moral obligation or discrimination and a principle of performance or execution").[25] From the point of view of the *Triebfeder,* Kant and Hobbes are not far apart on the duty to uphold the rule of law. In each case, material incentives provided by the state, such as the threat of punishment or the lure of honors, ensure that the legal system functions. From the point of view of the general justification of the rule of law itself, however, the two social contract theorists part ways. To be sure, Hobbes provides different sets of incentives to individuals outside and inside the state; natural law and its recommendation to seek peace are supplanted in civil society by positive law and its threat of punishment. But both sets of incentives are material, and neither would count as moral for Kant. Though Kant provides material legal incentives to uphold the rule of law in particular instances, he also grounds a general moral duty to promote justice in an application of the categorical imperative (in its formulation as a universality test)[26] to the realm of external actions: "Any action is right if it can coexist with everyone's freedom in accordance with a universal law, or if on its maxim the freedom of choice of each can coexist with everyone's freedom in accordance with a universal law."[27] Thus, while from within the sphere of legal justice (what Kant calls "strict right") only material, nonmoral incentives are appropriate, both the justification of the rule of law itself and the individual duty to uphold the civic order are part of the moral sphere and subject to the strictures of morality, such as nonmaterial incentives and the universality test.

Fortunately, Kant did not require his readers to struggle with the difficult distinction between *Triebfeder* and general principles of moral obligation in order to identify questions of legal right versus those of moral virtue. In addition to the rule dividing the two realms between internal and external actions and motives, Kant provided a third standard. In cases of legal right, it is always possible for a judge to render a just decision. By contrast, in those cases mixed with moral virtue or other nonlegal elements, no definite judgment may be pronounced.[28]

Kant illustrates the use of this standard in his discussion of "ambiguous [*zweideutigen*] right."[29] In cases of ambiguous right, the situation seems to require that morality be brought to bear; properly viewed, however, these cases have solutions from the realm of strict (legal) right. In strict right, only the formal, legal relations among people are considered; consequences, general objects, or other ethical considerations, even if universally agreed upon as morally desirable, are not valid in cases of legal right. The problem with all cases of ambiguous right is that no judge on earth may decide such a case justly. The reader is reminded that the most important thing about the rule of law is that under it all disputes ought to be able to be resolved without reverting to the state of nature (that is, to violence).

For example, Kant's second example of ambiguous right, the supposed "right of necessity," has to do with a case in which no juridical incentive could possibly motivate the actor in question: a shipwrecked sailor pushes someone else off a floating board in order to save himself. Kant agrees that no law could effectively prevent such action. The material legal incentives that enforce the law, such as the threat of punishment, are outweighed by the immediate danger of drowning. But he denies that the action is therefore just: "The deed of savings one's life by violence is not to be judged *inculpable (inculpabile)* but only *unpunishable (impunibile)*."[30] Mere empirical necessity cannot trump the "universal principle of right," which requires external legal rights to be universalizable (that is, consistent with the freedom of everyone).

More interesting for the purposes of my argument is Kant's first example of ambiguous right, the "right of equity." Cases of equity are those in which everyone would recognize that a situation is unfair, but in which no law or contract has been broken. Kant's example is of a servant whose annual wages are paid in a currency that has lost value over the year. Legal right, Kant argues, has nothing to do with the matter of a dispute, only with its form; the lost value is a question of empirical, material outcome, while the formal letter of the contract was upheld.[31] Moreover, he argues, no civil judge of equity can be found. He writes: "But this ill cannot be remedied by way of what is laid down as right, even though it concerns a claim to a right; for this claim belongs only to the *court of conscience* [*Gewissensgericht*] (*forum poli*) whereas every question of what is laid down as right must be brought before *civil right* [*bürgerliche Recht*] (*forum soli*)."[32] Here is another example of Kant's extremely careful distinction making between strict, or legal, right, which excludes general moral or material elements from consideration, and the common concept of right more generally, which does include moral and material elements. (In the case of ambiguous right, Kant calls this second category "ius latium," in contrast with strict right.) Kant is not excluding moral considerations from political life in general (hardly), only from the adjudication of the strictly legal rights enforced by the sovereign. As he indicates in this aside to his discussion of ambiguous right, there is another forum for bringing ethical questions about political life: the court of conscience, or public opinion.

Provisional Acquisition

Kant's concept of provisional right is rooted in his account of "provisional acquisition" in the *Rechtslehre,* concerning private rights.[33] As does Locke, Kant begins with basic property rights, establishing the civil state and its prerogatives on this ground. Unlike Locke, however, Kant insists that there can be no rights to things as such; rights for Kant are strictly a kind of relation among persons. Kant makes light of the view that rights inhere in things rather than between persons:

> Someone who thinks that his right is a direct relation to things rather than to persons would have to think (though only obscurely) that since there corresponds to a right on one side a duty on the other, an external thing always remains under obligation to the first possessor even though it has left his hands. . . . So he would think of my right as if it were a guardian spirit accompanying the thing, always pointing me out to whoever else wanted to take possession of it and protecting it against any incursions by them. It is therefore absurd to think of an obligation of a person to things or the reverse, even though it may be permissible,

if need be, to make this rightful relation perceptible by picturing it and expressing it in this way.

And also: "Speaking strictly and literally, there is . . . no (direct) right to a thing."[34]

Thus, what looks to Locke like a right to a thing with which one has mixed one's labor looks to Kant like a state of affairs in which each has the obligation to respect all his fellows' rights to use what is theirs unmolested. Of course, this leaves Kant in a worse position than Locke with regard to accounting for the origin of private property. With Rousseau, Kant assumes that the world belongs originally to all in common. From his deduction, he claims to establish the possibility of "merely rightful" ownership (that is, possession not dependent upon the owner's physical hold on the object). Finally, he distinguishes between property acquired originally (previously owned by no one else) and property acquired by contracting with other persons. Although Kant maintains his position that property rights are relations among persons, not things, he brings an element of Locke's solution to the problem of original appropriation by including the "capacity to use" the object as one of the three requirements for just original acquisition.[35] These rights of persons against each other are one practical application of the "universal principle of right: "Any action is right if it can coexist with everyone's freedom in accordance with a universal law, or if on its maxim the freedom of choice of each can coexist with everyone's freedom in accordance with a universal law."[36] Kant claims to have deduced property rights from this principle, as I shall discuss later in this chapter. What matters for now is that Kantian property rights are, first, based on relations between persons rather than between persons and things and, second, divided between provisional and conclusive rights.

As he also does later, in the section on public right, Kant distinguishes here between provisional and conclusive rights. "*Conclusive* acquisition takes place only in the civil condition," whereas provisional acquisition takes place "under the idea" of civil right (though not the reality of it). Kant's distinction between provisional and conclusive acquisition is not the same as his distinction between empirical and rational (intelligible) title to an object, though they are related to each other. Having empirical title to an object means having physical possession of it. Only with a rational title to an object does it remain mine even without my physically holding it (for example, my house remains mine when I am not at home). Gregor conflates empirical and provisional possession in her introduction to *The Meta-*

physics of Morals. She writes that for Kant "simple physical (empirical or phenomenal)" possession "can exist in a Hobbesian state of nature, but only provisionally, that is, only as long as one has the physical power to repel all claimants."[37] Provisional possession for Kant is indeed possession in the absence of a rightful civil condition, but rather than merely physical possession, it refers to ownership "under the idea" of rightful (intelligible) ownership. All existing civil societies fall into this category: their people are not in a state of nature, but they do not enjoy a just legal system as sketched in Kant's image of the ideal republic. Thus property rights in these intermediate societies, which include all real ones, are always both provisional and rational, since they do not depend on physical possession of an object.[38] These distinctions follow the ground-breaking distinction from *Critique of Pure Reason* between the perspectives of the noumenal and phenomenal realms:

> I call acquisition *ideal* if it involves no causality in time and is therefore based on a mere idea of pure reason. It is nonetheless *true,* not imaginary, acquisition, and the only reason I do not call it real is that the act of acquiring is not empirical . . . [all types of ideal acquisitions] can, indeed, take effect only in a public rightful condition, but they are not *based* only on its constitution and the chosen [*willkürlichen,* better: "arbitrary" or "particular"; in other words, promulgated] statutes in it; they [ideal acquisitions] are also conceivable a priori in the state of nature and must be conceived as prior to such statutes, in order that the laws in the civil condition may afterwards be adopted to them.

Kant thus needs to prove that merely rightful possession, that is, possession that does not depend on empirical considerations, is possible in order to proceed toward justifying the coercive power of the state.[39] He will argue that since rightful possession of external objects is possible, and since such a right on the part of one person implies complementary restrictions on the rights of every other person, the concept of *possessio noumenon* leads directly to the necessity of legal justice administered by a central authority.

In the *Rechtslehre,* Kant is attempting to ground a system of legal rights on irrefutable rational principles. In other, less formal, political works, Kant is willing to make arguments on an empirical basis, citing either past experience or likely outcomes in support of elements of his political doctrine. For example, in *The Conflict of Faculties* he affirms that the current government of Great Britain, outward appearances notwithstanding, is in fact an absolutist regime; this case is cited in support of Kant's argument that transparency is essential to legitimate government.[40] In the *Rechtslehre,* however, Kant will attempt to base his arguments on conclusions drawn from a few rationally defended premises, such as the moral necessity of freedom and the "fact of reason," which Henry Allison nicely glosses as "our common consciousness of the moral law as supremely authoritative."[41]

Evident from the outset is the tension between Kant's philosophical commitment to formal principles (that is, to the exclusion of empirical examples, which are necessarily particular, and thus weaker grounds for legitimation) and his need to refer to the historical world of politics in a work of political philosophy. In the preface to *The Metaphysics of Morals,* Kant explains his choice of title: the first part of the book is called "Metaphysical First Principles of the Doctrine of Right," not simply "Metaphysics of Right," because it aims to construct a system of rational principles of right but must "look to practice" for the application of any such principles. Since legal right, though it is based on a priori principles, applies only to experience, and since "what is empirical cannot be divided completely," the first part of *The Metaphysics of Morals* is incomplete by the usual standards of Kantian philosophy. As I have mentioned already, Kant clearly intended to maintain a strict separation between the a priori and the empirical elements of the work. In the preface, he writes that "that right which belongs to the system outlined a priori will go in the text, while rights taken from particular cases of experience will be put into remarks, which will sometimes be extensive."[42] Such a plan would have been consistent with Kant's repeated position on the use of examples in philosophical argument, namely, that they muddy the otherwise clear waters of formal reasoning but are sometimes needed to enlighten the obtuse. However, the separation of merely rational elements from empirical elements in the *Rechtslehre* cannot be maintained even through the first section on private right, and it is completely given up by the second half.

The two tasks confronting Kant as he wrote were not completely compatible: the *Rechtslehre* was to be both a work of political philosophy and a work that holds a place in the system of Kantian metaphysics. The *Rechtslehre* belongs on a shelf with the other classics of social contract theory— *Leviathan, Two Treatises of Government, On the Social Contract*—and with the commentators on law and natural right whose works Kant used as university textbooks, including those of Grotius and Achenwall. However, the *Rechtslehre* is also one of a series of works expounding Kant's critical philosophy in as systematic a manner as possible. Straightforward deductions from principles based on the categorical imperative might not have yielded positions on a number of topics that such a work of political philosophy would be expected to address. In the end, not only the conclusions but even the structure of the *Rechtslehre* seem much more influenced by Kant's predecessors in social contract theory than by his metaphysical presuppositions. Kant's ethical premises could have led to any number of alternative doctrines of political right—and, in fact, they have done so, in the form of modern-day applications of Kant's ethics to questions of contemporary political relevance.[43] The fact that Kant used these ethical premises to ground a particularly modern version of social contract theory has more to do with Kant's commitment to political enlightenment in general than with any natural tendency of transcendental idealism toward a particular form of ideal government. Indeed, if Kantian philosophy were more compatible with Kantian contract theory, the reader would have been spared a number of tortuous efforts to outfit the foregone conclusions of a moderate republican political theorist with appropriately a priori premises. The *Rechtslehre* as he wrote it is a social contract theory like those of his predecessors, but with a number of "Kantian twists" courtesy of his critical philosophy. His more interesting, original, and substantial contributions came not from his static theory of political right but from his dynamic accounts of the public sphere, revolution, federalism, and regime change.

Kant's deduction, in the *Rechtslehre,* of the possibility of external property rights is perhaps his least successful deduction. Even before the reasoning of the deduction itself could be examined by the reading public, the text was sprinkled with errors probably derived from misunderstandings between Kant and his copyist.[44] Kant did not review the published text to ensure that the argument proceeded in the order that he had intended; later scholarship has established fairly securely that most of what, in most texts, immediately follows the first paragraph of the deduction does not belong there.[45] Even so, scholars who have analyzed the reconstructed deduction are nearly unanimous in their disapproval of Kant's reasoning.[46]

Kant would not attempt to make a theoretical deduction of the possibility of property, as he did of the possibility of synthetic a priori knowledge in *Critique of Pure Reason.*[47] Instead, he took his cue from *Critique of Practical Reason* and provided a "practical" deduction of "the concept of merely rightful [that is, not simply empirical] possession of an external object (*possessio noumenon*)." Kant's practical deduction proceeds "by subtraction," that is, Kant removes in thought all empirical elements of the concept of possession, leaving only the abstract, generalizable concept of intelligible possession of any external object. What such a deduction aims to do is establish a postulate (in this case: "It is possible for me to have any external object of my choice as mine"), which itself is derived from the concept at hand (in this case, the concept of intelligible possession of an external object).[48] This is not to say that the postulate to be established is related analytically to the original concept; if it were, there would be no need of a deduction to ground its validity. But the original definitions, of possessing an external object and of intelligible (merely rightful) possession as opposed to simple physical possession, are marshaled, along with the postulate to prove its possibility, as follows:[49]

1. Postulate: It is possible legitimately to possess an external object of my choice.
2. If it were not possible to possess an external object of my choice, then the rightful maxim regarding property would be: external objects of choice can belong to no one.
3. But since intelligible possession of external objects of choice has to do only with formal, rational principles, one must abstract from every aspect of the object except that it is an external object of choice.
4. Thus in the object itself there can be no prohibition against its use.
5. #2 contradicts #4: there can be no prohibition against use of an object of choice.
6. Therefore, it must be possible to possess an external object of my choice rightly.

The first thing to be said about this deduction is that even if it were valid, it would not provide the ground for entry into civil society that Kant wants it to. Kant must prove that private property must be possible, since he will argue that the need to appropriate objects, combined with the necessity of interaction with others who also need to appropriate objects, leads ineluctably to the obligation to unite via a social contract.[50] Rather than proving that private property is rationally necessary, Kant's deduction would establish only that having a thing for one's use is not necessarily contrary to everyone else's rights. (Though Locke's legitimation of private property in the *Second Treatise* is on far less universalistic and rational grounds, as he bases his account on a claim about God's will for his creatures, it does have the advantage over Kant of doing what it sets out to do.) Having something external for one's use need not occur in a classic, natural rights-style private property regime.[51]

Second, the deduction is not valid, by Kant's own standards. #2 is not a contradiction of the postulate to be proven but is only a contrary statement.

In other words, it is possible for both the postulate (#1) and its contrary (#2) to be false. For example, external objects of choice could be used by people as allowed by a central absolute authority, who retained all rightful possession of objects. In this case, the objects would not belong to no one (they would belong to the authority), but people could use them as allowed. If a supporter of Kant were to object to this example that by definition an external object of choice implies that the chooser of the object must also be the owner of it, then I would reply that under such a definition of "external object of choice" (*äußern Gegenstand meiner Willkür*), the outcome of the deduction is presumed (in other words, Kant would be guilty of circularity).

Kant's assimilation of the disparate methods of traditional social contract theory and Kantian critical philosophy is more successful in the next section, where he applies the results of his deduction (the "proof" of the possibility of private property) to experience. Here Kant improves upon his predecessors by demonstrating that property rights are relations among willing subjects, essentially agreements to refrain from interfering with things rightfully possessed by others. Whereas in the last section Kant attempted a deduction of a postulate, here he resolves an antinomy in the manner familiar from the first *Critique:* he distinguishes between the two standpoints of intelligibility and empiricism. As Robert Paul Wolff argues, Kant's argument for property must come down to a conclusion drawn from the fact of a human being's physical nature. Since we must appropriate objects, and since the way in which we must appropriate objects necessarily excludes others from appropriating those same objects, for beings like us some form of private property must be necessary.[52] Of course, Kant could not have made such an argument explicitly, at least not in the text (as opposed to the "remarks") of the *Rechtslehre,* since no a priori postulate may be based on anthropological fact. Nonetheless, Kant's arguments on the basis of more "noumenal" qualities, such as the end-directedness of rational agents (it is this end-directedness that grounds the necessity for me to have objects "of my choice," clearer in the German *Gegenstand meiner Willkür*), come down to the same thing.

From Provisional Acquisition to Provisional Right: The Social Contract

Kant's view, set out in the *Rechtslehre,* of the relationship between the state of nature and the civil condition is obscure because he makes two different arguments simultaneously. In the first place, Kant argues for the requirement to exit the state of nature based solely on the need for a common judge of the right (as Locke would put it). In the second place, however, Kant argues for a transition not merely to an orderly state but to republican governance, including not only common authority but also respect for human rights.

In the first case, the difference between the state of nature and the civil condition is that the civil condition includes a judge to adjudicate disputes among citizens. For Kant the duty to enter this civil condition is an a priori duty, and it would apply even to those who are in fact doing no injustice to each other.[53] No matter how peaceful interactions actually are, no formal procedure exists in the state of nature for adjudicating disputes.[54] Even if all members of a community do what seems to them to be right and just, without legitimate autonomy they remain outside the civil condition, and thus only the arbitrary methods of personal persuasion or actual violence exist to settle disagreements. Entering the civil condition, then, means giving up one's personal right to judge any case of interaction among agents. (Kant insists, as is well known, that in all cases one retains one's right to judge all matters internal to oneself, such as matters of conscience.) In this first story, it does not seem to matter much whether the judge's authority is arbitrary or not: these problems with the state of nature could be resolved by any central authority with the ability coercively to enforce common judgments, in the manner of Hobbes.[55] Kant, however, offers a second version of the transition to the rule of law.[56] The civil condition described by Kant is no mere police state but a republic. Along with the a priori duty to submit to a common authority in cases of necessary interaction (Kant's rationale for leaving the state of nature) come other a priori aspects of that common authority, such as respect for individual moral autonomy. The second half of the *Rechtslehre* outlines these a priori elements of the ideal republic, which Kant envisions as the destination for those leaving the state of nature.

Two Versions of the Transition from the State of Nature

The two stories of the exit from the state of nature—one account of the duty to submit to some common authority, and one more purely Kantian account of the ideal republic—do not fit together very well. The disjuncture between Kant's two versions of the story makes it very difficult for the reader to determine exactly where the state of nature leaves off and the civil condition begins. In some places Kant seems to be distinguishing between the state of nature as an idea, on the one hand, and the civil condition, on the other, a line of reasoning that successfully justifies the coercive state but does not specify what kind of state it ought to be (this would be the first story). For example, in the first paragraph of section 41, "Transition from What Is Mine or Yours in a State of Nature to What Is Mine or Yours in a Rightful Condition Generally," Kant distinguishes between two types of political condition: countries that have institutions for distributive (in the sense of "promulgated," that is, not merely natural) justice and those that do not. "A court itself is called the *justice* of a country, and whether such a thing exists or does not exist is the most important question that can be asked about any arrangements having to do with rights."[57] Elsewhere, however, Kant seems to increase the number of stages in the transition from the state of nature to the civil condition from two to four, with the first and the last being merely ideal: (1) the pure state of nature, (2) societies with rules but no public law (such as paternal societies),[58] (3) orderly but arbitrary states, which have public law but do not conform to the ideal civil constitution, and (4) the ideal state, which exists only as a norm for all other states (this would be the second story, which differentiates between mere constituted authority and an ideal republic).

Though Kant nowhere explicitly subscribes to a fourfold differentiation of types of state according to the degree of rightfulness each embodies, there is textual evidence supporting this resolution of the problem of the boundaries of the state of nature, public right, and the civil constitution. For example, Kant concludes his reply to Friedrich Bouterwek's review of the *Rechtslehre* with a discussion of the citizen's obligation to obey existing authority despite its arbitrariness. Here he restates his view of the establishment of public right, in a way that supports a reading that allows even actual imperfect states to make a claim to it. No real state can withstand moral scrutiny of its empirical origins, argues Kant, since all states are begun by someone "seizing supreme power and so first establishing public right . . . although no example in experience is *adequate* to be put under this concept [the idea of a civil constitution], still none must contradict it as a norm."[59] Thus, as Kant clarifies the confusing division between states of nature and of public right he makes use of the concept of provisional right—though no empirical state under a perfect civil constitution exists, still the idea of that state holds as a norm for all states of public right.

This reading would argue that public right, as public order, may be guaranteed by any universal coercer, but (importantly for Kant) regardless of the failings of any particular state, the very existence of public right implies respect for the more stringent requirements of the ideal civil constitution. Introducing a series of specifications for a civil constitution, for example, Kant writes: "A *state* (*civitas*) is a union of a multitude of human beings under laws of right. Insofar as these are a priori necessary as laws, that is, insofar as they follow of themselves from concepts of external right as such (are not statutory), its form is the form of a state as such, that is, of *the state in idea,* as it ought to be in accordance with pure principles of right. This idea serves as a norm (*norma*) for every actual union into a commonwealth."[60] It looks as if the reading closest to Kant's text must include two kinds of state under the rule of public right: all actual states with universal coercive apparatuses in place to adjudicate disputes, on the one hand, and the ideal state with its civil constitution guaranteeing not only orderly resolution of conflicts but also republican government, on the other.

Provisional Right

In contrast to Kant's account of public right, his account of provisional right is consistent throughout the text: provisional right applies in the absence of conclusive right (that is, in both the state of nature and the orderly but arbitrary state). Kant's shifts in position in paragraphs 8 and 9 of part 1 (on private right) of the *Rechtslehre* illustrate nicely the difficulty of using a single line of reasoning to establish, on the one hand, the duty to submit to a common authority and, on the other hand, the necessity of a civil constitution going far beyond mere establishment of such an authority. Throughout these shifts, however, Kant maintains that where conclusive rights backed by a legitimate constitution are absent, provisional right prevails.

The chapter heading to paragraph 8 introduces the problem in classic Hobbesian terms: "It is possible to have something external as one's own only in a rightful condition, under an authority giving laws publicly, that is, in a civil condition."[61] Although Kant is interested here more in property rights than in personal safety, the arguments are similar to Hobbes's. Kant has established that ownership of property must be possible (in the deduction preceding these paragraphs); he has also set out the distinction between natural and positive rights, concluding that the only natural right is to one's freedom (in the sense of autonomy: freedom from others making choices for one).[62] In paragraph 8, then, Kant continues the argument with the point that for property and personal autonomy to coexist, no one should have to acknowledge anyone else's property without guarantees that his own property will be acknowledged in exchange. Otherwise, the only existing natural right would be violated, since the individual who acknowledges others' property will have to rely on the others' presumed good will for the security of his own property (and will thus enter a condition of heteronomy).[63] Furthermore, Kant argues, only a "collective general (common) and powerful will" can provide the guarantees necessary for this property rights regime to exist, since a "unilateral will" (any will less than general) cannot command anyone's obedience without infringing on autonomy.[64] Kant concludes, as would be expected from Hobbes's similar conclusion following similar argumentation, that entry into a common civil constitution is mandatory for persons who might interact with each other and thus expect to enjoy respect for each person's property.[65] In other words, if property rights are necessary, and if these rights are only possible in a civil condition, then entry into the civil condition is necessary.

If Kant's "collective general will" means nothing more than Hobbes's, that is, if Kant would accept universality and equality of coercion as the only conditions needed to separate legitimate from illegitimate authority, then his two accounts of the entry into the civil condition should be easy to reconcile. Even as he disagrees with Hobbes about the source of the need for a central authority (Hobbes cites distressing facts of human psychology, while Kant relies on a priori arguments), Kant could conceivably agree with Hobbes about what kinds of authority are legitimate. The answer to this point of interpretation depends upon what Kant means by "civil constitution" and "collective general will." He gives the reader some hints on this question in the next paragraph.

In the subject heading to paragraph 9, Kant seems to retreat from his previous claim that property rights are only possible in the civil condition: "In a state of nature something external can actually be mine or yours but only *provisionally.*" Without this last clause, Kant would have had to retreat not only from his categorical statement about the necessity of a civil condition for property rights but also from the conclusion he drew from it; namely, that we are obliged to enter into the civil condition. Such a move would delegitimize the coercive power of the state, and Kant does not make it. Instead, he introduces the concept of provisional right: "Possession in anticipation of and preparation for the civil condition, which can be based only on a law of common will, possession which therefore accords with the *possibility* of such a condition, is *provisionally rightful* possession, whereas possession found in an *actual* civil condition would be *conclusive* possession." And further: "In summary, the way to have something external as one's own *in a state of nature* is physical possession which has in its favor the rightful *presumption* that it will be made into rightful possession through being united with the will of all in a public lawgiving, and in anticipation of this holds *comparatively* as rightful possession."[66]

Why would Kant introduce such a concept here? The notion of a provisional right seems to fly in the face of such Kantian precepts as procedural justice as the cure for the arbitrary rule of empirical happenstance. Why not follow Hobbes in his view that the state's universal coercion makes property rights possible in the first place? The answer is that Kant could not follow Hobbes's view because he could not accept a Hobbesian state, with its arbitrary if universal rule, as the alternative to the state of nature. Mere provision of order, mere enforcement of reciprocal rights, without respect for the natural right of autonomy, could not satisfy Kant's conditions for entry into the civil condition. Had Kant been willing merely to justify the coercive power of the state, he could have stopped at paragraph 8, with its account of the duty to submit to a common authority for the reciprocal protection of everyone's property. (Such an account would have been compatible with the neo-Hobbesian account of the exit from the state of nature that Kant gives in the first part of section 41.) To raise the civil condition beyond mere universal coercion, however, Kant has to identify a third condition between the "pure" state of nature and the rule of law: the orderly but arbitrary state, which has systems of rights but no promulgated respect for a priori law. In the neo-Hobbesian account, such a state would be outside the state of nature. For Kant, however, the state of nature includes both the orderly but arbitrary state and conditions without any common rules. Both situations lack justice, but in each case provisional right is possible (and with this claim, of course, Kant departs definitively from Hobbes). In Kant's final account, possession ought to be respected if it promotes the possibility of eventual rightful (*rechtlich*) possession under a just civil authority.

Final Version of the Transition from the State of Nature

Confused though Kant's divisions between the state of nature and the civil condition may be, he gains a number of advantages for his theory over the simpler Hobbesian distinctions. In the first place, Hobbes's theory of the "right to everything" in the state of nature forces him to argue that even the killing of a person who has done no injury is permitted, so long as the killer has some reason for believing that his own life will be made more secure by the other's death.[67] Hobbes (famously) cannot account for the fact that interactions rarely occur in a social vacuum, from which it follows that the reputation one acquires in social life renders a potential killer's calculations of his interest uncertain. In a Kantian orderly but arbitrary state, on the other hand, attention to the future consequences of one's actions is built into the prevailing standard, which is the principle of provisional right. Kant applies this principle, for example, on the international level, to sovereign states that find themselves in a state of nature with regard to one another. Even in the international state of nature, Kant argues, wars of extermination or subjugation cannot be permitted, no matter how the aggressor state calculates its interests. Kant admits that each state is permitted to "preserve what belongs to it," but he adds that this right cannot justify "one state's increase of power [that] could threaten others." While in the short run such action may seem to serve the interests of the aggressor state, in the long run the state's sullied reputation and excessive projection of power will cause other states to refuse to cooperate with it. In short, pursuit of a war of extermination, analogous at the individual level with killing a nonaggressor, violates the principle that all reasonable actors in a state of nature must follow: act such that you promote the possibility of entering a rightful condition.[68]

Second, Kant's account of provisional property rights avoids the Rousseauian specter of a wholesale redistribution of property at the advent of the republican state. As I have already mentioned, Kant was consistently in favor of gradual transitions as opposed to radical revolutionary change: "A public can only achieve enlightenment slowly."[69] Under a simple distinction between a state of nature and an orderly, property-guaranteeing regime, no property rights are worthy of respect outside the rule of the just state. Given Kant's implied point that all actually existing states do not provide any genuine "civil condition" but in fact belong in the category of a late stage of the state of nature, a theory respecting only the conclusive property rights of the just state would encourage radicals to hope for redistribution of property under a new regime. Instead, Kant insists that while property in the state of nature cannot be conclusively owned—since no universally agreed contract to respect it exists—nevertheless de facto property rights must be respected insofar as they are consistent with the eventual advent of the civil condition.[70] Rousseau praises Lycurgus's redistribution of property possessed before the founding of Sparta's new institutions. "Despite all the labors of the wisest legislators, the political state always remained imperfect, because it was practically the work of chance . . . they should have begun by clearing the air and putting aside all the old materials, as Lycurgus did in Sparta."[71] Kant, on the other hand, would have property that was possessed provisionally under the old regime be respected under the new laws. In fact, Kant complains about the failure of the French revolutionaries to respect the continuity of property rights.[72]

In addition to the continuity of property rights, moreover, provisional rights in general head off the argument that in the absence of the just state anything is permitted. Instead, acts of possession and all other interactions are to be judged according to whether they permit the possibility of an eventual republican regime. Kant pursues a similar argument with regard to provisional right in the international arena. National states with no means of adjudication among themselves are obligated to leave this state of nature (which is a state of war) and to enter a civil union (or state of peace). Yet, Kant argues, a perfect international union, complete with universal coercion, is not possible, for reasons he discusses in the *Rechtslehre*, such as the unwieldiness of any global union. The right that prevails among states is thus always provisional, never conclusive. Perpetual peace is an impossible goal, but it is also an obligatory one: states must act on principles that "always leave open the possibility of leaving the state of nature among states (in external relation to one another) and entering into a rightful condition."[73] Kant's argument here is slightly different from the one he makes on the same topic in *Perpetual Peace*. The formulation of the impossible but obligatory goal is confusing, since of course an individual cannot be obligated to do what is out of his or her power. Nevertheless, moral reason sets the pursuit of political ideals as a goal for individuals, while providing maxims that take into account the fact that these goals may only be approximated, never fully achieved. Kant concludes: "So the question is never whether perpetual peace is something real or a fiction . . . we must act as if it is something real, though perhaps it is not; we must work toward establishing perpetual peace and the kind of constitution that seems to us most conducive to it (say, a republicanism of all states, together and separately)."[74]

Though there is no wholly authoritative source of adjudication in the (broad) state of nature, there is a standard of judgment: that of provisional right. For example, in defending his famous view that active resistance to existing authority is never permitted, Kant takes for granted both the ideal nature of civil society and the provisional nature of actually existing states: "The *idea* of a civil constitution as such, which is also an absolute command that practical reason, judging according to concepts of right, gives to every people, is *sacred* and irresistible. And even if the organization of a state should be faulty by itself, no subordinate authority in it may actively resist its legislative supreme authority."[75] Until a perfect state exists, "faulty" states will be the norm. In such cases, which include all cases, right applies provisionally.

Solving the Problem of Who Is Party to the Contract

Recognizing the importance of the concept of provisional right allows a resolution of previously difficult problems in understanding Kant's political theory. For example, Kant seems to commit himself to the sophisticated contractarian view—shared by Hobbes, Locke, and Rousseau—that the original contract is made among the people themselves: it is the act by which a people constitutes itself as a civil society. In some sophisticated contractarian accounts (for example, that of Hobbes), a separate sovereign does rule over the people; he has obligations, but not from the original contract. In Locke's case, the sophisticated social contract is even more apparent, as the people first contract among themselves to form a society, and only after that do they arrange for the presence of a universal coercer to adjudicate disputes. Less sophisticated theorists imagine a contract between a people and a separate sovereign, whose rule is justified so long as he abides by the "contract" which is supposed to guarantee that the people's interests are served. The problem for readers of the *Rechtslehre* is that by the end of the book, as he discusses more concrete, less formal aspects of his political theory, Kant writes as if he subscribes to the less sophisticated view that there is an original contract between the people and the sovereign.[76] In places Kant reminds the reader that the people and the sovereign are one, and that the everyday business of governance is done by another party, the "ruler." For example: "Even if the organ of the sovereign, the *ruler,* proceeds contrary to law, for example, if he goes against the law of equality in assigning the burdens of the state in matters of taxation, recruiting, and so forth, subjects may indeed oppose this injustice by complaints . . . but not by resistance."[77] In discussions of the duty to obey existing authority, Kant is very clear that the social contract is among the people, not between the people and the sovereign.[78] Elsewhere, however, he writes about the various roles of the sovereign without differentiating between sovereignty and rulership. Kant provides such details, for example, as the determination that the "sovereign" has the right of inspection of associations but not of private residences.[79]

Given that Kant explicitly distinguishes between the two political entities, and that he has committed himself to the sophisticated view of the original contract, such apparent lapses seem to present a problem for the reader. If, however, one keeps in mind that Kant is discussing both the structure of the ideal republican state and the vagaries of already existing provisional states, this problem disappears. When the ideal state is at issue, Kant consistently holds the sophisticated contractarian view: the people and the sovereign are one, and the original contract unites the people. On the other hand, in discussing provisional right in actually existing states, Kant admits that the sovereign usually rules over, not for, the people. In these cases, which include all real polities, the original contract is only an ideal, and thus the maxim for rulers is merely to behave such that the possibility of the ideal republic based on an original contract is not excluded.

APPLICATIONS OF PROVISIONAL RIGHT: RIGHT OF NATIONS

The most straightforward application of the concept of provisional right in Kant's *Rechtslehre* is to the "right of nations" (Kant uses the traditional term, though he notes that "right of states" would be a more accurate phrase).[80] The arguments for a Kantian doctrine of rights among states proceed primarily by analogy to those among persons, except that Kant claims that a just world government is impossible (while ideal republican states are in principle possible, though empirically absent). Just as Kant has argued regarding individuals in the previous chapter, national states with no means of adjudication among themselves are obligated to leave the state of nature (which is a state of war) and to enter a civil union (or state of peace). But since, argues Kant, a perfect international union, complete with universal coercion, is not possible (for reasons I discuss below), the right that prevails among states is always provisional, never conclusive. In the *Rechtslehre*, though not in *Perpetual Peace*, perpetual peace is an impossible goal, but also an obligatory one: states must act on principles that "always leave open the possibility of leaving the state of nature among states (in external relation to one another) and entering into a rightful condition."[81]

Kant is widely recognized as an important contributor to the theory of liberalism in international relations. As the concept of provisional right is essential to Kant's explanation of international rights in both the *Rechtslehre* and *Perpetual Peace*, one might be surprised at the almost total lack of coverage of the concept in the relevant literature. In the case of international relations, however, the omission is more understandable than in other areas of inquiry. After all, Kant's more important work on the right of nations, *Perpetual Peace*, was published two years before Kant had written anything explicitly concerning the concept of provisional right (see chapter 3).[82]

The most serious difference between the theories of international right in the two works is that *Perpetual Peace* envisions an eventual advent of world peace under the voluntary union of republican governments, while the *Rechtslehre* argues that such an outcome, while desirable, is impossible: "*Perpetual peace*, the ultimate goal of the whole right of nations, is indeed an unachievable idea. Still, the political principles directed toward perpetual peace, of entering into such alliances of states, which serve for continual *approximation* to it, are not unachievable."[83] The argument of the *Rechtslehre* runs as follows:

In a state of nature among nations, in which no judge of the right is available, all states, even those subscribing to republican principles, will have to resort to the arbitrary makeshifts of persuasion or war in cases of dispute: "In a state of nature among states, the right to go to war . . . is the way in which a state is permitted to prosecute its right against another state, namely by its own force, when it believes it has been wronged by the other state; for this cannot be done in the state of nature by a lawsuit (the only means by which disputes are settled in a rightful condition)."[84] However, as with Kant's complex account of the state of nature among individuals, the state of nature among nations is not without at least provisional rules. Kant in fact lists a number of rules for permissible warfare in the state of nature among nations, such as the stipulation that the war must be in the interest of the people of the country, not just in the interest of the ruler, and that the use of assassins and snipers violates the right of war.[85]

Kant recognizes that it is hard even to conceive of right during war, and he provides a maxim for right in the state of war: states ought to act on principles that "always leave open the possibility of leaving the state of nature among states (in external relation to one another) and entering into a rightful condition."[86] Thus a policy of assassination, for example, might be advocated as defensively necessary, but it is nonetheless disallowed because its practice would disqualify the state for future entry into a rightful condition.[87] Even in the state of nature, without any positive law among nations and no central authority to enforce such law, provisional right exists and is recognized, at least indirectly, by individual states, just as provisional right exists in the state of nature between individuals. By analogy to his previous claims in the case of private right, Kant argues here that disobedience of the precepts of provisional right constitutes a self-contradiction on the part of any state, in that the maxim under which such a state operates could not hold as a universal law: "But what is an *unjust enemy* in terms of the concepts of the right of nations, in which—as is the case in a state of nature generally—each state is judge in its own case? It is an enemy whose publicly expressed will (whether by word or deed) reveals a maxim by which, if it were made a universal rule, any condition of peace among nations would be impossible, and, instead, a state of nature would be perpetuated."[88] The arguments for legal order among states are the same as the arguments for legal order among individuals: (1) given the *globus terraqueus,* no state can exist in isolation; (2) among interacting states, contract keeping is necessarily desirable; (3) even in a world of well-meaning, peaceful states, disputes about right will arise; (4) therefore, all states necessarily ought to submit to the judgment of a neutral, universal arbiter. Now, in the case of individual agents, this arbiter ideally backs its judgments with universal coercion.[89] Kant does not advocate such a powerful judge of international right, however; rather than world government, Kant argues for a limited, voluntary "congress" of nations, along the lines of the States General at the Hague after the War of Spanish Succession (to which a number of European national states brought their differences, to be resolved under the principle that peace is guaranteed by a balance of power).[90]

Kant provides two main lines of argument for limiting international adjudication to a congress of nations: first, such a large area would be ungovernable and, second, without the right to withdraw reserved to member states, such a world government would interfere with the republican rights guaranteed by those states to their citizens. In the first line of argument, Kant simply accepts the then prevailing Montesquieuian notion that only a small state can succeed at republican governance.[91] He adds that order could not be maintained effectively over such a large area, and so breakaway regions would always exist, rendering the goal of uniting under a common global authority impossible.[92] In the *Rechtslehre* chapter on the right of nations, Kant provides only the beginnings of the second line of argument against world government. He writes: "By a *congress* is here understood only a voluntary coalition of different states which can be *dissolved* at any time, not a federation (like that of the American states) which is based on a constitution and can therefore not be dissolved.—Only by such a congress can the ideal of a public right of nations be realized, one to be established for deciding their disputes in a civil way, as if by a lawsuit, rather than in a barbaric way (the way of savages), namely by war."[93] On this basis, Kant could argue (though he does not so do explicitly here) that individual states protect the rights of individuals, and thus must be held more sacred than any international body. The basis for any legitimate use of coercive force, after all, is the will of individual human agents to interact according to contractual rather than arbitrary and violent standards. Thus an institution that threatens this fundamental ground of all political right would not be legitimate, provision of peace notwithstanding.

Significantly, in his writings on international peace Kant never praises the Pax Romana, or any other stability-providing hegemon. Kant's institutional solution, a voluntary federation which may be dissolved at any time, certainly suggests this sort of prioritizing; that is, with such a system Kant chooses to privilege the institution charged with protecting individuals (the national state) at the expense of world order, since he does not allow that any coercive authority at the international level is able by itself to prevent a relapse into the state of war. Kant's use of the lawsuit analogy also supports this reading of his second argument against world government; just as the right to sue preserves an individual's civil rights, often against democratic majority will, so the lawsuitlike procedure offered by a quasi-judicial congress of nations would protect an individual state's rightful interests against those of the whole. For Kant, the justification for governance comes from the protection of individual autonomy—"so that they may enjoy what is laid down as right"—rather than from any pragmatic achievement of a commonly held goal, however lofty.[94] When, in the conclusion to the *Rechtslehre*, Kant makes his famous plea for peace, he justifies it on the basis of ethical laws that affect us on an individual level, rather than making one of the many possible humanitarian arguments for the superiority of peace to war: "Now morally practical reason pronounces in us its irresistible *veto: there is to be no war*."[95]

So, for at least a couple of reasons, Kant argues for a noncoercive congress of nations to adjudicate disputes at the international level.[96] Though Kant has his reasons, his proposal for promoting international peace has one glaring fault not found in his promotion of peace at the state level: without a universal coercer, the autonomy of member states cannot be guaranteed. By analogy with the argument legitimating coercive adjudication at the state level, without such a guarantor each member state would be dependent on the (contingent and arbitrary) good will of the other member states for its security. As Kant argues with regard to individuals under the rule of a state, if one person respects the judgment of some outside authority without any guarantee that others will respect the same authority, then that person has given up his natural right to defend his interests while gaining nothing in return. Kant draws a strong conclusion: if we are to have property rights at all, then each person must have the right to constrain everyone else with whom he might interact to submit to a common judge of these rights, that is, "to enter along with him into a civil constitution."[97] How can Kant make an argument that the combination of individual property rights and inevitable interaction necessarily requires a universal coercer, without making the analogous argument that the same combination on the international level necessarily requires a world government with enforcement powers?

There are two possible answers to this question. Commentators on Kant's theory of international relations have noted that in his other writings on the topic he does call for world government. Conceding the point, I would nonetheless add that Kant's advocacy of world government is never without a touch of irony. Kant does emphasize, after all, that the innkeeper's sign with the words "Zum ewigen Frieden" (toward perpetual peace) was illustrated with a picture of a graveyard.[98] Where Kant expresses here the possibility of world government, he couches these hopes in conditional remarks about the limits of human understanding. For example, in the first supplement to the articles of peace in *Perpetual Peace,* Kant argues that eventual world peace is the final end toward which the human species naturally and inevitably strives: "Perpetual peace is guaranteed by no less an authority than the great artist Nature herself." This bold assertion is followed by a full paragraph of caveats, including the comment that we "cannot actually observe such an agency." The paragraph concludes with a cautionary reference to "the wings of Icarus."[99]

Rather than argue around Kant's account in the *Rechtslehre,* however, I shall give a different answer to the question of how Kant could argue for a world government without enforcement powers: his concept of provisional right allows him to circumvent this problem with regard to international right, just as the concept of provisional right allows him to assert that property rights must be respected in states with less than ideal governments. In the section on private property rights, Kant does make a strong case for the necessity of a universal coercer. Nevertheless, he follows that strong case (made in paragraph 8) with an account (in paragraph 9) of how property rights may exist provisionally in the absence of such a guarantor.[100] Discussing the right of nations, Kant rehearses similar arguments:

Since a state of nature among nations, like a state of nature among individual human beings, is a condition that one ought to leave in order to enter a lawful condition, before this happens any rights of nations, and anything external that is mine or yours which states can acquire or retain by war, are merely *provisional.* Only in a universal *association of states* (analogous to that by which a people becomes a state) can rights come to hold *conclusively* and a true *condition of peace* come about. But if such a state made up of nations were to extend too far over vast regions, governing it and so too protecting each of its members would finally have to become impossible, while several such corporations would again bring on a state of war. So *perpetual peace,* the ultimate goal of the whole right of nations, is indeed an unachievable idea. Still, the political principles directed toward perpetual peace, of entering into such alliances of states, which serve for continual *approximation* to it, are not unachievable. Instead, since continual approximation to it is a task based on duty and therefore on the right of human beings and of states, this can certainly be achieved.[101]

The case of international right, then, provides a particularly clear example of how Kant imagined provisional right would work in practice. As with the legal standards that operate on individuals, only external (nonmoral) considerations are needed as incentives to conform to the norms that make an approximation of world peace possible. A state would decide to forgo assassination as a foreign policy weapon, for example, not because assassination is immoral but because under the regime envisioned by Kant the use of assassination would have negative practical consequences for that state (it would no longer be trusted to play by the rules, and its own officers would no longer be safe). Importantly, however, the driving force behind the empirical disincentives facing states considering immoral politics is the public sphere, itself driven by individual-level moral considerations. Given the lack of universal coercion among states, some might break the rules and suffer no immediate consequences, but over the long run, Kant hopes, provisional international peace should provide its own positive feedback mechanism. Rather than make a sharp and hopeless distinction between an international state of nature and a peace guaranteed by world government, Kant invokes the concept of provisional right. In the absence of a coercive judge of the right, states seeking to adjudicate conflicting claims can argue before a world congress of nations: a public forum in which claims of right are judged according to commonly held standards, which, Kant would argue, are more or less explicitly related to the "moral law within us."[102] Even in the absence of such a forum, states may make provisional judgments of right on the basis of their fitness for holding as a universal law; these claims will be subject to public acceptance or rejection, the closest approximation available to an absolute judge of the right.[103]

APPLICATIONS OF PROVISIONAL RIGHT: REVOLUTION

Kant puts his would-be moral citizen in a tight spot. In the first place, the citizen's moral reason tells him that no disruption of any constituted authority can be permitted. At its most basic, the justification for this position runs as follows: Political right for Kant is grounded in natural principles of respect for human agency and autonomy. Because human beings are agents, they must have the use of the things that further their ends (and because they are moral agents, it must be possible for this possession to be legitimate). Having the use of a thing means that all other agents must agree to refrain from interfering with one's possession. But no agent would make such an agreement unless it was reciprocal, for to do so would interfere with one's own autonomy. Finally, without a universal coercer guaranteeing the arrangement, Kantian agents would be forced to rely on the arbitrary good-will of their fellows for secure possession. Thus, in order to secure their status as autonomous agents, human beings who interact with one another must submit to a common authority. To undermine this authority, then, would be to attack the delicate basis of peaceful coexistence, denying all participants even a chance at secure agency and autonomy—however meager their current status as autonomous agents might be.

To this version of social contract theory Kant adds his own arguments about the limitations of human knowledge of politics. Not only does our reason tell us that obedience to constituted authority is mandatory, but this reason is our only reliable judge of the right. Qua reason, it can compare particular historical situations with universal precepts but can never tell us anything about the pragmatic path toward a better world. Thus Kant argues (in the *Rechtslehre* and elsewhere) that moral reason provides an absolutely reliable model of perfect governance, and he recognizes that no really existing state adheres to these norms. But at the same time Kant claims that we cannot know what actions would take us closer to the ideal state, and that even if we did know, we could not recognize the ideal state with any certainty. "Reason is not sufficiently enlightened to survey the series of predetermining causes that would allow it to predict confidently the happy or unhappy results of human actions. . . . But it throws enough light everywhere for us to see what we have to do in order to remain on the path of duty."[104]

Given these severe limitations on possibly moral political action, it is not surprising that Kant is frequently mistaken for a political stoic. One might think that the Kantian moral agent, despite the agent's rational awareness of the discrepancy between the corrupt present and the ideal republic, ought simply to avoid following maxims inconsistent with the categorical imperative (in a policy that would boil down to "do no harm"). The combination of the fragility of peaceful coexistence and the impossibility of knowledge of consequences seems to exclude any substantive political action on the part of the citizen.

A simple prohibition on political action would be less a "tight spot" than a reduced horizon for the moral citizen. However, Kant is no simple political stoic, and his moral agents are not allowed to content themselves with taking the world as they find it. As Kant explains in "Theory and Practice," "without some end there can be no *will.*" Moral agents must presume "a good that is the *highest good,* in the world and also possible through our cooperation." Furthermore, "*if* we stand in certain moral relations to things in the world we must everywhere obey the moral law, and beyond this there is the added duty to bring it about as far as we can *that* such a relation (a world in keeping with the moral highest ends) exists. In this the human being thinks of himself by analogy with the Deity, who, although subjectively in need of no external thing, still cannot be thought to shut himself up within himself but rather to be determined to produce the highest good."[105] The highest political good ought to be plain to anyone with common moral understanding: people must become self-ruling; to be self-ruling, they need a free public sphere, republican democratic politics, and a peaceful international federation. Kant lists a few of the political principles that function, he argues, as norms for all political organization:

1. The *freedom* of every member of the society as a human being.
2. His *equality* of with every other as a *subject.*
3. The *independence* of every member of a commonwealth as a *citizen.*[106]

Thus as moral agents, and not merely passive reasoners, human beings according to Kant are obligated to pursue the highest good as an end; political republicanism is one element of this highest good.

Now we can see why Kant's moral citizen is in a tight spot. On the one hand, Kant argues strongly against any disruption of the constituted order, despite its manifest shortcomings as compared to the ideal republican state. On the other hand, Kant requires moral citizens to set political progress toward that ideal state as their personal ends. Kant argues in a number of places outside the *Rechtslehre* that human beings have only limited political knowledge, and are thus precluded from making accurate predictions about the empirical effects of their actions. However, he also argues that such an empirical limitation cannot cancel a moral agent's duty to pursue the highest good. Instead, agents must *assume* that progress is possible: "For it would not be a duty to aim at a certain effect of our will if this effect were not also possible in experience (whether it be thought as completed or as always approaching completion)."[107]

What, then, is a moral citizen to do? Kant clearly believes that obedience to constituted authority is a duty. But how can the performance of such a duty coincide with the imperative to pursue political progress, which empirically speaking would mean (at least in Kant's context) the transition from absolute to republican rule? Kant gives us a hint at the end of "Theory and Practice," in a discussion of the goal of universal peace and how finite individuals can possibly promote such an end: "[The principle of right] commends to earthly gods the maxim always so to behave in their conflicts that such a universal state of nations will thereby be ushered in."[108] This is a gloss of the principle of provisional right: act in such a way that the highest good remains possible.

Provisional right, then, ought to help people to live together while respecting each other's autonomy, and it ought to help them make progress toward institutionalizing such a community, in the absence of the just state that would guarantee it. When Kant writes about revolutionary actions, he considers only revolutions that promote ideals founded on what he regards as absolutely solid moral grounds. And yet he consistently denounces such actions, despite their admirable aims. Kant insists on holding both to the standard of decent respect for citizens' autonomy and to the standard of collective progress for the polity as a whole. As revolutionaries tend to discount the former in favor of the latter, Kant opposes his own concept of provisional right to their views on political change.

Kant is famous for denying the right to revolution. Even accounts of his political theory that portray Kant less conservatively than usual emphasize that Kant consistently holds that active disobedience to constituted authority is impermissible.[109] Most repeat Kant's neo-Hobbesian arguments for the necessity of undivided sovereignty (roughly: individual rights to enjoy property require entry into civil society and thus submission to a universal coercer. But any power to which the universal coercer might be responsible would then itself be sovereign. Thus the power of the order-guaranteeing authority must be absolute, at least in all areas having to do with external laws). Kant makes this argument, for example, in his discussion in the *Rechtslehre* of the rights of the head of state, where he is thinking particularly about the executions of Charles I and Louis XVI in the English and French revolutions: "The reason a people has a duty to put up with even what is held to be an unbearable abuse of supreme authority is that its resistance to the highest legislation can never be regarded as other than contrary to law and indeed as abolishing the entire legal constitution. For a people to be authorized to resist, there would have to be a public law permitting it to resist. . . . This is self-contradictory."[110]

If civil instability is bad in itself, a violation of the most basic human right to contract keeping guaranteed by a common authority, then why not ban revolutionary expression as well as action? By the argument for undivided sovereignty, no threat to constituted authority ought to be permitted. Yet Kant consistently reserves to the people the right to reason publicly about political matters. Occasionally he makes the argument that the use of public reason is no real threat to sovereign power (in, for example, "What Is Enlightenment?"). But clearly the constituted authorities in Kant's day perceived it as such, as Kant himself knew only too well.

The concept of provisional right gives a much better explanation than the argument for undivided sovereignty for why no revolution is permissible: provisional right requires that citizens act to promote the eventual advent of the just state, and, argues Kant, disruption of public right will always work against such a goal. Like the state that breaks international norms by choosing assassination as its foreign policy weapon, individuals choosing to undermine the current order rather than work for reform are entering into a deadly contradiction. They may believe that their actions will lead to good results (the removal of a dictator, say), but the costs of these results are too high, as they will have shown themselves incapable of respecting the most basic rights of their fellow citizens. Revolutionary activity violates the maxim of provisional right: always leave open the possibility of entering into a rightful condition.[111]

Both direct revolutionary action and (relatively indirect) revolutionary speech are seen *by rulers* as threats to the constituted order of a society. Kant's weak argument against revolutionary activity—that it contradicts the principle of undivided sovereignty—makes sense from the perspective of the ruler. But it cannot account for Kant's very different treatments of revolutionary speech and revolutionary action. The stronger argument against revolutionary action is based on Kant's theory of provisional right, which does successfully distinguish between direct, destabilizing action and the public use of reason. Any regime guaranteeing the sanctity of contract is a precious thing for Kant, because by allowing human agents to interact in a way that does not violate each other's basic rights, such a regime retains the possibility of eventual improvement toward the ultimate goal of an ideal republican state. Violation of what Kant saw as a fragile structure of civility in a mostly chaotic and violent world constitutes a much greater injustice than suppression of some other rights, all of which are, for Kant, dependent on initial order in the first place: "The attempt to realize this idea [the rule of law] should not be made by way of revolution, by a leap, that is, by violent overthrow of an already existing defective constitution (for there would be an intervening moment in which any rightful condition would be annihilated). But if it is attempted and carried out by gradual reform in accordance with firm principles, it can lead to continual approximation to the highest political good, perpetual peace."[112] Thus direct revolutionary action cannot be permitted. For Kant, reform rather than revolution is the road to the ideal republican state.[113] While maintaining the orderly state without which just civil relations are impossible, Kantian reformers will exercise their public reason in trying to improve that state. Elsewhere in his work, Kant argues that the mere exercise of public reason will act as an engine promoting civil reform toward republican government.[114] Thus the principle of provisional right, which is the standard that applies to all citizens of imperfect states, provides a blueprint for appropriate political behavior, according to Kant: "'Obey the authority that has power over you' . . . and though you can indeed reason publicly about its legislation, you cannot set yourself up as an opposing legislator."[115]

Why, then, ought the moral citizen to obey constituted authority, even when it is manifestly unjust? Applying the rule of provisional right, the moral citizen is enjoined to act in order to promote the possibility of political progress. Kant argues, in the *Rechtslehre* and elsewhere, that revolutionary action, in the form of disruption of the constituted order, will not achieve this end. Political stoicism will not extricate our moral citizen either; Kant insists that moral citizens take responsibility for moving humankind in the right direction. Moral citizens are obligated to provide the constituted authorities with the results of their reasoning about matters of common interest, and to do this in a public forum. The moral citizen must remain a "non-resisting subject," but at the same time, the citizen ought to "make known publicly his opinions about what it is in the ruler's arrangements that seems to him to be a wrong against the commonwealth."[116] Though the moral citizen cannot know what the pragmatic results of his public reasoning will be (as indeed we cannot know what the results even of revolutionary action will be), the citizen is nonetheless responsible for promoting the possibility of political progress by means of public comparison between the constituted authority and the ideal republican state.

APPLICATIONS OF PROVISIONAL RIGHT: HUMAN RIGHTS

In his "popular" political essays and the late work *The Conflict of the Faculties,* Kant sets forth a number of ideas about just how the exercise of public reason might lead to progress toward the ideal state. From the early and extremely cautious version of the public sphere in "What Is Enlightenment?"

to the post–French Revolution account of public judgment in *Conflict*, Kant develops a theory of the long-run effects of ideas of political right on pragmatic political institutions. He has less to say on this topic in the *Rechtslehre*, both because it has been covered elsewhere and, more important, because Kant defends his theories of ideal-driven progress mostly with relatively weak speculation about the course of history. As I have argued, however, stronger Kantian defenses of the pragmatic effects of public reason are available in the *Rechtslehre*. In this work on the a priori principles of political right, Kant strongly defends the rights of citizens to express themselves politically, but he says less about the details of how this publicly authorized sphere of discussion might in fact lead toward republican governance.

Reasoning in Public

On the face of it, the theory of provisional right makes no sense without a concomitant theory of publicity. "Act such that you promote the possibility of the advent of the ideal state" and its corollary principle that one must avoid disrupting the constituted order together imply that there is some force for political change beyond the violent, contingency-driven change with which we are all familiar.[117] Here Kant presumes (and elsewhere he argues) that this force for positive political change without violence is the free use of public reason. Citizens must be allowed to make comparisons between the ideals available to them, via natural reason, and the faulty situations in which they necessarily find themselves. Such arguments, presented to the world on their own merits (that is, without any authority deriving from the status of their authors), ought to encourage reform toward republican governance. In *Conflict*, Kant even implies that publicity can force rulers to improve their practices.

Most of the arguments on this topic in the *Rechtslehre* take the form of declarations of the right of citizens to complain but never to rebel. The Kantian right to reason publicly about political matters is not the same as the freedom of political speech as we understand it today. For example, Kant argues that citizens ought not to inquire into the origins of currently existing authority, since this could only serve to undermine such authority, and thus the result would not be in keeping with the rule of provisional right (to serve the goal of promoting the advent of the ideal state).[118] Instead, the right to use one's public reason exists only in the name of political progress (even though, of course, no individual user can know with any certainty at all whether his use promotes or hinders development toward the ideal state). The role of the public reasoner, then, is to "oppose . . . injustice by *complaints* (*gravamina*) but not by resistance."[119]

Declarations of War

In the *Rechtslehre*'s chapter on the right of nations, Kant argues that rulers have no right to send their unwilling subjects into battle.[120] This should surprise his reader, as Kant has earlier argued quite strongly for the duty of subjects to obey constituted authority, even arbitrarily constituted authority.[121] The reader might be excused for reasoning that military authority as commander in chief is part and parcel of sovereignty (represented by a ruler), and thus (by a Kantian argument against infinite regress) the supreme commander must have the final military say, or else not be the representative of sovereign authority.[122] However, Kant himself makes no such argument. Nor does he consider the right of individual conscientious objectors, only that of the people, taken as a whole. In his long "General Remark" on the rights of the head of state, Kant makes numerous references to the role of the ruler as administrator of military force, and even to the right of the ruler to require military service of subjects, but there are no references to any right to declare or prosecute war. To the contrary, Kant claims that the "supreme command of the sovereign" does not exert sufficient authority to send subjects to war. Instead, the people must "give their free assent, through their representatives, not only to waging war in general but also to each particular declaration of war."[123]

At this point in the text, Kant makes few positive arguments for his position, choosing instead to refute a false "deduction, as a mere jurist [that is, someone interested in the actual state of positive law, rather than in a priori laws of reason] would draw it up." Kant's mere jurist argues as follows: The state provides the security under which a people can flourish. Conversely, a people in the state of nature would be poor and few. Therefore, the state has a right to dispose of those products of its efforts—the people—as it sees fit. Kant summarizes the argument of the mere jurist: "Now just as we say that since vegetables (e.g., potatoes) and domestic animals are, as regards their abundance, a human *product*, which he can use, wear out, or destroy (kill), it seems we can also say that since most of his subjects are his own product, the supreme authority in a state, the sovereign, has the right to lead them into war as he would take them on a hunt, and into battles as on a pleasure trip." Not surprisingly, Kant refutes the mere jurist's argument with ease, noting that human beings, unlike animals and other things capable of being treated as property, must be regarded not as means but as ends in themselves.[124]

Kant's mere jurist makes a poor argument, but upon reflection its refutation is perhaps worth the trouble. After all, the idea that subjects owe their lives to the state, and thus the state has the right to ask anything of them, is not entirely foreign to contemporary political discourse in Kant's time or in ours. Here we have another in the series of Kantian arguments against making moral judgments based on empirical origins (such as the material conditions of one's existence). For Kant, moral arguments may be founded only on a priori, nonhistorical, noncontingent principles. Human beings, therefore, have the same dignity regardless of their origins, exalted or base.

By refuting the argument that rulers have rights over the lives of their citizens analogous to rights over property, however, Kant has not finished defending his position that rulers can have no right to send subjects into battle without their consent. At the heart of the matter is the difference between the decision to commit troops to battle and other decisions of state, such as to tax at a certain rate, to grant clemency to a particular criminal, or to provide charity to a group of needy subjects. What is it, then, about going to war that excludes it from the usual Kantian argument about the necessity for subjects to obey constituted authority?

In his political essays, Kant defends this distinction with a pragmatic argument about the institutional conditions conducive to peace. War interferes with trade and never benefits the majority economically, Kant claims. Modern warfare especially tends to empty state coffers and to require rulers to tax the people ever more heavily. Thus, in a world of republican governments, war would rarely if ever occur, since those who would be most harmed by it would decide whether to commit themselves to it. This argument, based as it is on an analysis of the likely interests of rational actors in the political sphere, carries no weight with regard to principles of political right, such as those discussed in the *Rechtslehre*.

Claims about the rights of rulers and subjects in time of war are necessarily made under the principle of provisional right. In an ideal world, disputes between states would be settled peacefully, under a legally constituted international authority, whose judgment would be taken as authoritative even though it would lack coercive enforcement powers. As Kant notes, it is strange even to consider the concepts of right and of war together, since they seem to contradict each other.[125] "Right during a war would, then, have to be the waging of war in accordance with principles that always leave open the possibility of leaving the state of nature among states . . . and entering a rightful condition."[126] Somthing about the treatment of subjects in war is more significant for the possibility of eventual republican governance (for provisional right) than the more mundane aspects of the ruler-subject relationship.

Discussing permissible and forbidden types of warfare, Kant provides some guidance to what might be especially important about the ruler-subject relationship during wartime: "A state against which war is being waged is permitted to use any means of defense except those that would makes its subjects unfit to be citizens . . . [such as]: using its own subjects as spies; using them or even foreigners as assassins or poisoners (among whom so-called snipers, who lie in wait to ambush individuals, might well be classed); or using them merely for spreading false reports—in a word, using such underhanded means as would destroy the trust requisite to establishing a lasting peace in the future."[127] Being constrained to pay an unfair tax burden, having to witness corrupt grants of clemency, or suffering under inadequate social welfare programs are all reasons for the citizens of the orderly but arbitrary state to complain. But none of these injustices is likely to undermine the citizens' ability eventually to rule themselves. Being forced to sacrifice social loyalty and individual morality to the interests of the state, however, would buy short-term collective security at the price of long-term unfitness for republican governance. Well ahead of his time, Kant makes a terribly accurate critique of totalitarianism, especially of the tendency of totalitarian rule to replace the fabric of social and political life with brittle and exclusive bonds between atomized individuals and the central authority.

Though Kant makes almost no direct argument for his position that rulers may not send subjects to war without their assent, his theory of provisional right can explain it. Subjects of imperfect states ought to tolerate faulty rule in nearly every sphere of life, in the name of the preservation of common authority and thus of some hope of eventual improvement. The case of war, however, is an exception, because the damage done to the polity through the prosecution of an unjust war is as bad as or worse than that done by political instability.

Kant does not intend for this limitation of the ruler's authority to denigrate in any way the sovereign authority of the state, which, after all, derives from the people even in imperfect states that do not consult them. The argument against unjust war does not apply to conscientious objectors, for example, whose refusal to fight a popular war would amount to defiance not of the ruler but of the people as a whole. Furthermore, even as Kant sets strict limits on the ruler's ability to wage war (insisting, for example, that no long-term, general authorization of war is possible), he is unwilling to require an actual vote of the people to determine their will. Apparently, much of the wrangling over whether a war is just or not may take place in the head of the ruler, since everything depends not on the actual opinion of the people but on how they are regarded by the head of state. The people "must always be regarded as colegislating members of a state," and, further, "the people will have to be regarded as having given its vote to go to war."[128] These limits on the right of the ruler to use his people as instruments of war are weak in an institutional sense, as there is no external check on the ruler other than a conscience prodded by the publicly expressed views of the people. But they are exactly the sort of limits compatible with Kant's theory of provisional right, in which both civil order and the possibility of progress must be maintained.

The foregoing exposition of the theory of provisional right shows us a Kant fundamentally concerned with political life in actual societies on earth, rather than ideal republics in books.[129] This contradicts a popular image of Kant as concerned primarily with constructing the ideal state (or worse, as preoccupied with philosophical arcana at the expense of political relevance). In Kantian political thought, however, ideals are important only as they are "schematized," that is, only insofar as they regulate action (or judgment of action) in the real, provisional world. Similarly, the state of nature and the original contract are mere conceptual touch points from which to argue. They are real, but not empirically real: they have authority and regulate rightful action, but exist in no concrete time or place.

A number of commentators, myself included, have sought to pull a unified political theory out of Kant's scattered writings.[130] If such a project is to succeed, it must include both the formal account of the just state from *The Metaphysics of Morals* and the theories of history, civil society, revolution, and the public sphere in the "popular" essays. As I have sought to show here, Kant's theory of provisional right and his account of publicity mutually imply each other; neither is complete without the other. For example, without Kant's explanation in "What Is Enlightenment?" that only by gradual enlightenment can a people hope to achieve lasting improvements, his objections to regime-threatening, even potentially revolutionary, behavior in *The Metaphysics of Morals* seem formalistic and even disingenuous. Not surprisingly, commentators focusing exclusively on these objections have frequently concluded that Kant's politics are too conservative, and especially that he is too easy on those in power.

The concept of provisional right in Kant's political theory provides a mechanism for progressive politics toward the ideal state. It is the formal, more strictly philosophical counterpart to the pragmatic account of publicity provided in the political essays. Both aspects of Kant's political philosophy aim to bridge the gap between freedom and nature. Provisional right provides a practical formula for acting rightly in a society that has absolute ideals but fails to realize them (that is, in any existing society of limited rational beings, according to Kant). The account of publicity also bridges the gap between freedom and nature, but does so via the slow education of humankind to enlightened governance, conducted in the public sphere. The theory of provisional right and the theory of publicity together constitute Kant's best effort to make the absolute ideals of political life—the truth of which he believes he has proved—relevant to the "bent wood" of all real societies.

Kant's system, as he sees it, is incomplete without such a bridge, though most commentators have focused on the account of the ideal state alone. Thus most works on *The Metaphysics of Morals* evaluate the coherence, correctness, or practicability of Kant's ideal principles of political right. While this aspect of his political theory is indeed important, by Kant's own standards it is incomplete. A mere image of a perfect state, however compelling, can make no claims on actual human beings without a necessary connection to them. This is why Kant's use of the phrase "Platonic ideals" in *The Conflict of the Faculties* with regard to his image of the ideal state is misleading.[131] Like Platonic forms, Kant's ideals provide true standards of rightness for comparison with the actual world; unlike them, however, ideals in the Kantian sense are supposed to have concrete effects. Once the comparison is made between historical reality and irrefutable ideals, according to Kant, action will necessarily (if, probably, slowly) follow. Kant's modern theory of political ideals, unlike that of the ancients, contains an account of human progress. It is no wonder, then, that Kant's political theory as usually presented in the literature has an odd, out-of-date, irrelevant flavor. Seen strictly in terms of the ideal state, without any connection to actual society, no number of key innovations (not even the principles of international right) can keep Kantian politics from seeming stale. Without the complementary accounts of provisional right and publicity, then, Kant's politics lose their relevance.

As numerous other commentators have noticed, one of the things that sets Kant's political theory apart is his designation of the republican form of government, based in an original contract, as an ideal. In Kant's philosophy, ideals have a special status: as models derived from irrefutable principles that all limited rational beings would acknowledge were they to reflect on them (in Kant's account), ideals justify themselves. The political ideal of republican governance carries the same special status in Kant's work as the ideal of the *summum bonum* (highest good), for example, or the ideal of the ethical paragon. As such an ideal, the republican state is categorically desirable; its structures, derived as they are from absolute principles of right, should upon reflection be as self-evidently correct as the categorical imperative itself. Kant's faith in this aspect of his theory is observable in his political essays, in which he frequently claims that both nations and their rulers will, once exposed to republican ideals in the public sphere, come to recognize their rightness (even if they do not promote them directly through their own actions). Not all contractarians make these kinds of claim. Locke, for example, uses Christian theology to defend the property rights on which his ideal government rests; Hobbes argues in instrumental fashion that the rational interest of subjects legitimates the absolute state.

Kant's version of social contract theory, then, with its republicanism treated as an irrefutable ideal, is indeed an interesting, and fairly original, contribution to the contractarian tradition, even without its account of the mechanism of progress toward the ideal state. Patrick Riley characterizes Kant as "the most adequate of the social contract theorists" with good reason.[132] However, Kant would not have been satisfied with this "thin" version of his theory, in which republican ideals are defended in a new and powerful way, but which lacks any guidance for political right in the imperfect world at hand and any account of a possible transition from absolute rule. Elsewhere in his work, Kant offers a pragmatic account of how progress toward enlightened governance might occur: this is his theory of publicity, including the mechanism of the public sphere. Here, in the formal, more critical of his political works, the *Rechtslehre*, Kant follows his standard practice of providing principles and suggesting maxims that link the ideal (in this case, republican governance) with actual practice. Where the essays provide an explanation of the connection between political ideals and historical reality in terms of a pragmatic account of the public sphere, the *Rechtslehre* attacks the same problem by different means.

This reading of the *Rechtslehre*'s concept of provisional right shows that Kant was in no way as unpolitical and uncompromising as he is often thought to be. A fundamental source of error on this point is, interestingly, a habit of taking Kantian distinctions too far. Most commonly, Kantian limits on the pretensions of human knowledge (epistemological limits) are mistakenly applied to the world itself (ontological limits), apart from our knowledge or perception of it.

Kant distinguishes between realms of freedom and nature, the noumenal and phenomenal worlds. But this distinction applies to our restricted human inquiry into human life, not to life itself. For example, Kant's three famous questions for philosophy—What can I know? What should I do? What may I hope?—notably exclude the question of being itself. Each question addresses the relationship between persons—as thinking subjects, agents, and believers—and the world. No question asks about the world itself. Commentators seem to forget the first lesson of Kantian method, which is that theoretical knowledge of the world around us is limited by our perceptive apparatus. (Kant does not claim that the world around us is itself limited by our perceptive apparatus.) The realms of freedom and nature, the noumenal and phenomenal worlds, are two standpoints from which to view one world, a world that cannot be seen whole by human eyes. But just because these realms cannot be united in our perception does not mean that they are not united in fact (only that we cannot know how this can be).

For example, Bernard Yack moves from a valid argument about Kant's derivation from Rousseau of the divide between humanity and human nature (a version of the freedom/nature dichotomy) to the claim that for Kant "our freedom cannot manifest itself or act as a force in the phenomenal world."[133] What Kant would really limit, however, is not freedom's manifestation in the world, in which he certainly believes, but the status of our knowledge of any such manifestation.

To summarize a complex topic: Kant would say that we can know freedom only indirectly, as the necessary condition of the "moral law within us."[134] Direct knowledge of freedom's causality would presuppose knowledge of the so-called noumenal world; since noumena are simply those aspects of the whole world that cannot be perceived by us as phenomena, and since for Kant direct knowledge of things must be based on perception of them, such knowledge of freedom's causality is clearly impossible.

But Kant does not extrapolate from his radical limits on possible human knowledge to radical limits on actual existence. Such ontological limits would be as unjustified an expansion of human perception as the ontological excesses Kant criticizes in his scholastic predecessors.[135] Rather than claiming to know the nature of the whole world (phenomenal and noumenal), Kant inquires whether there are any principles about this world that justify our holding them despite the impossibility of theoretical knowledge of their truth. In so doing, Kant introduces a number of lesser types of scholarly inquiry, none of which carries the degree of certainty accorded to a priori knowledge of nature. These types of inquiry are accorded different statuses in Kant's system, according to how well he can justify their conclusions with a priori principles. They include: theoretical principles based on mere experience (such as the physical law that every action has an equal reaction);[136] practical knowledge (of ethical truth, derived from the moral law);[137] reflective judgment; applications of formal theoretical and practical principles to particular material conditions (such as the application of practical principles of right to historical situations in the *Rechtslehre*); and "ideal history" (which, though Kant compares the practice of ideal history to augury, nevertheless provides a scholarly window into the concrete reality of freedom in the world).[138] This common misapplication of Kant's limits on human knowledge to the world at large, a confusion between epistemological and ontological limits, is at least partly responsible for the lack of coverage of the concept of provisional right in the commentary on the *Rechtslehre*.

5

the judging public

In Kantian political theory, provisional right provides the standard by which really existing political institutions may be judged; the public sphere provides the mechanism by which actual institutions may be improved. Though Kant's writings provide the foundation for our modern concept of a public sphere, he is not the only one to have studied the concrete effects of public ideas on practical politics. In fact, recent political science boasts a number of interesting new lines of research on the function of publicity. The vast literature on the public sphere attests to the fact that modern publicity takes many forms, not all of them benign; any general conclusions one draws about the effects of the public sphere on practical politics must respect the context of that sphere's operation.

A recent and fine example of the sort of political science that should interest Kantian political theorists is the work by Margaret Keck and Kathryn Sikkink on transnational advocacy groups.[1] Keck and Sikkink do not refer directly to Kant's philosophy; their work, however, builds on and contributes to some of Kant's most interesting lines of reasoning. The authors argue that a new, important, and poorly understood entity has emerged in international politics: transnational advocacy networks. These networks, linking activists in different countries interested in moral causes, such as human rights and environmental protection, can be shown to have concrete political effects under certain conditions. Keck and Sikkink identify, for example, a set of conditions leading to a "boomerang effect," in which domestic activists faced with an unresponsive government are able to work with international activists who put pressure on their more responsive home governments, which in turn are able effectively to pressure the originally unresponsive state.[2] What sets transnational advocacy networks apart from more traditional political agents is primarily their commitment to "principled ideas," which they use to attempt to change perceptions of interest among more powerful actors.[3] Keck and Sikkink use classic comparative methodology to examine their object of inquiry, setting up structured comparisons, for example, between failed and successful campaigns by advocacy groups.[4] The logic of transnational advocacy groups' activity, however, was set out more than two hundred years ago by Kant in his theory of the concrete political effects of speech in the public sphere. Keck and Sikkink's empirical findings on the effectiveness of transnational advocacy groups complement recent work in Kantian political philosophy on the norm of reciprocity and its political function.[5] Their findings about the transcultural value of the concept of human dignity (as opposed to the more culturally specific concept of human rights) have interesting implications for liberal theories of overlapping consensus.[6] In fact, Keck and Sikkink themselves draw some broad and interesting theoretical conclusions from their empirical findings: "Liberalism carries within it not the seeds of its destruction, but the seeds of its expansion. Liberalism, with all its historical shortcomings, contains a subversive element that plays into the hands of activists."[7]

Keck and Sikkink's boomerang model of the concrete effects of the public sphere is only one among several competing models of publicity available to contemporary political science. For example, Peter M. Haas and others have outlined a theory of "epistemic communities" that operate by a Kantian publicity logic, but in issue areas, on institutional targets, and by a form of authority that all are different from those of Keck and Sikkink's transnational advocacy groups. If Keck and Sikkink's transnational advocacy groups resemble what I call Kant's "judging public," made up of cosmopolitan actors moved by moral principle, Haas's epistemic communities resemble another of Kant's models for publicity, the rule of experts. Like Kant's philosophical faculty (see below), Haas's knowledge-based communities affect the decisions of state policy makers by providing authoritative information, framing the terms of debate, and institutionalizing their knowledge-providing role. Haas cites the sometimes determinative role played by communities of scientists and other policy experts on issue areas that satisfy two conditions, namely, that they require international coordination and that they are fraught with uncertainty. The problem of the thinning of atmospheric ozone above the earth is one such issue area, and epistemic communities do seem to be exerting an unusually powerful, if not determinative, policy effect in that arena.[8] Both Kant in his late political work and political science today struggle with competing models of the operation of the public sphere. In both cases, however, the basic logic of publicity's concrete political effects is enhanced rather than undermined by these multiple illustrations of the power of ideas in action.

Kant's early defense of free public expression did not develop into a full-fledged theory of the role of the public sphere for more than a decade. Between 1784 ("What Is Enlightenment?") and 1798 (*The Conflict of the Faculties*),[9] the public debate sparked by the French Revolution provided Kant with a renewed empirical model for his mature account of the public sphere as an agent of progress. The world of letters had provided an image of the public sphere for his early essay on enlightenment. *Conflict* contains three separate examples of a possible functioning public sphere: the philosophical faculty of the university, the members of an idealized version of the British Parliament, and the judging public. I argue here that Kant's best account of a model of a public sphere—according to internal standards of coherence and external standards of plausibility—is that of the judging public, based on the example of some brave and public expressions of sympathy for the ideals of the French Revolution.

THE JUDGING PUBLIC IN *THE CONFLICT OF THE FACULTIES*

Kant was impressed by the willingness of writers in the public sphere to address themselves to political topics even when such expressions endangered them personally. He praises, for example, Prussian sympathizers of the French Revolution, who air their republican sympathies even at the risk of "great disadvantage to themselves."[10] Kant was not, of course, sympathetic to the more violent aspects of the French Revolution; his denunciation of the treatment of Louis XVI is particularly famous.[11] Nevertheless, Kant was fascinated with political action that seemed to be motivated purely by general conclusions about political right. He was especially interested in the sometimes dangerous public discussion in Prussia on French revolutionary affairs. As in the rest of his popular political writing, Kant comments here on the affairs of his native state by means of indirect, frequently veiled references.

The central question of the second part of *Conflict* is whether humankind is making progress toward its perfection. Kant looks for a "sign" that might indicate such progress. A little too fortunately for his argument, he is able to say that there has been a historical sign of the tendency toward self-betterment that reason tells us should be evident in human history, and that the sign is the "attitude of the onlooker." Prussian spectators observing the French Revolution expressed sympathy for the causes of national self-determination and for the reduction in wars of aggression that, Kant believes, naturally follows the establishment of a republican constitution.[12] Like the public of "What Is Enlightenment?" these sympathetic public partisans of the republican cause judge political institutions and events disinterestedly, according to universal standards of right. Significantly, Kant represents the public observing the revolutionary action across the Rhine to the civil authorities as harmless; from the point of view of the ruler, their talk should be considered "innocuous political twaddle."[13] These judges in the public sphere are described as witnesses to events which are beyond their control and in which they have no material interest. Their accounts are therefore especially reliable.

If the judgment of the public is really powerless, however, it is hard to see how this public sphere can fulfill its role as the mechanism of human progress toward perfection. Addressing potential censors, Kant argues that public deliberation on political matters cannot have any concrete effect, at least not in the short run. As he writes in "What Is Enlightenment?" a ruler with a large, well-disciplined army can afford to tolerate public political discussion. Furthermore, just as in "What Is Enlightenment?" Kant in the second part of *Conflict* is as concerned to protect the authority of the public's judgment from the corrupting influence of power as he is to convince prevailing despots of their harmlessness. Thus the firewall between public judgment and political power seems at first to protect both the moral authority of the judging public and the political authority of the state. Provisionally speaking, Kant considers such a firewall absolutely necessary. Over the long run, however, judgments made in public do have concrete effects on political life. Using this distinction strategically, Kant can argue seriously that local enlightened absolutist rulers have nothing to fear from "innocuous political twaddle" in the marketplace of ideas, while at the same time identifying the public sphere as an agent of changes that, over the long run, will depose those rulers. Furthermore, as Kant has argued in the *Rechtslehre*, such progress necessarily leads to cosmopolitan republican governance (progress as such would bring the actual world closer to the ideal image generated by the moral principles shared by all; these principles demand respect for human rights, among other republican ideals). Besides his claims about the harmlessness of public deliberation in the near term, then, Kant must make equally strong claims about the effects of public judgment in the long term.

Up to this point in his work, the problems set for Kant by his predecessors in social contract theory—of finding an authoritative judge of public right on earth, and of retaining that judge's authority while allowing the judgments to have some effect—remain unresolved (see chapter 4). In *Conflict,* however, he does propose a solution to these questions. Judges in the public sphere derive their authority from the special qualifications Kant outlines in "What Is Enlightenment?" and elsewhere; these qualifications ensure that such judges take their standard of right from universal reason alone. Public judgment may not be conditioned by any contingent factor (only the object of judgment and the partisan's own sympathy are provided by experience). Once expressed, however, public judgment becomes a concrete force in the world.

Kant offered an early, very moderate account of the power of public judgment in "What Is Enlightenment?" (see chapter 1). In the 1784 essay, Kant imagines a situation in which the people object to a change in religious regulations: they should be allowed to discuss the matter freely, and if after a while no relief is given, the public may, Kant concludes, bring its suggestion before the throne.[14] A decade later, however, Kant has been deeply disappointed by Frederick II's cynical use of enlightened trappings for the policies of *raison d'état.* By the time Kant witnesses the outpouring of public sympathy for the republican cause in France, he is willing to make much stronger suggestions about the force of public judgment. In a note to *Conflict* Kant asks: "Why has a ruler never dared openly to declare that he recognizes absolutely no right of the people opposed to him, that his people owe their happiness solely to the beneficence of a government which confers this happiness upon them, and that all presumption of the subject to a right opposed to the government . . . is absurd and even culpable? The reason is that such a public declaration would rouse all of his subjects against him."[15] Kant's claim that the disputes of scholars should be tolerated by the state as harmless now sounds somewhat disingenuous. Their disinterested inquiry according to standards of reason allows members of the public sphere to claim "right" in the sense of correctness; however, they also acquire "right" in the sense of moral authority. Moral authority, Kant insists here and throughout his political work, has concrete effects in the world, however difficult it is for human beings to perceive them. The mechanism for these effects is the institution of publicity. Thus for Kant the public sphere, merely through its judging function, and without any coercive apparatus, constitutes a powerful agent of historical progress.

TEXTUAL BACKGROUND

The publishing history of *Conflict* is both curious and well documented.[16] Two different controversies surrounded its appearance. First, there was a dispute and then a lawsuit between two publishers, each of whom had been given at least indirect permission by Kant to publish some of what eventually became *Conflict*. Second, and more important, Kant's publication of *Conflict* required him to repudiate the promise he had made to Johann Christoph Wöllner, minister of ecclesiastical affairs under Frederick II's successor Frederick William II, not to publish any more tracts on religion. Kant had come under attack by Wöllner and his colleagues as perhaps the most prominent philosopher associated with the Berlin Enlightenment.[17] Kant's promise not to publicize his philosophy of religion was extracted under the threat of "unpleasant circumstances," as Kant shows in the preface to *Conflict*, where he published both the order and his response to it.[18] Kant wrote in the preface that after Frederick William II's death he deemed himself released from his promise to refrain from publishing on religion, as the promise was a personal one to the king.[19]

The three essays that make up *Conflict* were written at different times and for different purposes. Kant appears to have been inspired by the circumstances of controversy surrounding his writings on these topics, as well as by a long-term interest in the issue of a necessary disagreement between the philosophers and the more state-centered "higher" faculties, to publish the three essays together as *Streit der Fakultäten*. Part 1 is concerned with the role of the state in regulating religious practice and the philosophy of religion; it arose out of the controversy surrounding the publication of Kant's *Religion within the Limits of Reason Alone* (1793).[20] Part 3 is a late essay of Kant's, written in response to a treatise on prolonging human life by Christoph Wilhelm Hufeland.[21] Part 2, which interests me here, was originally an essay on the possibility of political progress, written at the same time as or shortly after "Theory and Practice."[22]

Several years passed between his writing of part 2 and the introduction, which attempts to tie the three parts of the book together by means of the unifying idea of a necessary dispute between the "higher" and "lower" faculties. In his introduction, Kant supports a reading of *Conflict* that emphasizes the role of the philosophers as judges of the right, at the expense of what I call Kant's "mature" account, which identifies members of the public sphere generally as the source of the best possible approximation of perfect political judgment. I argue below that while the example of the "lower" faculty serves to illustrate a number of important matters, especially Kant's point that interests other than the interest of reason necessarily corrupt the search for truth, the philosophers can nonetheless be no more than an inferior exemplar of the judging public.

THE CONFLICT BETWEEN THE PHILOSOPHICAL FACULTY AND AGENTS OF THE STATE

Kant follows the traditional division of university faculties into the "higher" departments of theology, jurisprudence, and medicine, and the "lower" faculty of philosophy (natural and moral). The former are concerned with pragmatic applications of knowledge in the service of the state, while the latter, comprising all natural and human sciences, concerns itself with knowledge for its own sake. By the time Kant writes the introduction, he has long been interested in the necessary disagreement that would arise from the circumstance that each higher faculty shares its object of investigation (religion, law, or nature) with the lower faculty, yet conducts its investigation according to completely different standards.[23] The lower faculty examines the world from the rational, a priori point of view, while the higher faculties see things from the empirical, worldly point of view. In the case of law, for example, a professor of jurisprudence will ask what existing positive law tells us is legal, while the professor of philosophy might ask what must be true according to natural right.

Though Kant does make some interesting arguments in the introduction to *Conflict*, the main contribution of this text is not its original arguments (most of which are made elsewhere in Kant's work, and with greater rigor) but its delightfully ironic and sometimes downright comical presentation. I mentioned in chapter 3 that attention to Kant's adoption and manipulation of the form of the peace treaty in his essay *Perpetual Peace* reveals a great deal about the way Kant addresses different arguments to different audiences. Similarly here, in a much less rhetorically beautiful work, attention to Kant's conscious adherence to the formulas of the advice-for-princes genre reveals the multiple targets of his claims. Incidentally, Mary Gregor's otherwise excellent translation obscures the humorous aspect of the work, as she tends to make word choices that smooth out Kant's often rough text. For example, she translates Kant's characterization in the introduction of the people as "Idioten" with the English "incompetent," which is in turn an exact translation of a Kantian technical term, "unmündig" (meaning incompetent to represent oneself legally, a minor). Gregor's translation does not convey a nice little running joke in Kant's text, whereby as he writes from the point of view of the interest of state, he uses correspondingly coarse language. The most generous way to read Kant's introduction is not by trimming the language but by leaving it in full rhetorical flower. In this way, the reader may decide whether Kant is employing an ironic if occasionally misfiring wit, in this case by writing from the adopted point of view of a representative of the state (the characterization of the people as idiots comes, after all, as part of an argument for why the state should tolerate free inquiry on the part of the philosophical faculty). This is of course a classic technique of the advice-for-princes genre: the author demonstrates the weaknesses of those in power while ostensibly pandering to their interests.[24]

Kant manages to make some important arguments while poking fun at those in power, however. For example, after making the familiar point that it would be beneath the dignity of the state to meddle in scientific matters, Kant adds that the people ("das Volk," that is, the common people) would be especially unpleasant toward any state representative playing the scholar, since the people cannot take a joke, and they lump everyone together. Next, however, Kant makes the important claim that not only ought the government, in its own interest, to leave off meddling in science but scientists, in their own interest, must relinquish all pretension to power: "Having no commands to give, [the learned community at the university] is free to evaluate everything." Kant deepens his standard argument that the most fruitful scientific inquiry must be free of government interference (which he cites in a note giving the classic story of the merchant who advised Colbert to "laissez faire") by adding the idea that to be free to pursue learning, the scientists must also avoid wielding any state power themselves.[25] There is a remarkable parallel between the conceit of the whole text—a conflict between philosophers and the other faculties—and Kant's mature argument about the judging public: philosophical faculty is simultaneously harmless to, and needs protection from, the power of the state. At the same time, however, philosophical faculty fulfills an essential, truth-finding function for the state, just because it is insulated from it.

By arguing from a point of view sympathetic to the government's interests, Kant is able to make fairly radical suggestions that would otherwise have been politically impossible. His standard argument for free philosophical inquiry, for example, is always flanked by two complementary points: first, that it is beneath the dignity of the state to meddle in scholarly matters and, second, that it is in the interest of the state to maintain a free realm of inquiry. This same reversal of the usual point of view of the enlightenment philosopher serves Kant's half-humorous, half-serious purpose in a note in the introduction on what counts as protected public speech (a topic dealt with much more seriously in part 2 and in "What Is Enlightenment?"). Kant denounces those members of the higher faculties, especially theologians, who would "illegally" bring a scholarly conflict before the people. The ostensible targets of Kant's denunciation are the "self-appointed tribunes of the people," who "stir up political struggles," in other words, those seen by the government as dangerous revolutionaries. But the "state of illegal scholarly conflict mentioned above" to which Kant refers is an instance *not* of revolutionaries seeking to overturn the government, but of representatives of the state-sponsored higher faculties using governmental power to suppress unpopular philosophical inquiry. Thus Kant demonstrates that the same reasoning which provisionally justifies government suppression of revolutionary rabble-rousing also withdraws legitimacy from state representatives who would criticize scholars from the pulpit.[26]

Aside: The Interest of Reason in Kant's First *Critique*

The most important argument, then, in the introduction to *Conflict* is that to remain authoritative, philosophers must be protected from both the encroachments of power and the dangers of wielding it themselves. The discussion of this same topic in *Critique of Pure Reason* has led some commentators to conclude that Kant's entire critical project is fundamentally political.[27] Such claims are based on an overestimation of the role of metaphor in Kant, and on a very broad definition of "political."[28] The first *Critique* is fundamentally concerned with establishing the limits of possible human knowledge. In the passages where Kant pauses to reflect on the effects of his work, he tends to speak metaphorically about the triumph of sound critical reason over, for example, the "despotism of the schools."[29] In the *Critique*'s "Polemic," Kant even describes a state of nature among inquirers and refers the reader to Hobbes's solution to the evils of the state of nature via the establishment of supreme authority. But while these comments are interesting for the light they shed on Kant's early political ideas, they in no way demonstrate any primacy of the political in Kant's thought.[30] The "state of nature" here is a metaphorical description of the state of philosophy before the critique of reason sets everyone straight: dogmatists on all sides of a debate, Kant complains, win temporary victories by the argumentative equivalent of brute force. The authority of reason's critique, Kant proceeds, provides a rational source of adjudication among points of view. Under the reign of critical reason, then, disputes may be resolved in the civilized manner of a legal contest according to universally accepted standards of reason, rather than by uncivilized and dogmatic recourse to authority. Even as Kant is using the language of social contract (and, in typical Kantian style, the language of several other metaphorical tropes, including, in this short section on polemic, war, fencing, house building, and road traveling in addition to state building), he is discussing metaphysics.[31]

The second essay of *Conflict*, which contains the political arguments of the book, is ostensibly concerned with the antagonism between the juridical and philosophical faculties. In this section Kant never once mentions such a conflict explicitly, and this is not surprising. After all, Kant wrote the essay perhaps three years earlier, with another purpose in mind.[32] However, the theme of conflict between the interests of the faculty of law and the faculty of philosophy is certainly relevant to the material Kant includes here. The higher faculties, concerned as they are with supporting the efforts of the state, take the positivist view of political possibility that Kant is eager to criticize, both in *Conflict* and elsewhere in his writings (especially *Theory and Practice*, written at about the same time). "One must take men as they are, [the politicians] tell us, and not as the world's uninformed pedants or good-natured dreamers fancy they ought to be. But 'as they are' ought to read 'as we have *made them* by unjust coercion.'"[33]

THE JUDGING PUBLIC AS ONE SOLUTION TO THE PROBLEM OF FREEDOM AND NATURE

The essay that became part 2 of *Conflict* is a complicated text. Though Kant's section titles announce an epistemological inquiry into the possibility of knowledge of human progress, the assertions made in part 2 seem to range far outside the limits of knowledge set by Kant in the first *Critique*. Kant seems to be grounding his assertions on both empirical and a priori bases. Twice in the essay Kant eliminates an area of possible knowledge and then returns to it as the solution to a given problem.[34]

Why is the account in *Conflict* so confused?[35] Here more than anywhere else in his political works Kant attempts to reconcile nature and freedom, and specifically to construct an account of human history that incorporates "human beings with even a limited will of innate and unvarying goodness" while remaining at least compatible with empirical historical inquiry. This seems impossible on the face of it, by Kantian lights: How can one demonstrate freedom's causality in the phenomenal world, if no knowledge of nonperceptible things is strictly speaking possible? True, Kant argues that rational beings must presume a number of things about the noumenal world for practical purposes, but he does not claim that these practical postulates achieve the status of knowledge. However, in the second section of *Conflict,* Kant attempts just that: he seeks to discover empirical evidence of a cause in human history that moves humankind toward the ideal state.

Were Kant's attempt to achieve a "prophetic history of the human race" successful, *Conflict* would be a much more widely read text than it is. As an essay in epistemology, part 2 of *Conflict* is not especially compelling. Perhaps Kant's best argument for his attempted synthesis of the empirical and the a priori, that one can predict the course of actions for which one is responsible, still rests on mere suggestive analogies rather than serious analysis.[36] The enduring achievement of part 2 is Kant's mature account of the problem of transition to republican governance, via the mechanism of the public sphere.

The Question of Progress

Kant begins the second section of *Conflict* with a "renewed attempt" to answer the question of whether mankind is progressing toward an ideal state, picking up a theme he addressed earlier in "What Is Enlightenment?" and again in "Theory and Practice." In the latter essay Kant makes the argument, familiar from his ethical works, that even though strictly theoretical knowledge of possible progress in human affairs is impossible, a rational person must assume that progress is possible. Briefly, the argument runs as follows. Kant has argued that any moral willing must have an object, that such an object of moral willing would be one whose necessity is grounded in principles of reason, and that therefore individuals have a duty to pursue such objects of moral willing. But one cannot have a duty to perform the impossible. Therefore objects of moral willing must be possible. Now Kant seems here to be repeating the error he famously refuted in Descartes, who argued that, by definition, a supreme being must contain the most perfect of all properties, and since existence is a more perfect property than nonexistence, the supreme being must exist.[37] Kant counters that existence is not a property; for Kant, we can have no knowledge of the existence of things outside the phenomenal sphere (of things that can be perceived), and thus we can have no knowledge, strictly speaking, of the existence of any supreme being. (Kant distinguishes between knowledge [*Wissen*] and cognition [*Erkenntnis*]; we can cognize nonphenomenal things, such as triangles. But cognizing something has no implications for a thing's existence or nonexistence, phenomenally speaking).

By refuting Descartes' proof of the existence of God, however, Kant does not necessarily support the opposing position, namely, the nonexistence of God. Instead, Kant proves that theoretical arguments for and against the existence of God share the same flaw: the would-be extension of human knowledge beyond the bounds of possible experience. What, then, of Kant's claim in *Conflict* to know that objects of moral willing must be possible? Would not such a claim fall under the same ax that Kant applied to Descartes, as an unauthorized excursion into the noumenal world? It would, if Kant in fact claimed to have theoretical knowledge of the object's possibility. But Kant makes no such claim. Instead, he relies on his well-known distinction between theoretical and practical reason: the possibility of objects of moral willing is practically, though not theoretically, necessary. Because human progress toward the ideal state is a necessary object of moral willing, Kant writes in "Theory and Practice," one is justified in one's presumption of it.[38]

In the second part of *Conflict*, Kant begins with the same question of the possibility of progress, but instead of deducing its practical necessity from the fact of moral reason, he approaches the question as a philosophical historian. The assumptions of "Theory and Practice" are based on postulates of practical reason, cognitions that Kant claims are necessary elements of our reasoning minds but are not objects of empirical inquiry. Here, by contrast, Kant asks what the historian can discover about human progress. Nevertheless, Kant's mode of reasoning in *Conflict* mirrors that of "Theory and Practice" in some respects. In "Theory and Practice" he begins with a fact of reason (our common recognition of the authority of the moral law) and derives practical postulates based on what must be necessary if the moral law is to hold. In *Conflict* Kant looks for "some experience in the human race" and derives the possibility of human progress from it.[39] Even as a historian Kant cannot relinquish the hypothetical mode of reasoning, since the objects of his inquiry are "beings that act freely, to whom, it is true, what they ought to do may be dictated in advance, but of whom it may not be predicted what they will do."[40]

Kant claims that previous thinkers have despaired of knowing anything about progress in human history, because knowledge of any such object presumes knowledge at least of the effects of free human will, which are notoriously unpredictable and imperceptible. Kant does not despair. In a familiar move, he suggests that if "the course of human affairs seems so senseless to us, perhaps it lies in a poor choice of position from which we regard it."[41] Invoking the famous image of the Copernican turn, Kant advises would-be historians to take a hypothetical approach: "If one were able to attribute to man an inherent and unalterably good, albeit limited, will, he would be able to predict with certainty the progress of his species toward the better, because it would concern an event that he himself could produce."[42] If, then, some piece of empirical evidence allows the philosophical historian to presume the existence of moral willing, then some knowledge of progress in human history will also be possible.[43]

In *Conflict,* then, Kant pursues his usual strategy of achieving practically if not theoretically necessary postulates based on some grounding fact, but in this case the grounding fact will be empirical and not ideal. The historian must look for an empirical event that would be a sign indicating that freedom is operating in the phenomenal world: this sign "points to the disposition and capacity of the human race to be the cause of its own advance toward the better, and (since this should be the act of a being endowed with freedom), toward the human race as being the author of this advance."[44]

Spectators at the Revolution: Kant's Best Example of a Judging Public

Proof, however indirect, of freedom's causality in the world is a tall order, and Kant comes up with a suitably momentous event to fulfill it. He writes, "Only nature and freedom, combined in mankind in accordance with principles of right, have enabled us to forecast [human progress]." Under the heading "An Occurrence in Our Own Times Which Proves This Moral Tendency of the Human Race," Kant cites his contemporaries' public expressions of sympathy with the French Revolution. Even though the revolution itself "may be so filled with misery and atrocities that no right-thinking man would ever decide to make the same experiment again," its stated aims are based on fundamental principles of right, such as the rule of law and the promotion of peace. Public expressions of sympathy for these principles, without any possible private motive and at considerable personal risk, "can have no other cause than a moral predisposition in the human race."[45]

The event to which Kant points as evidence of the causality of freedom in the world looks a great deal like an instance of his public sphere at work, familiar from "What Is Enlightenment?" and elsewhere: "We are here concerned with the attitude of the onlookers as it reveals itself *in public* while the drama of great political changes is taking place: for they openly express universal yet disinterested sympathy for one set of protagonists against their adversaries, even at the risk that their partiality could be of great disadvantage to themselves. Their reaction (because of its universality) proves that mankind as a whole shares a certain character in common, and it also proves (because of its disinterestedness) that man has a moral character, or at least the makings of one. And this does not merely allow us to hope for human improvement; it is already a form of improvement itself." Here is Kant's version of the unimpeachable source of political judgment sought by social contract theorists as the worldly substitute for divine authority on matters of right. Real-world partisans of the French Revolution, safe from the corrupting influence of the possibility of actual power thanks to the absolute monarch under whom they live, mediate between the ideal and actual worlds by pronouncing judgment on current events. By exercising their public reason in a realm not only free of but also probably counter to their own private interests, these sympathizers of the republican cause gain extraordinary moral authority. Kant's members of the judging public make themselves virtual ambassadors of the noumenal world to the phenomenal realm, to put it a little grandly. Their circumstances—free of all but the interests of reason—allow them to approximate the impossible point of view of perfect judges of political right.

It is important to note that Kant expresses no admiration for the French revolutionaries themselves. His point of view toward the revolution is the same in *Conflict* as elsewhere in his work: the aims of the revolution (human rights, republican government) may be those dictated by reason, but the means taken by its participants are both immoral and unlikely to succeed. Privately, too, Kant is said to have been enthusiastic about events in France.[46] Rumors of Kant's supposed Jacobinism were so widespread that he was asked to advise the revolutionary government itself, a request he turned down. But although Kant's philosophy was publicly associated with the revolution (to the extent that Heinrich Heine famously called Kant's first *Critique* the spiritual analogue to the material revolution in France),[47] in print he opposed all revolutionary activity except the public use of reason. Even unjust authority must be obeyed. In *Conflict*, Kant maintains the same account of provisional right in the absence of the just state that he does elsewhere (most importantly in the *Rechtslehre*).[48] Referring to his own Prussian people, he writes that those under a monarchy do not have the right to overthrow it in the name of republican government.[49] Morality forbids endangering the established order, and progress in any case can be expected only via top-down gradual reform, rather than bottom-up revolution for which the people are "unripe."[50] Throughout this section, Kant uses the distinction familiar from "Theory and Practice" between republicanism as opposed to despotism, on the one hand, and republicanism as opposed to monarchy, on the other. In the provisional state between disorder and ideal republican rule, monarchs may rule in a republican manner: "It is provisionally the duty of the monarchs, if they rule as autocrats, to govern in a republican (not democratic) way, that is, to treat the people according to principles which are commensurate with the spirit of free laws (as a nation with mature understanding would prescribe them for itself), although they would not be literally canvassed for their consent."[51] Even though circumstances may not allow for the institution of republican governance in its ideal form, the possibility of progress toward that state must be preserved by means of the protection of the public sphere.

The Kantian public sphere needs to be protected from two sorts of dangers: its existence must be secured (protection from censorship), and its members must be allowed to make judgments free of all but the interests of reason (protection from the corruption of power). Regarding the first danger, of censorship, Kant writes that public expressions of judgment on matters of common interest must be legal and that he therefore opposes any "prohibition of publicity."[52] Kant does not simply argue that censorship interferes with the free exchange of ideas that is most likely to result in truth, though he does make that argument as well. He also offers an analysis of the detrimental effects of censorship on what we might today call the sociology of knowledge. Censorship forces the public expression of ideas underground, where it suffers from the constant threat of exposure to state punishment. Even more seriously for Kant, the very atmosphere of secrecy, apart from any concrete danger, interferes with the pursuit of knowledge. Secret societies, veiled and dissimulating publications, diversion of the interest of reason—these are symptomatic of the breakdown of the public sphere occasioned by state censorship. As early as the first *Critique,* Kant writes that the danger to knowledge from the state is not just direct interference but a poisoning of the atmosphere in which inquiry flourishes.[53]

Regarding the second danger to the public sphere, Kant claims it must be protected from corruption by private interest. For Kant "private" denotes that which is not universal, and thus the sphere of private interests includes the particular interests of the state as well as the usual interests of individuals, corporations, and so forth.[54] Judges in the public sphere deserve protection because they express judgment that is both universal and disinterested. Neither "monetary rewards" nor "even the concept of honor" can alter the universal and disinterested views expressed in the public sphere.[55]

Kant does not expect that every expression of judgment in the public sphere will be an accurate rendering of the necessary universal interest of humankind. Participants in the public sphere are ordinary individuals, and are as such subject to error. Though Kant does not imagine that participants in the public sphere will provide an exact substitute for divine judgment, he does hope that they will be able to approximate it as well as is possible in the world, because their circumstances relieve them of the ordinary impediments to free public reason. In the first *Critique*, Kant argues that the interplay of unimpeded points of view subject only to the critique of reason will inevitably lead to enhanced understanding.[56] In *Conflict*, Kant makes a different argument for the power of the public sphere to approximate ideal judgment: only the inspiring power of purely moral ideals, such as the concept of right, could possibly lead to such enthusiastic public expressions of sympathy for such a dangerous cause as the French Revolution.[57] In both cases, public expression in the name of universal principles succeeds because private interests are shut out.

The Happy Consequences of an Epistemological Problem

How, then, can Kant expect that the judgments of the public sphere will have concrete political effects? In order for the judges to retain their authority, they must be protected not only from interference from state censors but also from the corruption that would accompany any direct power on their part. How do concrete political effects follow from necessarily powerless judgments? In "What Is Enlightenment?" Kant has no answer to this conundrum. By *Conflict*, however, he does. Judges in the public sphere do cause changes in the empirical world by means of their expressions of the right, but they cannot themselves become aware of their own effectiveness. The gap in time that separates the determination of a judgment in public with its eventual effect, in combination with innumerable other expressions of judgment, makes it impossible for any particular (human, fallible) judge to experience these effects personally. In the short run, public expressions of the right can have no concrete effect (since inciting revolutionary change cannot be the result of any rational deliberation). Over the long run, however, the cumulative effects of these judgments in public provide the motor of progress toward the ideal state. This same necessary ignorance of one's own place in human history that makes Kant's epistemological task in part 2 of *Conflict* so difficult also makes Kant's account of the judging public coherent. To know where one is in the course of history requires the assumption of a standpoint impossible for limited rational beings like ourselves. The philosophical historian is left with a mere approximation of this standpoint, to be made by way of the interpretation of "signs" and "prophetic history." But what is a handicap for the historian is a virtue for members of the judging public, who may hand down their powerful judgments in happy ignorance of their particular consequences.

Kant's Three Examples of Publicity in Action

Kant provides three main examples of the public sphere operating in the world. First and most important, Kant offers the reader the example of the sympathetic partisans of the French Revolution, who express themselves despite evident dangers. The mediation between ideal principles and actual political life provided by the judging public is supposed to have concrete effects over the long term. The determinations on the part of disinterested spectators that the ideals of the French Revolution express universal principles should stand as examples in the minds of all future peoples: "For that event is too important, too much interwoven with the interest of humanity, and its influence too widely propagated in all areas of the world to not be recalled on any favorable occasion by the nations which would then be roused to a repetition of new efforts of this kind."[58]

In his second example of a functioning public sphere, Kant illustrates the actions of the "free teachers of right, i.e., the philosophers," whose influence comes not from their effects on the people at large, who ignore scholarly disputes, but from the "respectful" applications of philosophers to the state.[59] Kant deploys the model of free teachers of right, rather than the more powerful model of the general public sphere, in order to address one of the most common worries raised against the Enlightenment: Will its progress corrupt the people?[60] No, Kant answers. The people will ignore the more radical propositions of the philosophers, and only those (sound) ideas that have withstood the test of critique in the scholarly public sphere are ever likely to trickle down to the masses. As Kant himself argues in the introduction to *Conflict*, the philosophical faculty has no direct connection with the people, and precious little influence on the state, in whose wisdom Kant has at any rate lost faith by the 1790s. The model of philosophers is thus better able to quell the fears of those worried about the destabilizing social effects of public reason. Moreover, the philosophical faculty plays an essential role in Kant's mature theory, as the arena most protected from outside influence and thus most able to pursue inquiries aimed at knowledge for its own sake. Finally, the philosophical faculty has naturally authoritative judgment insofar as other societal groups seek to adjudicate among differing positions by appeal to it. However, the philosophical faculty *cannot* be the motor that drives progress toward enlightened governance. This role is reserved for the public at large, who make comparisons between morally justified ideals and empirically given circumstances. The incentives motivating the judging public are different from those that face members of the philosophical faculty. The judging public experiences "enthusiasm" based on awe before the moral law, whereas the philosophical faculty ought to be moved purely by thirst for knowledge (the former incentive is practical, while the latter is theoretical). Moreover, as the ultimate arbiter of claims of knowledge, the philosophical faculty must be kept behind an extrathick firewall, as it were, to protect their truth-seeking from the corrupting influence of power. In the introduction to *Conflict*, though not in part 2, Kant seems to be thinking of the general judging public as a sort of mediator between the philosophers and the state, so as to keep the lower faculty safe from any contact with the state.[61]

Third and finally, Kant makes a counterfactual case for political representatives as a kind of judging public, by arguing that Great Britain lacks a true public sphere. In Britain, he claims, an absolute monarchy rules under the name of mixed government. The members of the British Parliament, Kant writes, do not actually limit the will of the monarch, who manipulates them by means of bribery, including his control over offices and honors. Anyone can see that the government of Britain is absolute, Kant argues, since an absolute monarch is one who may go to war on his own authority, and "the monarch of Great Britain has waged numerous wars without asking the people's consent." The occasional instances of disagreement between king and Parliament are explained by Kant as a sort of conspiracy "to furnish ostensible proof of parliamentary freedom." But this is a "mendacious form of publicity." Were the British government to be subjected to true publicity, Kant argues, "this corrupt system" would certainly fall.[62]

The example of the British government is problematic for Kant. In the first place, it is odd that he would associate Parliament with publicity, since even though both institutions are supposed to represent the general will, any actual power on the part of judges in the public sphere would (Kant usually argues) corrupt that sphere by providing an incentive other than the pure interest of reason. Even if all members of Parliament were perfectly moral, their legitimate interests in the immediate welfare of their constituents would cloud their judgments about long-run ideal principles. Part of what makes the judgment of the public so authoritative is its very separation from power of any sort, even from legitimate representative power; public judges are answerable to reason alone. Though Kant is by no means clear on this point, the separation of publicity from power explains why he never mentions the public sphere as part of the ideal republic: ideally, there would be no need for an external judge of the right. The public sphere is required provisionally, to ensure humankind's progress toward the ideal state. Leaving aside the problem of the inappropriateness of any parliament as a public sphere in the Kantian sense, we can follow Kant's point: the intrusion of private interest into the public sphere is fatal to its authority.[63]

KANT'S MATURE CONCEPT OF A JUDGING PUBLIC

In all three examples of a functioning public sphere, the basic mechanism of progress is the same: timeless principles of universal right are interpreted by speakers in the public sphere, who use them to measure the worth of their own institutions. Kant writes that the perfect constitution may be called a "Platonic Ideal (*respublica noumenon*), [which] is not an empty chimera, but the eternal norm for all civil organization in general."[64] This basic formulation echoes Kant's previous discussions of the public sphere, even the very meek version set out in "What Is Enlightenment?" In fact, Kant's second example in *Conflict* of a functioning public sphere closely resembles that of the 1784 essay, in that the philosophers, as "free teachers of right," may humbly present their findings to the state and hope for enlightened rule. Kant has clearly not abandoned his "evolution, not revolution" model of progress in *Conflict*.

Toward the end of part 2, Kant puts forward an even more gradualist answer to the question of public enlightenment and the hope for political progress than the one he has published in his previous essays. Not only must all political change come "from the top downwards," but now, unlike in "What Is Enlightenment?" Kant's expectations for progress from a gradually educated general public are meager indeed. "To expect that the education of young people . . . will not only make them good citizens, but will also bring them up to practice a kind of goodness which can continually progress and maintain itself, is a plan which is scarcely likely to achieve the desired success." Kant follows this dour prediction with what looks, in Nisbet's translation (from the Reiss edition) at least, like an even less optimistic one: "In view of the frailty of human nature . . . we can expect man's hopes of progress to be fulfilled only under the positive condition of a higher wisdom (which, if it is invisible to us, is known as providence); and in so far as *human beings* can themselves accomplish anything . . . it can only be through their negative wisdom in furthering their own ends."[65]

Elsewhere, Kant has expressed the view that some progress toward enlightenment can be achieved in the near term via reform "from above." In this context, he praises the achievements of Prussia's enlightened absolutist ruler Frederick II (the Great), whose government provided Kant some measure of intellectual freedom until his death in 1786. Shortly thereafter Kant's freedom to publish was restricted under the administration of the fanatical Frederick William II and his minister Wöllner. By the 1790s and the publication of *Conflict,* Kant has become embittered about the possibility of enlightened state-led reform.[66] He seems to abandon the goal of state-led reform here, to rest his all hopes for progress on the purposiveness of nature, which guides human destiny without any conscious participation (and thus without any moral willing) on the part of individual beings. The account of progress toward social harmony emerging paradoxically out of the selfish private motives of individuals ("a negative wisdom"), is typical of Kant's teleology. Though this segment of *Conflict* cannot be saved from a general tone of pessimism about an agency-centered account of human progress, Kant's view is actually more ambiguous than Nisbet's translation implies. Where the English reads "a higher wisdom," (which implies divine, and thus unavailable, judgment) Kant's original reads "wisdom from above," repeating the formula that introduced this segment, "progress . . . from above" (implying the judgment of an actual head of state). Thus, reliance on providence may be for Kant here only a last resort, if no other, worldly "wisdom from above" is available. Admittedly, in the brief conclusion to part 2 Kant refers exclusively to the teleological account of the explanation of possible progress: "I blame no one when, considering the ills of the state, he begins to despair of the health of humanity and its progress toward the better," writes Kant, concluding that some (perverse!) optimism may be gained from the terrible costs of modern warfare, which may thus provide natural (that is, interest-based, not rational) incentives to promote more peaceful, republican governance.[67]

The conclusion of Kant's text does not contain his most conclusive arguments. If the Kant of the 1790s has lost his faith in enlightened absolutism's tendency to promote political reform, he has gained some confidence that lasting political authority depends on support from public moral authority. Though he never recommends revolution, or for that matter any action that might disturb the provision of public order, Kant in fact expects that public discontent with the gap between ideal and reality will force political change. The power of enlightened ideas, not the hidden plan of nature, provides Kant's best account of the motor of progress toward the ideal state.

Kant's best account of the public sphere is also his most politically radical, and the climate of Prussia on the eve of the Napoleonic Wars was very dangerous for this sort of opinion. Matthew Levinger has demonstrated that Kant was aware of the scrutiny his views on political change would undergo, both from a suspicious and religiously fanatical ruler, on the one hand, and from an ever more deeply radical reading public, on the other.[68] Kant was unwilling to give the Prussian government cause to limit the freedom of expression any further than it already had. Though the practice of reading secret messages into the writings of those under political pressure is, I think, never likely to produce enlightening interpretations, and though in Kant's case such a reading would be particularly inappropriate, given his deep and well-argued aversion to partial or secret expression, it does make sense to draw the most coherent conclusions from Kant's *Conflict* without necessarily expecting him to repeat them in the conclusion, or to announce them in the introduction.

Kant did announce the main intention of his investigation at the outset of part 2: to answer the question of whether the human race is improving.[69] The mechanics of transition from the provisional (and in Kant's case, absolutist) state are at issue: How can a people emerge from political tutelage with the hope of progress intact (a hope that, Kant argues here and elsewhere, is erased by the violent overthrow of the state)? The precise constitution of an ideal state matters less than the transition to it: "It is certainly *agreeable* to think up political constitutions which meet the requirements of reason (particularly in matters of right). But it is *foolhardy* to put them forward seriously, and *punishable* to incite the people to do away with the existing constitution."[70] The concrete effects of public judgment on political matters, that is, transition to (at least a more) republican rule, then, is Kant's main concern.

Kant considers three possible mechanisms of such transition: the hidden hand of nature (teleological history), enlightened absolutist reform, and the pressure of public judgment. Of these three possible motors of political progress, the latter two rely on the concrete power of ideas in the world as a driving force, while the first excludes that possibility. In the case of teleological history: taking all moral willing as insignificant, and in any case unmeasurable, superstructure, one could support the account of the purposiveness of nature, relying on the telos provided by providence to move humankind toward the ideal, with or without their willing it.[71] The only examples of this kind of quasi-natural mechanism of progress given in *Conflict* are Kant's suggestions about the relationship between republican government and peaceful conduct: "Gradually violence on the part of the powers will diminish and obedience to the laws will increase. There will arise in the body politic perhaps more charity and less strife in lawsuits, more reliability in keeping one's word, etc., partly out of love of honor, partly out of well-understood self-interest. And eventually this will also extend to nations in their external relations toward one another up to the realization of the cosmopolitan society, without the moral foundations in mankind having to be enlarged in the least."[72] Kant seems to have viewed this version of the mechanism of progress less as an alternative to those that consider willed action than as a story told from a different point of view. As he indicates at the beginning of this passage, Kant is only discussing physical causes in the phenomenal realm.[73] It could be that Kant means the judging public to be a mere sign of the inevitability of human progress, while the mechanism of that progress is the purposiveness of nature described in his teleological history. This is how one would have to read *Conflict* in order to make it compatible with Kant's theory of the purposiveness of nature in his teleological history. As I argue in chapter 2, however, this cannot be Kant's definitive solution.

The problem of free will versus determinism cannot be resolved here. Yet it is just this problem that leads Kant to offer two apparently incompatible theories of progress throughout his work, most confusingly in *Conflict*. On the one hand, Kant argues that the motor of human progress is the power of ideas, exerted either by an elite or by a would-be enlightened ministry, or in the form of a public sphere where rational and disinterested political judgments may be reached. On the other hand, Kant says that no matter what actual human beings do, nature has arranged the world in such a way that progress toward the ideal republican constitution is inevitable; the very opposite of the object of any goodwill, namely, wars of aggression, inexorably pushes humankind toward republican government.

Even in this mature work Kant jumps back and forth between those two alternative explanations. No sooner has Kant argued (in section 6) that public expressions of ruling maxims contrary to right would result inevitably in the ruler's fall (a strong case for the efficacy of ideas) than he reverts (in section 7) to the teleological language of mankind's "intended constitution" and the "ultimate purpose of creation."[74] By section 10, Kant appears to have given up the efficacy of publicity in favor of providence's plan, brought about by the interplay of unconscious, self-interested human actors.

What is at stake here is nothing less than the causality of freedom. If the ideals expressed by the judging public have the power to promote concrete progress in human affairs, then freedom is not merely an internal experience but a force in the world. Knowledge of freedom's causality, though, as any sympathetic reader of Kant's first *Critique* would reflexively insist, is impossible. We have, according to Kant, indirect knowledge of freedom's reality by means of our experience of the moral law (the moral law is the *ratio cognoscendi* of freedom, in other words). But we cannot have knowledge of freedom's causality, of its effects in the phenomenal world. Instead, the phenomenal world as we experience it is complete in itself; every physical occurrence has in principle a physical explanation.[75]

Kant never adjudicates between these two points of view. Within the narrow limits of our rational capacities, he argues, human beings may neither affirm nor deny any wholly empiricist (or idealist) ontology. We may, however, speak hypothetically about what conditions would be necessary for other things—perception, practical reason, human progress—to be possible. Kant is able to draw some surprisingly strong conclusions using this metaphysically modest method. As Henry Allison notes in his superb analysis of Kant's theory of aesthetic judgment, for example, while for Kant one may never determine moral truth from empirical human characters (cannot move from "is" to "ought"), "the reverse is possible, at least with regard to the 'consequences that the concept of freedom has in nature.'"[76] If we are to consider ourselves moral agents, we must *presume* a causality for freedom that we can never *know*. This practical presumption need not disturb our theoretical presumption that empirical explanations be, at least in principle, complete, since the phenomenal effects freedom is presumed to have are themselves part of the empirical world. Kant may require two standpoints—theoretical and practical—but he does not need two stories—teleological and agency centered—to make sense of human freedom in the world. The consequences of the necessary presumption of agency do the work that Kant sometimes, regrettably, assigns to teleological history.

The history of humankind's transition to republican rule might appear, then, as one led by an invisible hand toward an ideal goal conceived by providence, but this is misleading. Kant's other two possible mechanisms for progress are agency-centered accounts that rely on the power of ideas to influence political change. In both cases the free interplay of ideas in the public sphere leads to gradual enlightenment; that is, the principles of political reason, such as the necessity of republican rule, the evils of war, and the sanctity of human rights, become more widely accepted. Then one of two things occurs: either representatives of enlightened thought appeal to the sovereign, provoking beneficent reform from above, or the very fact of widespread public comparison between rational ideals and an imperfect government somehow forces change on the state, willing or not. As I discuss above, by the time he writes *Conflict* Kant has lost some of his early enthusiasm for the progressive possibilities of enlightened absolutism. Instead, Kant implies at several points that publicity itself has the power to force political change, even without a sympathetic ruler. The mere public articulation of the rights of man, Kant implies in a note, shatters old-regime opposition "like brittle ice."[77] At two places in *Conflict*, in the criticism of Great Britain and in the note on the power of "true enthusiasm," Kant claims that unjust governments require secrecy in order to maintain their regimes. "This corrupt system must naturally be given no publicity if it is to succeed." That this remark, and Kant's previous one about the fact that no ruler would dare openly to proclaim the rights of citizens null and void, are both made in notes to the main text is attributable to Kant's political caution rather than his view of the importance of the arguments. For Kant is here claiming that publicly articulated principles of right have a driving power of their own, independent from the existence of an enlightened or unenlightened ruler. In any regime, political power ultimately rests on the consent of the governed, who cannot submit, at least not over the long run, to the violation of fundamental principles of right. This is what Kant means when he remarks that all "forms of state are based on the idea of a constitution which is compatible with the natural rights of man, so that those who obey the law should also act as a unified body of legislators."[78]

What separates Kant's theory here from those of his fellow social contract theorists is the word *idea*. Kant cannot be satisfied with the mere construction of an image of the perfect republic. Nor can he advocate revolutionary change, such as the immediate implementation of the vision of the ideal state would require. Instead, he concerns himself with how real-world societies may move toward approximating an ideal state. In his best account, the agents of this change are Kant's judges in the public sphere, who expose the disparity between their provisional states and the ideal republic. These members of the judging public ought to inspire "true enthusiasm" but not be corrupted by any interests other that those of reason, even the honorable interest in the public good.[79] The power of ideas must be exercised over the very long term, in order to allow fallible human judges in the public sphere to approximate perfect judgment: change must come by evolutionary, not revolutionary, means, over a considerable time.[80]

Kant's theory of the public sphere in *Conflict* is at once more radical and more conservative than its predecessor in "What Is Enlightenment?" Kant's

Conflict provides an example of judges in the public sphere directly addressing political issues, including even such a dangerous one as revolution. Unlike their weaker counterparts in "What Is Enlightenment?" the fiery public partisans in *Conflict* openly compare current political conditions to absolute standards of moral right, even when those comparisons threaten the ruling regime. At the same time, in the process of clarifying the question of how a morally authoritative public sphere could also promote political progress, which Kant left open in the earlier essay, he further restricts any immediate pragmatic effects the public sphere might have. In "What Is Enlightenment?" Kant recognizes the state's interest in stability by restricting "private" speech, while protecting "public" discussion in the interest of progress. By *Conflict,* he makes explicit what was only implied in "What Is Enlightenment?": political action of any sort other than speech is reserved to the state. Two consequences follow from the fact that Kant is speaking strictly of the provisional state and not of the ideal republic, and thus of a government composed of fallible human beings ruling over a less than perfectly enlightened people. The acts of the government, as acts of men, will always remain subject to public criticism. However, the state will always have some legitimate interest in restricting potentially dangerous speech.[81] The state, though moved to gradual reform by the stimulus of ethical truth made public by partisans of right, retains its monopoly on action to the last: progress proceeds not *"from bottom to top,* but *from top to bottom."*[82] The task of bringing the actual state in line with the precepts of moral right is "an *obligation,* not of the citizens, but of the sovereign."[83]

Such a conservative move, disheartening as it must have been to Kant's more revolutionary contemporaries, answers the questions about the relation between the public sphere and the state left at the end of "What Is Enlightenment?"[84] First, the authority of Kant's judges in the public sphere is now safe from corruption by contact with the coercive power of government, for all such force is reserved to the state. Along the same lines, Kant adheres to the precept of moral right that forbids citizens from endangering the state, even if it is unjust, so long as it preserves civil order. Second, Kant reveals the mechanism whereby the public sphere is supposed to have a pragmatic effect on political life: comparisons between ideal and actual political life made in the public sphere will, slowly, influence the people and with them those in charge of the state. These leaders may make progressive reforms: "It might well behoove the state likewise to reform itself from time to time and, attempting evolution instead of revolution, progress perpetually toward the better."[85] The ruler may be forced to respond to public outrage ("such a public declaration [contrary to right] would rouse all of his subjects against him").[86] What insulates the authority of the public sphere from the potentially corrupting influence of its pragmatic effects is the slow pace of reform, which ensures that participants in the public sphere will be unable to observe any direct results of their suggestions. Their sole motivation ought to be the universalistic interest that invested the public sphere with its moral authority in the first place—the interest shared by all "rational beings as such" in ethical right.

Taking the short view of ordinary provisional politics, Kant has taken a circuitous route back to the same "inconvenience" suffered by the early social contract theories of Hobbes and Locke (the lack of an authoritative judge of the right). Kant has ruled out the state as a possibly authoritative judge of public right, but he has also eliminated the public sphere from consideration as a legitimate wielder of coercive political power. From the perspective of day-to-day governance, the Kantian political system subjects citizens to the provisional rule of an unpredictable human sovereign, without even the redress offered by Locke in the form of a right of revolution. In this light, the innovation of a modern sense of civil society, seen as a source of authority separate from the state, appears stillborn: the public sphere is the pure, but powerless, source of political judgment.

The long view presents a more optimistic picture. Kant's theory of the public sphere resolves the old problem of the social contract theorists by locating an authoritative source of political judgment in the world. While retaining the old ideal of a *societas civilis* legitimated by conformity with the general interest, Kant's account of the source of this interest provides a theory of civil society in the newer sense of the term, as organized society outside the state. Moreover, Kant's public sphere constitutes a potentially workable, if extremely slow, mechanism for the application of ethical precepts to political practice. "All politics must bend the knee before right, although politics may hope in return to arrive, however slowly, at a stage of lasting brilliance."[87]

conclusion: a kantian theory of citizenship

With chapter 5's analysis of *Conflict*, my reading of Kant's politics is at least provisionally complete. In this concluding chapter, I shall suggest some lines of application of Kantian political theory to issues of interest to contemporary political scientists. Earlier in the book, I argue that present-day readers of Kant must make choices about which elements of his political theory might prove most fruitful, since some aspects of Kant's political writing (most notably his teleological theory of history) are incompatible both with the rest of his political theory and with modern day political science. Here, I shall move even further from fealty to the sage of Königsberg, taking inspiration from Kant's most interesting lines of argument (but dropping some of the least productive), even where they are not incompatible with the rest of his work. Kant himself argues that no one could rightly construct a dogma definitive for all time, as such intellectual closure would violate the dignity of all who are supposed to inherit it. In this spirit, I offer the following preliminary arguments for a Kantian politics in the present day.

From Kant's theory of provisional right (chapter 4), I take the general maxim for a mid-range theory of pragmatic politics that incorporates ideals of human rights: always act such that you preserve the possibility of progress. Most neo-Kantian political theory has, as I discuss in the introductory chapter to this book, taken as a starting point Kant's ethics, rather than his political writings. Thus neo-Kantian theorists of many different stripes, from Rawls to the deliberative or discursive democrats of the 1990s, have taken the justification of state action against individuals or groups as their primary question. Neo-Kantian theorists can give us advice about whether the state may interfere in the religious upbringing of children, the decision of women to end their pregnancies, or the lifestyle choices of those who receive public funds. Not surprisingly, many neo-Kantian political theorists focus their arguments around the U.S. Supreme Court and its decisions, as the place where the conflict between the good of the majority represented by the state and the right of the minority represented by the individual or group receives the most public scrutiny. Kant's ethical theory as interpreted and elaborated upon by his modern-day successors has much to contribute to these important debates. Unfortunately, however, these juridical-limit cases have overshadowed the arguably more fundamental contributions of Kant to political theory, especially his dynamic theory of political progress. Kant's system as I read it integrates ethical norms as a fact about human beings living interdependently on what he calls the "globus terraqueus" with the pragmatic realities of political influence and regime change. All too often, the study of politics is divided between practitioners of normative theory investigating the ethical limits of state authority in particular cases and practitioners of materialist or realist theory investigating distribution, development, and regime change. As some scholars of international relations have recently argued, however, norms of human rights and the public spheres that transmit them can have quite significant concrete effects.[1] Kant's political theory, as opposed to his ethics, is not concerned with establishing the right application of conclusive principles of justice to tricky individual cases. Instead, a Kantian political theorist should be interested in establishing the conditions under which an actually existing public might apply such principles itself. In other words, the Kantian political theorist does not attempt to settle particular issues of justice, but attempts to enable real citizens freely to determine the effects of their principles themselves. This is not to say that Kantian political theorists will not have concrete policy proposals, for indeed they will. However, such specific proposals are made in a Kantian spirit of preserving the possibility of political progress, and thus limit themselves to establishing the conditions under which real people acting by their own lights may collectively determine their political fates.

The reader may have noticed that this attitude toward politics entails a greater respect for decisions made in the marketplace (as opposed to decisions made centrally, whether by democratically or autocratically selected representatives) than has often been the case for Kantian political theorists, at least in recent years.[2] A Kantian politics of provisional right looks at the norms of process rather than anticipating any particularly just outcome for a given policy question.[3] Kantian politics are antipaternalistic: they promote, as Kant would put it, the emergence from tutelage of all kinds. Thus no Kantian political theorist may replace old-regime tutelage with a new form of paternalism, even one whose benefits are widely distributed. Given that no policy prescription, regime, or political institution may be deemed conclusively just under this theory, the Kantian theorist would look instead to the preconditions of just processes of decision making.

Two potential misunderstandings should be addressed at this point. First, a focus on process does not ally Kantian politics with civic republicanism or any other theory that promotes the value of political participation as a good in itself. Kantian provisional politics asks the citizens to make their own determinations of the good, while requiring that the form of collective decision making allow continued progress toward universal freedom. For example, one could imagine a provisionally right system that delegates nearly all day-to-day governance to a small group of representatives, so long as the values of publicity, transparency, information, accountability, and responsiveness were given their due. Kant does not agree with Rousseau that representation as an institution is equivalent to periodic slavery.[4]

Second, respect for decisions made by large numbers of freely acting citizens is not the same as the libertarian respect for the economic marketplace (though in any particular provisional regime respect for economic decisions made in the marketplace could be high or low). In the *Rechtslehre*, Kant argues for respect for the status quo in property rights, but not for any Lockean reason (see chapter 4). Provisional respect for the status quo preserves the degree of order necessary for substantive improvement to be possible, according to Kantian political theory. Once the maintenance of the rule of law is ensured, however, there are no Kantian barriers to collective interference in the marketplace.[5] Kantian political theory is suspicious of any central decision maker whose determinations are not subject to public accountability and feedback mechanisms. This suspicion, however, applies equally to public and private (in the modern sense) institutions: to one-party distributors of tax revenue, and to small groups of technocrats running any enterprise without accountability. A Kantian respect for aggregate decisions would provide just as much critical purchase against failures of accountability in the private sector, such as the Enron Corporation and Long-Term Capital Management debacles of recent years, as it would against overcentralized governmental entities.

In the rest of this chapter, I shall apply Kantian political theory to contemporary questions of democratic citizenship. In so doing, I shall rely on the reading of Kant developed in the preceding five chapters. In the following list, I have summarized the bare outlines of a dynamic Kantian theory of politics, for reference. Based on this theory, I argue that the development of a maximally autonomous citizenry on a global basis should be the standard by which the political actions of states and other entities are judged.

PRINCIPLES OF KANTIAN POLITICAL THEORY

General maxim: "Preserve the possibility of progress"

1. Kantian politics is a mid-range, dynamic theory of the preconditions of possible (though not inevitable) transition from less freedom to more freedom.
2. There are no conclusive political answers: all political right is provisional.
3. Therefore, institutions guaranteeing the preconditions of freedom, including substantive citizenship, open societies, and human rights generally, take precedence over institutions that aim for specific policy results.
4. A commitment to the possibility of progress under conditions of uncertainty entails the promotion of a substantively autonomous citizenry.
5. Kantian antipaternalist politics is suspicious of, though not conclusively opposed to, aggregation of power, wheresoever it may be found.
6. Inclusiveness beats exclusiveness.
7. Publicity is the mechanism of progress. From which follows the value placed on: freedom of expression, transparency, freedom of information transmission and reception, inclusiveness, freedom of association, freedom to demonstrate and petition, and so forth.
8. Publicity is the best source of political judgments, as the public sphere reaps the benefits of expertise without submission to it. Multiple overlapping sources of information are therefore essential.
9. Cosmopolitan citizenship is necessary and possible. The primary responsibility of the state to its citizens is to preserve possibility of progress. When Kant was writing, the national state was the only possible provider of such a service. These days, multilayered, functional, overlapping citizenships are necessary to make the same essential guarantees.
10. Gradualism under conditions of order beats revolutionary change.
11. Ideals matter.

A KANTIAN EXPANSION OF MARSHALL'S TRINITY

T. H. Marshall gave a famous lecture on citizenship and social class at the University of Cambridge in 1949. Grounding his case on the modern history of Great Britain, he argued that citizenship rights ought to be considered in three separate and historically successive categories: civil, political, and social. Marshall's threefold typology was meant to describe democratic citizenship as it could be realized in the mid-twentieth century; it was not supposed to be definitive for all time. In fact, Marshall argued that even "this [third, social] phase will not continue indefinitely."[6]

Marshall was right. Though I agree with Jytte Klausen and others that his conceptualization of citizenship is imperfect, Marshall did correctly see that there would be new phases in the development of democratic citizenship.[7] Conflicts over the establishment of civil, political, and social rights are of course still with us, and the contents of these conflicts vary according to the stakes at hand. But substantive democratic citizenship now requires a *fourth* set of enabling conditions, which I call rights of autonomous citizenship.

For Marshall, each phase of citizenship develops out of conflicts in realizing the demands of the earlier phases. Similarly, I argue that under current conditions not even substantive civil rights (to say nothing of rights of political and economic participation) can be established without institutions guaranteeing some degree of citizen autonomy. Democratic theory makes a number of assumptions about citizen capability (to participate in public debate, to identify and act on interests, to make use of the legal apparatus for the protection of rights, and so forth). As political science has not tired of telling us, these ideals are rarely realized in practice. But citizen incapacity is usually conceived of either as a necessary evil or as a by-product of unfinished social rights business. I argue instead that the realization of the civil, political, and social promises of liberal democracy depends on the creation of institutions guaranteeing a fourth element of substantive citizenship: autonomy.

Kant's dynamic and underappreciated political theory provides a useful account of citizen autonomy in progress toward realizing the promises of freedom and equality. As should be clear by now, I distinguish this theory from the usual reception of Kant by political theorists, who tend to interpret Kant through his ethical works. Kant's political theory, as opposed to his ethics, is a dynamic theory of political progress based on the application of provisional rather than conclusive right. A Kantian extension of Marshall's trinity of citizenship rights illuminates some important contemporary political problems. After brief looks at some topics in the literature on citizenship, I conclude that Marshall and Kant point us to a new theory of citizenship that transforms formal into substantive citizenship by adding autonomy to the familiar goals of civil, political, and social rights.

MARSHALL'S LEGACY

Marshall divided democratic citizenship rights into types (civil, political, and social), and he placed the battles for these rights in three successive stages of the history of Great Britain. One important consequence of Marshall's typology is that it transfers battles about economic redistribution from the sphere of democratic electoral politics to the sphere of citizenship-based rights talk. Of course, in modern democracies we have electoral battles about the meaning of citizenship: in Germany about the extension of voting rights to supposedly temporary guest workers, in Norway about the trade-offs between transnational citizenship and national sovereignty, in California about whether the provision of health care to children is a basic or a citizen's right, and many other instances. But the political discourse in which these battles are conducted constrains the actors and their arguments. Marshall reconfigures the conflict over redistribution as part of the fight for full citizenship rights, and in so doing, he makes the provision of social policies like insurance and education an inevitable part of the modern (or even, formerly, "civilized") state's repertoire.

Klausen complains about just this aspect of Marshall's legacy, arguing that "it is erroneous to regard social citizenship as the equivalent of civil and political rights and that instead it is necessary to distinguish between rights and redistribution."[8] Redistributive issues belong in the democratic electoral arena, Klausen argues, and not in the (relatively) depoliticized realm of citizenship rights. Furthermore, Klausen points out, making social rights part of citizenship actually leads to less rather than more inclusiveness, since citizenship tends to be defined against newcomers (such as migrant workers and asylum seekers, among others). Surveying Scandinavian welfare policies, Klausen notes that the language of social citizenship was adopted strategically by parties interested in redistribution and was dropped when the political climate changed.[9] "It can in fact be argued that the Scandinavian welfare states are as much examples of closure and exclusion as they are examples of welfare state inclusion. Which feature predominates depends upon one's vantage point, particularly whether one is a citizen or an alien."[10]

Klausen is right to be suspicious of any political discourse that recommends transferring important decisions from the many to the few. Moreover, decisions about redistribution of national resources certainly ought to be submitted to the electorate and its representatives in any democratic polity. But though these starting points ring true, as does Klausen's related critique of social scientists' rather uncritical celebration of Scandinavian welfare policies, they do not resonate with her attack on Marshall and his successors. Marshall himself is responsible for some of the confusion about social citizenship.[11] Marshall's postwar enthusiasm for the welfare state led him to exaggerate the redistributive elements of his theory. As Anthony Rees suggests, Marshall's 1949 "statement that twentieth-century capital-ism and citizenship were 'at war' was profoundly misleading."[12] Social rights are essentially about the preconditions of substantive citizenship; while some redistribution is likely to be part of any state's social policy, it is a means to an end rather than an end in itself. As Ralf Dahrendorf said in a lecture honoring Marshall, "Modern social conflict is about attacking in-equalities *that restrict full civic participation* by social, economic or political means, and establishing the entitlements that make up a rich and full status of citizenship."[13]

At the heart of Klausen's critique of Marshall and his successors is an ar-gument against replacing classic democratic conflicts with rights-based ar-guments about the state's obligation to its citizens. As I discuss below, Robert Putnam and the civic engagement theorists raise similar concerns about a troubling shift from collective decision making in the name (at least) of the common good, toward rights-based claims on the state at-tached to a proliferating number of subnational identities. Klausen cites, among other examples, the shift in the discourse over health care in the United States from a debate about the best use of national resources to one about health care as a right of citizenship. Will Kymlicka's theory of multi-cultural citizenship has come under similar fire for using rights language in cases that have traditionally been viewed as straight intergroup conflict.[14]

From a conclusive rather than a provisional perspective, Klausen's and others' worries about the advance of rights-based claims in the contempo-rary democratic arena are indeed troubling.[15] Liberal theorists have been trying without success to ground political right on something incontrovert-ible for quite a while now. Wouldn't the addition of rights for health care, minimum income, leisure, and other apparently secondary goods dilute what case there is for defending first-order human rights like freedom of movement or political expression? By insisting on social rights, Klausen and others ask, are we not conflating claims we make against each other (redis-tribution) with our legitimate rights against the state?[16]

Two responses may be made here, both from the point of view of provisional rather than conclusive right. Kymlicka's theory supplies the first response: there are, he argues, no neutral states, and thus no status quo that does not harm some and benefit others. Therefore, redistributive policies, especially those redressing concrete injuries suffered on the basis of one's identity, are not "Robin Hood" policies as Klausen characterizes them. Instead of maintaining a mythical neutrality that serves the interests of the dominant groups, liberal states should endeavor to include all citizens as fully as possible in collective life. Depending on the particular group in question, inclusion in full citizenship may require the state to add new official languages to its repertoire, broaden its views on what constitutes proper citizenship, and even grant some local control to regional entities.

The second response to Klausen and others concerned about the expansion of rights talk is related to the first one.[17] The policies of social citizenship that would address states' real failures of inclusiveness are indirectly redistributive, in that some would lose resources they are used to enjoying while others would gain resources they have not previously enjoyed. However, social citizenship policies do not *replace* the bargaining and electoral competition that characterize democratic politics. Instead, they *enable* genuine democratic politics to occur, by including previously excluded groups. Klausen worries that social citizenship policies would replace democratic politics; where this is so, as in some of the civic engagement literature's examples, it is indeed worrisome. However, a substantively democratic politics must begin with substantive inclusiveness to which social citizenship policies are essential.

Taking Dahrendorf's characterization as a starting point, one can view social rights not as an illegitimate transfer of redistributive debates from the electoral arena to the discourse of citizenship rights but instead as a set of policies (Marshall cites education and social insurance) aimed at guaranteeing substantive citizenship on a broad basis. However, as political scientists are beginning to understand, substantive citizenship at the beginning of the twenty-first century requires more than civil, political, and even social rights. Contemporary challenges to effective participation—such as the shifting locus of decision making from the national state to supranational and quasi-private organizations, the shift in modes of effective democratic participation from federated mass-membership organizations to single-issue professionally directed pressure groups, and many others—are setting new preconditions for substantive citizenship. If today's citizens are not to suffer what Kantian theory would call substantive heteronomy while enjoying merely superficial citizenship rights, we must follow Marshall's directive and expand his trinity to include the next set of rights and institutions, and the battles that seek to establish them: rights of citizen autonomy.

SUBSTANTIVE CITIZENSHIP IN THE SOCIAL CAPITAL AND CIVIC ENGAGEMENT LITERATURES

Communism is a judgment against our failure to make democracy real.
—*Martin Luther King Jr.*[18]

Kantian political theory enjoins us to make the conditions of political progress real. Given the permanence of political uncertainty, the corruption of judgment that accompanies even legitimate power, and the danger of tyranny that accompanies the concentration of political authority, Kantian theory recommends the achievement of substantive citizen autonomy rather than any particular slate of policies to be carried out by the state. This substantive autonomy should not be confused with individualist autarky, libertarian minimalism, Jeffersonian localism, or any other view that celebrates independent individuals apart from their social and political relations. Unlike most liberal social contract theorists, Kant does not view the autarkic individual as the politically relevant unit of analysis. As I discussed in chapter 4, Kant faults Locke for failing to recognize that the most basic political right, to property, ought to be conceived in terms of *relations* among autonomous subjects, rather than as a right held by a lone individual. For Kant, the *globus terraqueus* represents the ground on which political right must be built.

If Kantian political theory may not be pressed into the service of the minimalist state, however, it should also not be seen as defending traditional strong-state democratic arguments. In chapter 4, I noted that Kant does not conclude his exposition of social contract theory with the obligation to submit to common order but insists in addition that states must move beyond mere order toward a condition of right. Kant never trusts the state, even a relatively republican state with a representative legislative branch, to make progress on its own toward perfection. Instead, he requires states to tolerate and even encourage alternative sources of political progress, including a free public sphere, an unfettered philosophical faculty, and an active and progressively more enlightened citizenry. Like Tocqueville, Kant is interested in the underlying structure of power; unmediated relations between ruler and ruled are dangerous for progress, however the ruler is selected. Thus, Kant criticizes the structure not only of absolutist monarchies but also of democratically controlled administrative states.

Writing sympathetically if skeptically about the prospects for left-wing liberalism in present-day American politics, Jeffrey C. Isaac criticizes progressives' often uncritical support of powerful administrative states: "To be blunt: Progressivism has always been relentlessly modernistic and technocratic. It has always been enthusiastic about human power, and it has always been enthusiastic about the beneficence of the power of the liberal state. But such enthusiasms can no longer be credibly indulged."[19] Isaac notes that present-day political cleavages cannot be reduced to dichotomies of the sort that used to mobilize progressives around the state. More fundamentally, Kantian political theory insists that alternative sources of political judgment are necessary to the very possibility of political progress. Neither the autarkic individual under the minimalist state nor the member of the mass public under a formally democratic administrative state has the potential to achieve what Kantian political theory regards as the sine qua non of good government: substantive citizenship.

Some present-day political scientists agree with the Kantian political theorist on the importance of substantive citizenship. Citizens possessed of substantive autonomy in present-day states will not be independent of the state, but neither may they be considered its clientele. Rather than focusing on the delivery of the policies that liberal philosophy determines are necessary for the people's happiness, and rather than expecting the free operation of the marketplace to produce citizens capable of enjoying the freedom promised by minimalist philosophers, advocates of substantive citizenship look to the state and to civil society for the preconditions of autonomous political activity. Some scholars, notably the theorist of social capital Robert D. Putnam, identify these preconditions mostly in basic social interactions below the level of formal politics. Others, such as the theorist of civic engagement Theda Skocpol, look to state-society relations for the preconditions of substantive self-rule. Both schools of thought, however, agree that good government in a liberal democratic sense rests on a social basis of empowered and capable citizens, organized in such a way that substantive self-rule, rather than mere exchange of ruling elites, is possible.

Social Capital

Putnam, in his study of patterns of decline in American communities entitled *Bowling Alone,* uses survey data unprecedented in scope and degree to document something many of us suspected already, namely, that there is a strong relationship between the health and vitality of a democracy and the health and vitality of its nonpublic social organizations.[20] By 1993, Putnam and his colleagues had already argued for this thesis in their careful comparative study of civil society in parts of Italy, *Making Democracy Work*.[21] The *Making Democracy Work* group measured the success of new regional governmental districts instituted in Italy in 1970 (comparing their achievements in delivering services to their citizens, levels of corruption, and so forth) and tried to account for the differences. The structure of government and most external factors were conveniently held constant, as each region interacted with the same central government and each had been given the same basic institutional apparatus. After testing a number of hypotheses, the team members were, as Putnam later describes it, forced to admit that what seemed to account for the different success rates was the level of civic vitality, which Putnam calls "social capital."[22] Institutional differences were held constant, and none of the other factors (political party in power, dominant ideology, population stability, and prosperity, among others) had consistently significant effects on governmental success. Where the new regional governments were most successful, Putnam and his colleagues found, they were relying on long traditions of civic organization. Putnam traces the histories of civil society in the successful regions back to their civic republican roots. The phenomenon of social capital as Putnam understands it works subtly, mostly as citizens build face-to-face relationships that are only indirectly political. As Putnam says, the Florentine choral singers get together because they enjoy music, not to strengthen the social fabric, even if that is an indirect result.[23]

In *Bowling Alone*, Putnam applies the same idea to contemporary American society, documenting simultaneous declines in traditional forms of civic participation, most forms of political participation, and political health generally. Recalling Tocqueville, Putnam uses his empirical observations to argue that the public's business is best done when that public is engaged, with citizens trained to think of themselves as participants in collective enterprises of their own choosing, organized to force elites to serve broad rather than narrow interests, and simply connected to each other in multifarious ways across narrow socioeconomic categories. In the introduction to a volume of studies applying the concept of social capital to eight countries, Putnam and Kristin A. Goss write that the "idea at the core of social capital theory is extremely simple: Social networks matter."[24]

Putnam and his colleagues studying social capital make a fundamental point of great interest to Kantian political theory: good government in a liberal democratic sense depends on an empowered citizenry. To be substantive citizens and not mere subjects, citizens must be linked to one another in social networks that both provide leverage against would-be oligarchs of all stripes and enhance each member's politically relevant skills. However, a Kantian perspective also highlights some serious shortcomings of the social capital point of view. As the strongest (nonteleological) reading of Kant's political theory has it, one may not expect citizen empowerment to arise on its own, without the agency of committed human beings in government ministries, in the public sphere generally, and even in philosophical faculties. Civil society in the weak sense can flourish even under absolutist political conditions ("Argue as much as you like . . . only obey," says Frederick the Great). Thus Kant argues that rulers interested in having done the right thing ought to promote, not just tolerate, the development of an enlightened, and by implication an empowered, citizenry. The lesson that present-day Kantian theorists may draw from Kant's argument—that enlightenment must be promoted by the state itself—makes even more sense under the conditions of complex, highly administered, advanced industrial states than it did in Frederick's Prussia. One ought not, as Putnam evidently does, expect private sector initiatives and local-level community building to bring about the conditions of the possibility of political progress.

Civic Engagement

Skocpol's analysis of the history of civic engagement in the United States supports the case for the necessity of participation by national states in any promising civic renewal. Contrary to popular wisdom and to social capital theory, Skocpol argues, "American civic voluntarism was never predominantly local and never flourished apart from national government and politics."[25] Her study of federated mass-membership organizations in the United States starts from the same empirical evidence—declining trust in government, civic activity, and political participation in the second half of the twentieth century—used by Putnam in his work on social capital. Civic engagement theory as practiced by Skocpol and her colleagues, however, looks at changes at the organizational level rather than the individual level, differentiating between face-to-face meetings that ultimately have political relevance (such as membership in huge national groups like the Knights of Columbus) and face-to-face meetings of lower political import (such as bowling leagues).

Skocpol, Morris Fiorina, and their colleagues tested the thesis that low civic engagement leads to democratic dysfunction in *Civic Engagement and American Democracy*.[26] Some of their most intriguing suggestions come from work that disaggregates general categories like "civic participation," breaking them down into types that reflect the complex reality of present-day life. For example, they distinguish between old-style "participation in federated mass membership organizations with lots of local level participation" and new-style "participation in national lobbying and interest groups with professional staff doing most of the work."[27] When looked at this way, civic participation in the United States shows a pretty solid decline in the former type but a steady rise in the size and influence of the latter. Thus, it may not be the quantity of public participation in affairs of common interests that has changed (after all, by many measures other than voting, public participation has risen in recent years, thanks to new governmental openness, among other institutional changes) but the quality of public participation. Where in the first two-thirds of the twentieth century in the United States we would expect civic engagement and public activism to meet at the union hall, the veterans' lodge, or the fraternal temple, today's civic engagement takes place in the electronic spaces of fax lines, e-mail in-boxes, and bank accounts, or in the Washington offices of professional lobbyists. What's more, it is likely to be done by and in the name of citizens with certain resources, not all of them economic (Robert Reich has usefully called this the new class of "symbolic analysts"). Robert Wuthnow's study of changes in the character of religious organizations and their interaction with government shows a similar pattern of changes: whereas the typical active member of a religious organization used to belong to a mainline Protestant church involved in externally directed charity activities, today there are fewer practicing that model of religious-civic engagement than fifty years ago, and more practicing a new style of evangelical church membership combined with (often very extensive) internally directed charitable activities than there once were.[28] Group activity in the United States has become less racially and sexually exclusive, but it is now deeply divided along class, religious, and geographic lines.

Not only has the shift from old-style to new-style civic activity made the civic universe "remarkably oligarchic," but the decline of opportunities for Americans to interact across social barriers has diminished that staple of social capital and civic engagement theory alike, public spiritedness: "Federations were especially vital in building an American democracy in which ordinary people could participate, gain skills, and forge recurrent ties to one another—not just locally but also across communities, states, and regions of a vast and expanding nation. Federations allowed ordinary Americans to interact with powerful societal leaders. And they nurtured a style of public leadership based on majority election and the responsibility of officeholders to engage and mobilize their fellow citizens."[29] By contrast, professionally managed associations structure themselves in ways that Kantian political theorists would find suspicious: masses of members are solicited individually by the center (usually, as Skocpol notes, located in Washington or New York); rather than meeting with each other, members participate by writing checks, reading reports, and occasionally participating in center-orchestrated mass mailing campaigns. The historical norm in politics, Skocpol reminds us, is elite cooperation and contention with one another "above the heads of most people living in their societies. Only in special circumstances do elites turn to democratic leadership."[30]

Skocpol illustrates her case that these changes matter for good government with a focused comparison between the passage of the G.I. Bill after the Second World War and the failed effort at health care reform under the Clinton administration. She notes that elite professionals in the 1940s tried to pass a much more limited piece of legislation than the one that ultimately provided education, business loans, and home ownership to a huge new group of middle-class Americans. The relatively modest original bill was challenged by the American Legion, which drafted an ambitious alternative piece of legislation and used its federated structure and mass-membership clout to encourage members of Congress to support it. By contrast, the failed effort of the Clinton administration in the 1990s to reform the provision of health care in the United States, where currently tens of millions are without any formal coverage, and millions more are underinsured, was a battle of elites among themselves. "The drafting of President Clinton's health security legislation was done by a secretive five-hundred-person commission full of self-appointed experts, which produced a 1,342-page bill that few could understand, let alone use to mobilize popular support."[31]

Skocpol is criticizing not the goals of the Clinton health care initiative but the structure of the decision-making power that promoted it. Like the social capital theorists, Skocpol finds that ordinary Americans' participation in public life has become so weak that their very status as citizens is threatened. In contrast to social capital theory, and like Kantian political theory, Skocpol's theory insists that the state must promote the preconditions of substantive citizenship, especially those that provide for an active, organized, public-spirited civil society. The mass-membership federations that were a staple of postwar American political and civic life were nurtured by government, and any new institutions and practices aimed at renewed civic engagement must also be.

Taken together, the studies that make up the social capital and civic engagement literatures suggest that norms and social institutions that are not expressly political, such as the norm of reciprocity and the institution of civic organization, can have profound political effects.[32] Both the deliberative democracy literature (see my discussion in the introduction to chapter 1) and the social capital and civic engagement literatures focus on reciprocity in particular as a necessary ingredient of political health. However, whereas the deliberative democracy theorists look at reciprocity as an intellectual norm to be consciously adhered to by citizens in disputes with one another, the civic engagement theorists look for the social roots of reciprocity as sort of Humean custom. Both the formal and the substantive elements of the principle of reciprocity are important in a polity that hopes to make progress toward realizing democracy's promises, though political theorists have tended to emphasize the former over the latter. Substantively autonomous citizens do not automatically emerge to practice reciprocity in an arena of deliberation. Instead, the formal norm of reciprocity must tacitly presume the social preconditions of substantive reciprocity in practice. When the social preconditions of autonomy are absent or waning, as the civic engagement literature suggests, substantive citizenship will be available only to a lucky subset of those to whom formal citizenship is guaranteed.[33]

This very preliminary look at some of the literature on civic engagement suggests that the Kantian political theorist interested in promoting progress toward better governance should look to institutions that encourage substantive rather than merely formal citizenship. While there are still a number of live and interesting issues around issues of formal citizenship rights, particularly in immigration policy and in municipal voting rights, these studies of civic engagement in the United States today demonstrate that formal democratic citizenship without the informal institutions that enable substantive participation fails to deliver on its promise of freedom and equality for all. Schattschneider's famous dictum—"The flaw in the pluralist heaven is that the heavenly chorus sings with a strong upper-class accent"—is as relevant today as ever, as are Marshall's and others' observations that formal citizenship without the social bases of meaningful participation means relatively little. But beyond complaints about the elite character of pluralist interest representation, a Kantian political theorist would ask how citizens today could move toward substantive freedom that entails the opportunity to exercise control over the decisions that determine people's collective fate. According to Kantian political theory, the theorist ought to focus on the mid-range problem of maintaining the possibility of progress, rather than on determining particular policy or even regime type outcomes and expecting the practical problems to be resolved separately.[34]

Thus the Kantian political theorist faced with the issue of ensuring substantive citizenship in the present day would ask under what conditions might we expect the possibility of progress. Given the uncertainty of the result of any particular policy, the Kantian theorist would insist instead on the maintenance of feedback mechanisms, including especially free and fair elections, transparency in both the public and private spheres as far as possible, and a vibrant, competitive, global public sphere. The theorist would assume that in the normal course of things, the power to make decisions over matters of collective interest tends to become monolithic and unresponsive, and thus that an important element of democratic political life is the maintenance of a viable opposition, and not just an opposition political party.[35] Kant's theory of the indirect power of publicity reminds us of the importance of a thriving public sphere. Publicity is part of what enables the creation of a substantively autonomous citizenry.

SUBSTANTIVE CITIZENSHIP IN RECENT FEMINIST SCHOLARSHIP

Students of the relationship between state policy and gender roles have been writing about the problem of substantive citizenship for more than a decade now. Like other disenfranchised groups, and following a course not dissimilar to Marshall's succession of civil, political, and social rights, feminist scholars and activists have discovered that the achievement of formal rights only initiates the process of achieving substantive freedom.[36] Although most of the formal rights are still incompletely won, even in developed countries like the United States, women are finding that those rights they have achieved formally require substantive backing before their promise may be realized. North American women, for example, have achieved some measure of equality with men in the areas of property rights, voting rights, rights of political participation, and so forth. Along with their male fellow citizens, they enjoy some social rights, such as retirement income and unemployment insurance, to complement their civil and political rights. This progress notwithstanding, it is easy to document women's lack of, for example, material success compared with men's; despite the passage and sporadic enforcement of laws against discrimination in education and hiring, for example, women's pay lags behind men's pay across nearly every industry. Women receive less than men do of nearly every valuable resource: less leisure time, less societal respect, and less money.

However, theorists interested in the achievement of substantive citizen autonomy may learn more from the past decade of feminist scholarship than the brute fact of relative deprivation.[37] If the promises of formal democratic citizenship in the civil, political, and social arenas are to be realized for women, scholars have been arguing, then the substantive preconditions of women's autonomy must be met. Nancy Fraser, for example, argues that democratic states need to stop presuming that most citizens fit the standard pattern "of male-headed families and relatively stable jobs."[38] In an earlier article, Fraser calls for the reconstruction of "androcentric institutions so as to welcome human beings who can give birth and who often care for relatives and friends, treating them not as exceptions, but as ideal-typical participants."[39] As the scholars of civic engagement have been documenting, participation as an autonomous citizen realizing the democratic promises of freedom and equality depends substantially on the social bases that enable this kind of citizenship. While the formal means for granting them full citizenship are available in many places, women have not realized their potential because the social institutions that support them are for the most part *un*available to them. The decline of leisure and the rise of two-income families only begin to tell the story, but they are vivid facts that indicate the seriousness of the problem. Without the social bases enabling citizen autonomy, full citizenship (for women and for men) will remain an empty promise.[40]

Kant's own rather dated theory of qualifications for citizenship at least recognizes this important point (that formal citizenship depends for its realization on social institutions). Though few would defend the notorious Kantian distinction between active and passive citizens, the reasoning behind Kant's distinction is interesting.[41] Kant argues for the institution of two tiers of citizenship, active and passive. Active citizens would be accorded full rights of citizenship, while passive citizens would have what we would now call civil rights, but no political ones. Only those with the means to support themselves without selling their labor would be eligible for active citizenship, though Kant makes an exception to this rule for university professors like himself. Excluded from active citizenship are farm laborers, workers, and women, among others. The intuition behind Kant's distinction, however irrelevant the distinction itself, is worthy of note. Participation in the institutions that enable self-rule requires not only formal membership in the polity but also the means to realize these rights and responsibilities. Kant was probably arguing on the basis of one of his most common presumptions, namely, that the autonomous exercise of public reason requires that it be separated from all (even unselfish) concrete interests. Though Kant certainly (and unfortunately) meant to divide citizens into those capable of active citizenship and those deserving mere civil protection, he does seem to recognize the contradiction between such a position and his antipaternalism. For example, Kant adds that in a just state all citizens must be able at least potentially to reach active status. The important conclusion to draw from Kant's dated theory of citizenship qualifications is this: without the social bases of autonomy, even people with formal citizenship rights cannot represent themselves actively or adequately.

In this concluding chapter, I have begun to develop a Kantian expansion of Marshall's theory of democratic citizenship. Along the way, I hope to have illustrated some of the usefulness of this book's new reading of Kant as a dynamic theorist of political change, rather than simply as a philosopher of magisterial, but static, ethical principles. More important, perhaps, is that this work should contribute to a growing literature on realizing the promises of liberal democratic citizenship. In a famous article a few years ago, Robert Kaplan asked whether "democracy was just a moment."[42] The answer, I think, is definitely no, but the challenges raised by Kaplan and others are real. In the field of citizenship theory, a changing political environment has led to a fourth requirement for substantive citizenship. States and societies need institutions that encourage citizen autonomy along with civil rights, rights of political participation, and the social basis of the use of these rights. As Dahrendorf writes, "It is difficult to think of human association without an element of domination. Where there is society, there is power."[43] With substantive heteronomy a constant problem, citizens need the means to assert their rights as much as they need the results of fights for civil and other rights. Kant's political theory of provisional right takes for granted a constant struggle between oligarchical and public control. The appropriate response to this fact of political life is the initiation of the battles for and the establishment of institutions to protect citizens' abilities to control their own collective destinies.

NOTES

Note. In notes referring to Kant's works, I cite a short title, then the volume and page numbers from the standard Preussischen Akademie edition of Kant's writings, followed by the page number of the relevant English translation. Most English-language citations are from *Immanuel Kant: Practical Philosophy* translated and edited by Mary J. Gregor (Cambridge: Cambridge University Press, 1996); also cited are: *Critique of Pure Reason* translated by Paul Guyer and Allen W. Wood (Cambridge: Cambridge University Press, 1998); *Prolegomena to Any Future Metaphysics* Carus translation revised by James W. Ellington (Indianapolis: Hackett, 1977); *Critique of Judgment* translated by Werner S. Pluhar (Indianapolis: Hackett, 1987); and *The Conflict of the Faculties* (Lincoln: University of Nebraska Press, 1979). Where I have used my own or another translation, I have mentioned this in the notes.

Preface

1 Alexander and Corrado, *Financing the 1992 Election.*

2 For an illuminating account, see Heider-Markel and Meier, "The Politics of Gay and Lesbian Rights."

3 Will Kymlicka has usefully drawn a distinction between the demands of minority groups for, on the one hand, inclusive citizenship rights and, on the other, limits of state harassment. The former type of policy battle involves changes in government policy that allow full, positive participation as members of the polity to minority groups or newcomers (Kymlicka's example is the desire of Sikh men to be exempted from the ceremonial headgear requirement for entry into the Royal Canadian Mounted Police). Admission to the military similarly constitutes a crucial part of substantive political citizenship, and thus the battle over equal access to military service is one for inclusion, rather than for exclusive (so-called special) rights. See Kymlicka, *Politics in the Vernacular,* 165.

4 See Rimmerman, Wald, and Wilcox, eds., *The Politics of Gay Rights,* especially chapter 11.

5 At the time, hardly anyone imagined that impeachment might be used against Clinton.

Introduction

1 Haas, "Epistemic Communities and International Policy Coordination"; Keck and Sikkink, *Activists Beyond Borders.*

2 Isaac, "The Strange Silence of Political Theory."

3 Shapiro, *Democracy's Place,* 5; Bell, *East Meets West,* 6.

4 To give only the most important of these publications, respectively: Hans Reiss's 1970 edition of Kant's political writings, Lewis White Beck's 1963 collection of Kant's writings on history, and Zwi Batscha's 1976 collection of Kant's politically relevant reflections, with commentary; Ronald Beiner and William James Booth's collection of

essays on Kant's political philosophy, James Bohman and Matthias Lutz-Bachmann's collection of essays on *Perpetual Peace,* and Mark Timmons's collection of interpretive essays on Kant's *Metaphysics of Morals;* Norbert Hinske's German-language collection and James Schmidt's English-language collection of essays around "What Is Enlightenment?"; Frederick C. Beiser's two works of intellectual history and his collection of the writings of Kant's immediate successors; Onora O'Neill's brilliant *Constructions of Reason,* Henry Allison's definitive *Kant's Transcendental Idealism,* Patrick Riley's two essential works, *Kant's Political Philosophy* and *Will and Political Legitimacy,* and the work of John Christian Laursen and others establishing Kant's pragmatic and engaged politics; Manfred Kuehn's authoritative *Kant: A Biography;* John Rawls's decreasingly Kantian series of philosophical works, Jürgen Habermas's increasingly Kantian series of works in philosophy and social science, and a number of significant theories in political science inspired by Kant, such as the work of Michael Doyle. Mika LaVaque-Manty's brilliant *Arguments and Fists: Political Agency and Justification in Liberal Theory* does not fall neatly into any of these categories; it combines historical analysis of liberal thought, particularly of Kant and Montesquieu, with consideration of contemporary philosophy of agency and applies the resulting view of liberal agency on the model of Kant's *Gelehrte* (scholar) to a focused comparison between two discourses of legitimacy in contemporary environmental politics.

5 See, for example, Cassirer, *Kant's Life and Thought.*

6 Here the good work of the past few decades on Kant's political theory has made rather little headway. Only a few commentators consider the dynamic aspect of Kant's politics, as opposed to the static conditions he sets for juridical perfection. Those who do investigate Kant's thinking on transition fall into two main categories: commentators on Kant's theory of the public sphere, and commentators on Kant's philosophy of history. I incorporate both of these perspectives within a general perspective on Kant's theory of provisional right.

7 O'Neill, *Constructions of Reason.*

8 "Rigorism" is a term sometimes applied to Kant's ethics in the philosophical literature. See, for example, R. F. Atkinson, "Kant's Moral and Political Rigorism."

9 Three excellent recent works explore this topic: Barbara Herman's *The Practice of Moral Judgment,* Christine Korsgaard's *Creating the Kingdom of Ends,* and Henry Allison's *Kant's Theory of Freedom.*

10 The review attributed to Christian Garve but written by both him and his editor, Johann Georg Heinrich Feder, makes this mistake. This tradition in misreadings of Kant is carried on in modern times by P. F. Strawson, in *The Bounds of Sense,* among many others. See Kitcher, *Kant's Transcendental Psychology,* chapter 1. See also Allison's *Kant's Transcendental Idealism* and the replies to his critics contained in *Idealism and Freedom: Essays on Kant's Theoretical and Practical Philosophy.* In reading Kant myself, I have continually been surprised at the persistence of the view that Kant posited two worlds rather than two perspectives. Even in his late works, Kant remains very careful to avoid such descriptions, always prefacing any possibly confusing sentence with "as it were" or

some other caveat. In a note to the preface to the second edition of *Critique of Pure Reason*, Kant compares his method to the experimental method of natural science: "Now the propositions of pure reason, especially when they venture beyond all boundaries of possible experience, admit of no test by experiment with their *objects* (as in natural science): thus to experiment will be feasible only with *concepts* and *principles* that we assume a priori by arranging the latter so that the same objects can be considered from two different sides, *on the one side* as objects of the senses and the understanding for experience, and *on the other side* as objects that are merely thought at most for isolated reason striving beyond the bounds of experience. If we now find that there is agreement with the principle of pure reason when things are considered from this twofold standpoint, but that an unavoidable conflict of reason within itself arises within a single standpoint, then the experiment decides for the correctness of that distinction." *Critique of Pure Reason*, Bxix; III.

11 Allison, *Kant's Transcendental Idealism*, 3–4.

12 Yack, *The Longing for Total Revolution*, 99.

13 Actually, in his later work Kant suggests several instances in which freedom's causality (for this is what is at issue here) is implied, if not directly observable, including the existence of consensus about the beautiful, and the expression of moral sympathy for the French Revolution.

14 Even Yovel, who reads Kant's works through the lens of teleological history, criticizes the version of teleology Kant puts forward in his "Idea for a Universal History" as incompatible with the rest of Kant's system. Yovel, *Kant and the Philosophy of History*, 154–55.

15 Studies of single works of Kant need not posit that the work contains the key to his whole philosophy. See, for example, Dieter Henrich's *Kant, Gentz, Rehberg: Über Theorie und Praxis*, and Georg Cavallar's *Kant and the Theory and Practice of International Right*.

16 See Kersting, *Wohlgeordnete Freiheit*; see also Mulholland, *Kant's System of Rights*. Mary J. Gregor's excellent translation of the *Rechtslehre*, which appeared in 1991, and in a revised edition in 1996, has been a boon to English-speaking scholars of Kant's politics.

17 Other commentators who take a developmental view include Yirmiyahu Yovel, Richard Velkley, Richard Zammito, and Werner Busch, among others.

18 The best book on Kant as a social contract theorist is Riley's *Will and Political Legitimacy*, but see also Cassirer's *Rousseau, Kant, Goethe* and Kelly's *Idealism, Politics and History*.

19 Skinner, *Reason and Rhetoric in the Philosophy of Hobbes*, 7.

20 Melvin Richter has made some of the work of the "Geschichtliche Grundbegriffe" group available to an English-speaking audience under the title *The History of Political and Social Concepts: A Critical Introduction*.

21 Pocock, *Politics, Language, and Time*, 11.

22 Pagden, *The Languages of Political Theory in Early-Modern Europe*, 2.

23 Ashcraft, *Revolutionary Politics and Locke's Two Treatises of Government*. The "Geschicht-

liche Grundbegriffe" project is a multivolume work of intellectual history that provides very thorough, sometimes book length, articles on the modern and contemporary histories of political concepts. Like their British and American counterparts, the German members of the "Geschichtliche Grundbegriffe" group study political vocabularies not to ascertain any definitive meaning for them but to trace their development through histories of political arguments and actions. Unlike their English-speaking counterparts, the "Geschichtliche Grundbegriffe" group members focus on a particular time period, the late eighteenth to early nineteenth centuries. See also Richter, *The History of Political and Social Concepts.*

24 Skinner, *Reason and Rhetoric in the Philosophy of Hobbes,* 8.

CHAPTER 1 Civil Society

1 See, for example, Rawls, "Kantian Constructivism in Moral Theory," and more recently *Lectures on the History of Moral Philosophy.* For Habermas's roots in Kant, see chapter 13 of *The Structural Transformation of the Public Sphere.*

2 Amy Gutmann and Dennis Thompson have written a now-classic expression of this view, *Democracy and Disagreement.* See also the collection edited by Bohman and Rehg, including especially the contributions of Joshua Cohen.

3 Shapiro, "Enough of Deliberation."

4 Ibid., 29–30.

5 Pagden, introduction to *The Languages of Political Theory in Early-Modern Europe.*

6 In the late work *The Conflict of the Faculties* (1798), Kant writes that imagining ideal states is pleasant, but he implies that the activity is ultimately irresponsible. *Conflict,* 7:92; 167.

7 See, for example, Kersting, *Wohlgeordnete Freiheit;* Williams, *Kant's Political Philosophy;* and Rosen, *Kant's Theory of Justice.* For studies that are at least partial exceptions to this rule, see: Langer, *Reform nach Prinzipien,* Cavallar, *Kant and the Theory and Practice of International Right,* and Riley, *Kant's Political Philosophy.* Laursen's study of the roots of Kantian publicity in his critical appropriation of the skeptical method provides a welcome exception. As Laursen points out, the "skeptical method in Kant's hands is rife with political implications, most of them pointing toward intellectual freedom" (Laursen, *The Politics of Skepticism,* 204). Since Kant accepted the skeptics' claims about the radical uncertainty that accompanies the search for political truth, but never accepted any "skeptical tranquility (*ataraxia*) in the face of doubt" (201), his politics of publicity provided a coherent means of accommodating fallibilism without succumbing to radical doubt.

8 Kant's *justification* of the ideal state is of course not typical of his contemporaries, as he bases his theory of legitimacy on his critical ethics. However, the constitutive *elements* of the republican state itself are not especially original. Those elements that are unusual, like his distinction between active and passive citizenship, are not especially appealing on their face, though they contain important insights about the necessary conditions of substantive autonomy (see the conclusion to this book). What makes Kant's

politics interesting is not his vision of the best state but his original account of political transition.

9 In some other works, notably in *Critique of Judgment* and in "Idea for a Universal History," Kant provides an alternative source of political progress: the purposiveness of nature. I argue throughout this book that the teleological history is the weakest aspect of Kant's political theory, both from the point of view of present-day philosophical relevance (evolutionary systems do not as a rule evolve toward any preordained goal) and from the point of view of internal coherence (the teleological history is not compatible with Kant's theory of publicity, despite the initial appearance of complementarity).

10 Laursen has called much-needed attention to Kant's theory of publicity in a number of important books and articles. In "Subversive Kant," he notes that scholarly focus on Kant's social contract predecessors and away from "contemporary German belles lettres and political journalism" has led commentators to miss the importance of publicity for Kant's political thought. I agree with Laursen that Kant turned to the terminology of Friedrich Just Riedel, Wilhelm Wekhrlin, and August Ludwig von Schlözer in "developing a political vocabulary that was subversive for its time" (599). However, Kant's use of contemporary political vocabulary, and even his clear engagement in contemporary political debates, were both secondary to the larger philosophical problems with which Kant struggled throughout his career. Politics and philosophy were never separate for Kant. In this case, he uses the contemporary institution of the public sphere to solve a problem in political philosophy, the mediation by human agents between theory and practice.

11 Stuke, "Aufklärung," 265.

12 Kant, "Theory and Practice," 8:299–300; 298.

13 Locke formulated the problem as follows: "Here, 'tis like, the common question will be made, who shall be judge whether the prince or legislative act contrary to their trust? . . . But further, this question (who shall be judge?) cannot mean, that there is no judge at all. For where there is no judicature on earth, to decide controversies amongst men, God in heaven is judge: he alone, 'tis true, is judge of the right." Locke, *Second Treatise of Government*, secs. 240–41.

14 "What Is Enlightenment?" translation from the Reiss edition, 54; 8:35; 17. These famous words and their translation have been fodder for much scholarly controversy. Hans Reiss rightly, if a bit strongly, criticizes James Schmidt's translation of "Ausgang" as "exit," arguing that it misses the sense of "Ausgang" as an ongoing project (Reiss, review of Schmidt, 265). For my purposes, the most important concept in Kant's definition is "immaturity," or "Unmündigkeit." Most translators, including Gregor, remind the reader that in German the word has definite legalistic overtones of "minority" in addition to the basic idea of being on the way to adulthood. Rüdiger Bittner cites recent philology to clear up a long-standing misapprehension shared by Germans and non-Germans alike, namely, that the root of "Unmündigkeit" is "Mund," or "mouth." This suggestive, but false, etymology leads to all sorts of nice interpretations about political freedom having to do with speaking for oneself. And in fact, as Bittner admits, though

Kant likely understood the correct origin of the word in an obsolete legal term ("munt") that means being one's own master, since he used it in that sense, the mistaken etymological if not political theoretical association of legal maturity with speaking for oneself may be found in works as established as those of Luther and Lessing. Bittner, "What Is Enlightenment?" in Schmidt, ed., *What Is Enlightenment?* 357–58.

15 Kant, "What Is Enlightenment?" 8:36; 17.

16 See, for example, Andreas Riem, "Aufklärung ist ein Bedürfnis des menschlichen Verstandes."

17 "What Is Enlightenment?" 8:37; 18.

18 "What Is Enlightenment?" 8:37; 18. Habermas interprets "What Is Enlightenment?" and its public/private distinction somewhat differently, asserting that what Kant called "publicity" is the same thing that Hegel later called "public opinion." "[The concept of publicity] in Kant lacked only the name of 'public opinion'" (Habermas, *Structural Transformation,* 108). Such a reading serves to keep the structure of Habermas's book coherent, since it moves from an account of the origins of publicity, through the representational aspirations of nineteenth-century democratic theory, to a critique of capitalist misuse of the institutions of publicity. However, for Kant publicity is precisely not the same as public opinion. Public opinion, as understood by the turn of the century, *represents* people's will on a topic (Hölscher, "Öffentlichkeit"). In "What Is Enlightenment?" Kant rejects this view of publicity, preferring to see it as a means to disinterested, universally applicable points of view. Public opinion is necessarily interested, and it often changes according to arbitrary or even no visible standards. Publicity for Kant, on the other hand, is supposed to approximate ideal judgment on earth.

19 Kant, *Rechtslehre* (the first half of *The Metaphysics of Morals*), in Gregor, ed., *Practical Philosophy,* 6:325; 467–68.

20 Hölscher, "Öffentlichkeit," 413 and passim.

21 Cited in Hinske, ed., *Was Ist Aufklärung?* l–li. An English translation by John Christian Laursen appears in Schmidt, ed., 87–96. Klein was coauthor, with Carl Gottlieb Svarez, of the Prussian Civil Code.

22 Interestingly, Kant twice refers indirectly to Julien de la Mettrie's notorious work *Man the Machine* in "What Is Enlightenment?" La Mettrie, an infamous freethinker, found refuge from persecution for his views at the court of Frederick II, who, while disagreeing with many of La Mettrie's ideas, personally defended his work in a eulogy. La Mettrie argues that human beings, far from having souls or any other insubstantial entity providing immortality, are in fact wholly material beings. Taking Descartes' characterization of plants and animals as living machines one step further, La Mettrie argues that human beings, too, are machines that reproduce. In the last sentence of "What Is Enlightenment?" Kant writes that a human being in the process of moral and political enlightenment will become "more than a machine," a strange locution unless one realizes that La Mettrie's notorious views had placed the metaphor in the popular imagination. Kant, "What is Enlightenment?" 8:42; 22; and see also 8:37; 18.

23 Kant, "What Is Enlightenment?" 8:37; 18.

24 Kant, "What Is Enlightenment?" 8:41; 21–22. For a different view, see Laursen, *The Politics of Skepticism*, chapters 8 and 9.

25 Kant, "What Is Enlightenment?" 8:38; 19.

26 Ibid. Nisbet translates this as "the essence of religion," which is correct, but which loses the sense, present in the German, that this essence is present *in the mind of the cleric.*

27 Kant, "What Is Enlightenment?" 8:38; 19.

28 Kant, "What Is Enlightenment?" 8:39; 20.

29 Ibid. In Kant's case, this will may be ideal rather than real. Thus an enlightened monarch might, as a matter of fact, legislate more justly than even a parliament or a democratic assembly.

30 Enlighteners like Johann Karl Wilhelm Möhsen argued that the state had an obligation to use its religious authority to dispel superstition, and criticized Frederick II for laxity in this regard. Knudsen, "On Enlightenment for the Common Man," 272.

31 Kant, "What Is Enlightenment?" 8:39; 20.

32 For a discussion of Kant's argument for separating the pursuit of true judgment from the exercise of representative power, see chapter 5.

33 Kant, "What Is Enlightenment?" 8:40; 21.

34 Ibid.

35 Kant, "What Is Enlightenment?" 8:41; 22.

36 Kant erects a sort of firewall between the public sphere and the practice of politics here. While comforting the enlightened absolutist for the time being, such a firewall would also protect the public sphere itself from corruption by private interests. See chapter 5.

37 This has interesting implications for Kant's theory of citizenship as well (see chapter 4 and the conclusion). To function publicly in Kant's sense, a speaker must enjoy independence from private constraints, perhaps including even the obligation to work for a living. Though Kant's distinction between active and passive citizenship is outmoded, the intuition behind it—that substantive autonomy is a precondition of political freedom—remains of interest.

38 Habermas addresses this problem in *Knowledge and Human Interests.* In this work, Habermas considers Kant's theory of moral motivation in terms more general than those of his earlier *Structural Transformation,* where the discussion of Kant is focused more tightly on the issue of publicity. Habermas highlights Kant's recognition of an interest of reason as a solution to the *Triebfeder* problem (that is, Kant's claim to have discovered a motivating interest for ethical action provided by reason itself, rather than by some contingent element of the empirical world). Kant and Habermas agree that while the pursuit of knowledge is never free of interests, these interests vary, such that some are legitimate and others are not. Their solutions to the problem of what Habermas calls "knowledge-constitutive interests" are different, however. While Habermas attacks "positivism" for refusing to recognize its necessarily interested position, Kant would have members of the public sphere consciously distance themselves as reasoners from all "private" (i.e., particular) interests, excluding especially interests dictated by social position or loyalty to the state.

39 Kant elaborates his position in the introduction to *The Conflict of the Faculties.*

40 See my discussion of *Conflict,* in chapter 5.

41 Elsewhere, Kant defines republicanism as "the political principle of separation of the executive power (the government) from the legislative power." Kant, *Perpetual Peace,* 8:352; 324. In contrast with despotism, under republican government the sovereign will of the people is represented to the ruling power charged with carrying it out. In his account of the ideal state, as with his account of the public sphere, Kant aims to protect the legitimacy of the public will by erecting a firewall between expressions of public judgment of right and actions based on that expression. Modern readers may find Kant's distinction between the form of sovereignty (democracy, aristocracy, autocracy) and the form of government (republican or despotic) confusing for two reasons. First, a modern reader might focus on the control of government by the popular will, while Kant is more concerned with the purity of the popular will being protected from the corruption of political power. Second, a reader might neglect the distinction between the provisional state and the ideal state, which Kant clearly has in mind as he writes (the admittedly initially cryptic statement) that monarchy is more conducive to republican rule than is either democracy or aristocracy (*Perpetual Peace,* 8:353; 325). No matter which body exercises sovereign power, the government may be republican or despotic, depending on whether its legislation reflects the will of the people. See my discussion in chapter 3.

42 Beiser, *Enlightenment, Revolution, and Romanticism,* 25 and 35.

43 Levinger attributes the common German overestimation of the power of the British monarch mainly to the influential publicist August Rehberg and his reading of Jean Louis de Lolme's *Constitution de l'Angleterre.* Levinger, "Kant and the Origins of Prussian Constitutionalism," 252. Interestingly, Kant criticizes the actual British monarchy for being absolutist (see chapter 4).

44 Kant, *Conflict,* 7:90; 163. Georges Lefèbvre argues, contra Kant, that the concept of enlightened absolutism could not apply to eighteenth-century England or Holland, since the commoners in both states held substantial ruling power. Lefèbvre, "Der aufgeklärte Despotismus," 80.

45 Levinger, "Kant and the Origins of Prussian Constitutionalism," 243. Levinger demonstrates that habits of Kantian thinking were widespread, if fairly superficial, in the upper levels of the army and bureaucracy in Prussia in 1806 and 1807. Especially entertaining is Levinger's account of a letter written by Major August Neithardt von Gneisenau from the front, a few months before the capitulation to Napoleon: "What can we believe, what shall we hope, what must we do? These three Kantian questions apply directly to us. If only the German were more vigorous. But he is stupid: he believes the French pretenses, he bears like a beast of burden, instead of rising up with flails, pitchforks, and scythes, and exterminating the foreigner from our land." Cited in Levinger, 248.

46 Kopitzsch, "Die Aufklärung in Deutschland," 18.

47 Knudsen, "On Enlightenment for the Common Man," 271.

48   The term *enlightened absolutism* was first used by historians in the nineteenth century, mainly to describe Frederick II of Prussia and Joseph II of Austria. Aretin, "Introduction," 11. See also Hartung, "Der aufgeklärte Absolutismus," 56. For interpretations of "enlightened absolutism," see Aretin, ed., *Der aufgeklärte Absolutismus.* See also Rosenberg, *Bureaucracy, Aristocracy and Autocracy,* and Koselleck, *Critique and Crisis.*

49   Not that Prussian kings ever surrendered their argument by divine right: Frederick William IV used the argument from divine right to refuse the crown offered by the German National Assembly in 1849. Levinger, "Kant and the Origins of Prussian Constitutionalism," 263.

50   Cited in Hartung, "Der aufgeklärte Absolutismus," 59–60. Kant spent much of his philosophical energy criticizing Wolffian reasoning. Despite being superseded in nearly every particular, Wolff's thought in general influenced a generation of German-speaking scholars to apply principles of rational explanation to the world, and thus promoted enlightenment (especially in the sense of dispelling superstition).

51   Cited in Hartung, "Der aufgeklärte Absolutismus," 60.

52   Hartung also cites Justi, Sonnenfels, and Martini as representatives of this view.

53   Rosenberg, *Bureaucracy, Aristocracy and Autocracy,* 150–57. Frederick William I promoted the interest of the absolute state by opening the ranks of the bureaucracy to talented commoners, and by securing for the central state a number of privileges previously held by other groups, such as the nobility and the church. His son, while aggrandizing the Prussian kingdom, also reinstated a number of privileges associated with the old corporate system.

54   Hartung, "Der aufgeklärte Absolutismus," 60–61. Maternal breast-feeding became an enlightenment cause after Rousseau pleaded for it in *Emile* (Rousseau, *Emile,* 44–47). See also Mary Trouille, "La femme mal mariée." I am not sure what was so dangerously unenlightened about Easter eggs, though the custom does date back to pre-Christian times.

55   Kopitzsch, "Die Aufklärung in Deutschland," 20.

56   See my discussion of this edict in chapter 5. Quoted by Kant, *Conflict,* 7:6; 11.

57   Kant, "Theory and Practice," 8:290–291; 291.

58   See, for example, Kant, "Theory and Practice," 8:290; 291.

59   Werner Kraus, quoted in Hinske, ed., *Was Ist Aufklärung?* xx. The *BMS* is available on the Web at: http://www.ub.uni-bielefeld.de/diglib/Berlinische_Monatsschrift (1998, Bibliothek der Universität Bielefeld).

60   The *BMS* was second only to the Jena-based *Allgemeinen Literaturzeitung* in subscriptions. Ilonka Egert, "Die 'Berlinische Monatsschrift,'" 131.

61   See Johan van der Zande's illuminating discussion in "In the Image of Cicero: German Philosophy Between Wolff and Kant," 420–21.

62   E. v. K., "Vorschlag, die Geistlichen nicht mehr bei Vollziehung der Ehen zu bemühen," *BMS* 2 (1783): 265–76; reproduced in Hinske, ed., *Was Ist Aufklärung?* 95–106. The author was probably Biester, who used the pseudonym "E. v. K." more than once. Hinske, ed., *Was Ist Aufklärung?* xxxvii.

63 E. v. K., "Suggestion," 95; 98; 102.

64 Hinske, ed., *Was Ist Aufklärung?* 107–33.

65 The Berliner Mittwochgesellschaft was a private group of scholars, men of letters, bureaucrats, and others who met on a regular basis to discuss social, political, and scientific policy from an enlightened point of view. Schmidt, "The Question of Enlightenment," 272. See also Birtsch, "The Berlin Wednesday Society."

66 Zöllner, "Ist es rathsam, das Ehebündniß nicht ferner durch die Religion zu sanciren?," reproduced in Hinske, ed., *Was Ist Aufklärung?* 107–16.

67 This topic was frequently discussed, for example, at the meetings of the Berliner Mittwochgesellschaft. Schmidt, "The Question of Enlightenment," 273, 278–80.

68 See Hinske, ed., *Was Ist Aufklärung?* xli.

69 Zöllner, "Ist es rathsam?" 115.

70 Zöllner, "Ist es rathsam?" 115. Of course, Zöllner was not the first person to ask this question. By the late eighteenth century, analysis of the process of enlightenment—true or false? elite or popular? subversive or loyal?—had established itself as one of the main topics of the new literary and political journals. While Zöllner's essay responds to Biester's suggestions on marriage, the question of enlightenment's definition refers to Johann Karl Wilhelm Möhsen's 1783 proposal to the Wednesday Society. Knudsen, "On Enlightenment for the Common Man," 271.

71 Reinhart Koselleck has described this period (1750–1850) as "*Sattelzeit,*" a time of tremendous conceptual flux during which the modern constellations of meaning for many social and political concepts were worked out. Koselleck himself used the term only casually. However, as his translator Keith Tribe has observed, *Sattelzeit* "has since become a concept in its own right." Keith Tribe, "Translator's Introduction," in Koselleck, *Futures Past,* x. Also cited in Richter, *The History of Political and Social Concepts,* 17–18. For an overview of the literature on the subject, see Strum, "A Bibliography of the Concept *Öffentlichkeit.*"

72 Bödeker, "Prozesse und Strukturen," 10–15. Bödeker cites the work of Rudolf Schenda, who estimates that about 15 percent of the public were potential readers in 1770, and about 25 percent in 1800.

73 What is remarkable in retrospect is the staying power of such an ideal image of the role of publicity in political life, despite political and social changes that eventually undermined its historical basis. Hölscher, "Öffentlichkeit." See also Kopitzsch, "Die Aufklärung in Deutschland," 9–10.

74 Hölscher, "Öffentlichkeit," 446–47; 432–36; 436. See also Dann, ed., *Lesegesellschaften und bürgerliche Emanzipation.*

75 Jürgen Habermas, *Structural Transformation.* For a critical introduction to the literature inspired by Habermas's study, see Calhoun, ed., *Habermas and the Public Sphere.*

76 See Muthu, "Justice and Foreigners: Kant's Cosmopolitan Right."

77 See, for example, Dahl, *Dilemmas of Pluralist Democracy.*

78 Rousseau, *Social Contract,* 148.

79 Up to the 1780s, writers in the social contract tradition used the term *civil society (soci-*

etas civilis) to designate the opposite of the state of nature: *societas civilis* was what human beings entered upon giving up their natural liberty in exchange for security. Toward the end of the eighteenth century, however, "civil society" came to mean something quite different. Rather than encompassing the entirety of a governed group, ruler and ruled alike, "civil society" began to stand for organized society outside the state. The question of the proper relationship between the state and civil society, which could not have been raised under the old conception of the term, became important: civil society was seen variously as being controlled by the state, using the state to represent its interests, criticizing the state, or legitimizing the state. For the sake of convenience, I shall use the Latin term *societas civilis* for the older sense of a governed body of people, leaving "civil society" to stand for the newer sense of the term. For the distinction between the old and new senses of "civil society," I am grateful to John Keane, "Despotism and Democracy." See also Riedel, "Gesellschaft, bürgerliche," 739, 741, 746–47.

80 In fact, when Locke speaks of a reversion to divine judgment on earth, he is referring to the resort to violent conflict among men, whose outcome can be assumed to be determined by God. Locke, *Second Treatise of Government,* secs. 222, 241; 227, 239–40.

81 Hobbes, *Leviathan,* part 2, ch. 18, 113; Locke, secs. 240, 239.

82 Hobbes, *Leviathan,* part 2, ch. 18, 117.

83 Riedel, "Transcendental Politics," 601–02.

84 Kant's spelling of the Latin term for "ideal state." In this and all subsequent quotations, emphases are in the original.

85 Kant, *Conflict,* 8:91; 165.

86 As is well known, for Kant philosophy is divided between theoretical and practical philosophy, the former answering the question "What can I know?" and the latter addressing itself to the question "What ought I to do?" "Practical" philosophy has to do with moral willing, and the human freedom that makes moral willing possible. Thus in this book the word *practical* is used in the technical, Kantian sense of having to do with moral willing, while the ordinary sense of the word is usually rendered with the admittedly less felicitous "pragmatic."

87 Kant, *Rechtslehre,* 6:220; 384–85.

88 Kant's ethical theory is based on the premise that all human beings (indeed, all limited rational beings of any kind) share a faculty of practical reason that allows them to discover moral truths and to apply them to everyday situations. As is well known, Kant argues that the formal test for whether a principle is a "moral truth" is whether it may hold as a universal law without coming into contradiction with itself. But ordinary people are not supposed by Kant to apply the categorical imperative consciously to their lives. Instead, most people simply recognize a few common moral precepts (such as honest dealing or doing no harm) as the basis for ethical interaction. In his ethical work, Kant tries to set these commonly recognized moral truths on a solid foundation in reason. Kant, *Groundwork,* 4:385–463; 37–108.

89 Kant, *Groundwork,* 4:412; 65.

90 Kant, *Rechtslehre,* 6:354; 491; 355; 491.

91 Kant, *Conflict*, 7:91; 165. Translation from the Reiss edition, 187.

92 Kant, *Rechtslehre*, 6:355; 491.

93 Ibid., 6:312; 456; 221; 376.

94 Kant, "Idea for a Universal History," in Reiss, edition, 41–53, 45.

95 Kant, *Conflict*, 7:90,163. Translation from the Reiss edition, 187.

96 In fact, Locke's separation of society and government with regard to the right of revolution might be seen as an early sign of the emerging new sense of "civil society," with the unitary commonwealth (societas civilis) breaking up into society and state.

97 Kant, *Rechtslehre*, 6:355; 491.

98 Ibid., 6:320–23; 463–66.

99 Kant, "What Is Enlightenment?" 8:36; 18.

100 Ibid., 8:41; 22.

101 Keck and Sikkink, *Activists Beyond Borders;* Pagden, "Introduction."

102 See Bartholomew, "Constitutional Patriotism and Social Inclusiveness."

CHAPTER 2 Political Judgment

1 Of course there are far too many good books to list here. However, much of the best new work on Kant's politics has been written by philosophers working in political science departments; including for example Katrin Flikschuh, whose *Kant and Modern Political Philosophy* is a tightly argued defense of Kantian metaphysics in political thought. The Austrian political theorist Georg Cavallar has written well on Kant's theory of international law in *Kant and the Theory and Practice of International Right.* Other recent contributions in political theory have appeared mainly in the form of edited collections or chapters in topical books, such as John Christian Laursen's *The Politics of Skepticism in the Ancients, Montaigne, Hume, and Kant* and Mika LaVaque-Manty's *Arguments and Fists: Political Agency and Justification in Liberal Theory.*

2 See, for example, Gutmann and Thompson, *Democracy and Disagreement;* or Walzer, *Just and Unjust Wars.*

3 Kant, "Idea for a Universal History," in Reiss edition, 45–46.

4 See Beiser, *Enlightenment, Revolution, and Romanticism;* see also Fleischacker, "Values Behind the Market: Kant's Response to the *Wealth of Nations,*" and, more recently, *A Third Concept of Liberty: Judgment and Freedom in Kant and Adam Smith.*

5 Contemporary philosophers of a liberal political bent, such as John Rawls and Jürgen Habermas, tacitly recognize this problem, either by ignoring Kant's clear expressions of support for teleological reasoning and focusing exclusively on his deontology, or by trying to extract the "good" deontology from the "bad" teleological system. Critics of the Kantian liberal tradition simply take the incompatibility of teleological reasoning for granted, as for example does Michael J. Sandel when he writes that in the liberal conception of a disenchanted world "the depth of opposition between deontological liberalism and teleological world views most fully appears." Sandel, *Liberalism and the Limits of Justice,* 175.

6 See Henry Allison's beautifully written, definitive interpretation of the first part of

Critique of Judgment, Kant's Theory of Taste: A Reading of the Critique of Aesthetic Judgment.

7 Pitkin, *Wittgenstein and Justice*, ch. 8.

8 Kant, *Critique of Judgment*, 5:196; 37. See also Fleischacker, *A Third Concept of Liberty;* Riley, *Kant's Political Philosophy;* Kelly, *Idealism, Politics and History;* Yovel, *Kant and the Philosophy of History;* Arendt, *Lectures on Kant's Political Philosophy.*

9 Kant, *Critique of Pure Reason*, A19/B33–A292/B349; 155–383. This and all subsequent quotations are from the 1998 Guyer and Wood translation.

10 Rawls, *Political Liberalism,* 258.

11 Two excellent recent English-language accounts of Kant's anthropology, including its implications for the relation between freedom and nature in his system, have followed Reinhardt Brandt and Werner Stark's 1997 edition of Kant's lectures on anthropology (in volume 25 of the *Akademie* edition of Kant's works): G. Felicitas Munzel's *Kant's Conception of Moral Character,* and John H. Zammito's *Kant, Herder, and the Birth of Anthropology.* See especially in this regard Zammito's chapter 7.

12 Kant, *Critique of Practical Reason*, 5:161–62; 269. Note also Kant's definition in *Judgment:* "The feeling that it is beyond our ability to attain to an idea *that is a law for us* is RE-SPECT" (5:257; 114; sec. 27). Of course, I am leaving out the more specific version of this argument, and probably the best one for the necessity of presuming some causality for freedom, namely, the insufficiency of efficient causal explanations. In other words, a "why" question is always possible for natural chains of events. In order to stop our reasoning questioner from infinite regress, it may be necessary to posit a final cause, which would by definition be something spontaneous. See especially Kant's treatment of the Third Antinomy in *Critique of Pure Reason*, A444/B472–A451/B479; 484–89. See also Allison, *Kant's Transcendental Idealism,* chapter 15.

13 I discuss this claim in chapter 5.

14 Kant, "Idea for a Universal History," 41.

15 Later in this chapter I discuss Kant's claim that the empirical investigation of nature, including humankind considered as nature, requires the presumption of purposiveness. Of course, both the teleological history and the agency-centered account of publicity make assumptions about the rationally necessary goals of human existence. However, the telos of the ideal state, according to Kant's second account, is pursued by enlightened individuals acting according to rational principles under the influence of public judgment about the right. In the teleological historical account, on the other hand, the motor of progress is not human willed action but the telos itself.

16 On compatibilism in the Third Antinomy (freedom's causality), see Allison's enlightening discussion in *Kant's Theory of Freedom*, 11–28.

17 Kant, *Rechtslehre*, 6:205; 3.

18 By "quasi-natural" I mean the motivations and institutions attributed to human actors without consideration of their conscious states of mind. For example, a theory that posits self-interested human individuals pursuing their passions and their rationally calculated, physically based needs is a quasi-natural theory. Such agents may well con-

struct an artificial institution for government, but they do so for what Kant would call "pathological" reasons. Another way to put the distinction is that natural action and quasi-natural action are based only on hypothetical principles (if I want *x*, I must do *y*). The freely willed action of moral agents, according to Kant, is, however, based not on hypothetical but on categorical imperatives.

19 Arendt, *Lectures on Kant's Political Philosophy,* 61.

20 Ibid., 33.

21 Kant, *Judgment,* 5:288; 153; sec. 36.

22 Vincent van Gogh, *A Glass of Absinthe and a Carafe,* 1887, Van Gogh Museum, Amsterdam, oil on canvas, 46.5 x 33 cm, F 339.

23 Kant, *Judgment,* 5:240; 90; sec. 22.

24 Ibid., 5:297; 164; sec. 41.

25 Ibid., 5:292; 158; sec. 39.

26 Rousseau, *Discourse on Inequality,* in Cress, ed., 54–55. Rousseau's version of this situation has the philosopher using abstraction to argue himself out of a natural human inclination to pity the suffering of another human being.

27 Arendt, *Lectures,* 54.

28 Ibid., 75.

29 Kant, *Judgment,* 5:229–30; 76–77; sec. 16.

30 Ibid., 5:261; 120; sec. 28.

31 Ibid., 5:300; 167; sec. 42.

32 He says that such judgment must be devoid of all private interest, but Kant's idiosyncratic definition of private includes all but the "interests of reason." See chapter 1.

33 Arendt, *Lectures,* 65.

34 Kant, *Judgment,* 5:222; 68; sec. 12. See also 5:274–75; 134–35, where Kant complains that the conflation of pure beauty with agreeableness leads people to "believe they are edified by a sermon that in fact builds no edifice (no system of good maxims), or are improved by the performance of a tragedy when in fact they are merely glad at having succeeded in routing boredom." See also 5:292; 158; 209; 51.

35 Ibid., 5:300; 167; sec. 42.

36 Ibid., 5:285; 149; sec. 34.

37 Arendt, *Lectures,* 73.

38 Kant claims that neither the teleological proof nor the moral proof is objectively necessary, but he makes strong hypothetical claims for them nonetheless.

39 Kant, *Judgment,* 5:226; 73; sec. 15; See also 5:240–41; 91–92. See Allison, *Kant's Theory of Taste,* 148–49.

40 In her discussion of Kant's doctrine of the sensus communis, Arendt says that she recognizes the difference between the *sensus communis* on the one hand, and "common sense" on the other (*Lectures,* 70–71). She nevertheless ignores the distinction, writing that by the "term 'common sense' [Kant] meant a sense like our other senses" (70).

41 Kant, *Judgment,* 5:293–94; 159–60; sec. 40.

42 Ibid., 5:293–94; 160; sec. 40.

43 Ibid., 5: 294–95; 160–61; sec. 40.

44 Ibid., 5:295; 162; sec. 40.

45 Ibid., 5:216; 60; sec. 8.

46 Ibid., 5:296–97; 163–64; sec. 41; 281; 144; sec. 31.

47 Ibid., 5:240; 90; sec. 22.

48 Obviously, Kant's political thought must incorporate some "teleology," since his theory of moral motivation accounts for human action in terms of its ends. What I mean by teleology here, however, is something very different than mere ends-orientation: the teleological view of politics posits a naturally given set of necessary ends toward which human action unconsciously and inexorably moves.

49 I do not mean to imply that all determinist arguments necessarily take what I in the following section call the "strong" teleological form. As any political scientist knows, there are modes of investigation that treat freedom as epiphenomenal while avoiding any talk of naturally determined ends. These are middle-range theories that hold macro-level questions (for example, "Is there a true universal morality?") and micro-level questions (for example, "Are people ultimately motivated by material self-interest?") constant while addressing issues at the institutional level, such as how a polity might democratize or develop economically.

50 What Riley calls "contractarianism" I call the realm of freely willed human actions. Riley turns the nicer phrase. The reason I stick with my cumbersome one is that contractarianism applies only to Kant's description of the political *ideals* shared by all reasoning beings, not to the whole sphere of political action. This broader political sphere includes ideals, but also the provisional, everyday political action of agents between the state of nature and perfect governance. See Riley, *Kant's Political Philosophy,* 170. Riley also recognizes that Kant's contractarianism is not a Hobbesian or Rousseauian contractarianism but a unique Kantian idealized construct. To this end he also considers reading Kant's politics as "quasicontractarian" (*Will and Political Legitimacy,* 131) or as contractarian "in a broad sense" (*Kant's Political Philosophy,* 8).

51 See Ameriks, *Kant and the Fate of Autonomy,* part 4.

52 Riley, *Kant's Political Philosophy,* 174.

53 See Atkinson, "Kant's Moral and Political Rigorism."

54 See, for example, Allison, *Kant's Theory of Freedom,* 184–91, and passim; Herman, *The Practice of Moral Judgment,* 216–21; and Korsgaard, *Creating the Kingdom of Ends,* 169 and passim.

55 "Judging a thing to be a natural purpose on account of its intrinsic form is something quite different from considering the existence of that thing to be a purpose . . . of nature" (translator's emendations omitted), Kant, *Judgment* 5:378; 258; sec. 67.

56 Riley, *Kant's Political Philosophy,* 170.

57 An acorn, to use a classical example, has an intrinsic end: to become an oak tree. But the mere reality of this intrinsic end does not entail its necessary success. The acorn, intrinsic end and all, may be eaten by a squirrel in the service of its own intrinsic goals.

58 Kant, *Rechtslehre,* 6:256–57; 44–45; secs. 8–9; 314; 91; sec. 46.

59 See for example, Riley, *Kant's Political Philosophy*, 173. See also Kant's argument in "What Is Enlightenment?" that any permanent settlement of moral issues would be "a crime against human nature [ein Verbrechen wider die menschlichen Natur]" (8:39; 20).

60 Riley, *Kant's Political Philosophy*, 174.

61 Ibid., 173.

62 Kant, *Critique of Practical Reason*, 5:161–62; 269.

63 The "nation of devils" argument is found in *Perpetual Peace*, 8:366; 335.

64 Kant, "What Is Enlightenment?" 8:39; 20.

65 Allison, *Kant's Theory of Taste*, 34–35.

66 Kant, *Judgment*, 5:379; 259; sec. 67.

67 See Pocock, *The Machiavellian Moment*, 79–80. See also Pocock, *Politics, Language, and Time*, chapter 8.

68 Kant, *Judgment*, 5:433; 320–21; sec. 83.

69 As Riley has explained very well in *Will and Political Legitimacy*.

70 Kant, *Judgment*, 5:436n.; 323n.

71 Ibid., 5:196; 37.

72 Ibid., 5:195–96; 36.

73 Ibid., 5:291; 156.

74 Ibid., 5:397–98; 280; sec. 75.

75 Ibid.. 5:411; 295; sec. 78.

CHAPTER 3 **Progress toward Peace**

1 Kant, *Perpetual Peace*, 8:348: 321.

2 James Bohman, for example, expresses surprise that Kant "leaves existing political and legal pluralism in place." Bohman's analysis rightly corrects the view that limits Kant to proposals for ideal politics, but it fails to understand that the two parts of Kant's analysis, ideal and provisional, complement rather than contradict each other. Bohman, "The Public Spheres of the World Citizen," 180.

3 Georg Cavallar divides the literature in this way, citing Howard Williams and Otfried Höffe, among others, in the first camp, and Karl Vorländer, Leslie Mulholland, and himself, among others, in the second. See Cavallar, "Kant's Society of Nations," 461. See also Cavallar, *Kant and the Theory and Practice of International Right*.

4 Rousseau took up St. Pierre's enormous unfinished work early in his career, intending to edit it into completion. Instead, he produced his own contribution to the eighteenth-century collective project of proposals for institutions aimed at ending the frequent, limited wars among states that had characterized the European international system since the peace of Westphalia in 1648.

5 Rousseau, *The Confessions*, book 9.

6 Williams, *Kant's Political Philosophy*, 257–58.

7 See Cassirer, *Kant's Life and Thought*, 371; Beiser, *Enlightenment, Revolution, and Romanticism*, 311–26 and passim.

8   Beiser analyzes the controversy around Garve's famous "Göttingen review" of *Critique of Pure Reason,* largely exonerating Garve of having been the author of the charge that Kant's idealism is warmed-over Berkeley (Garve claimed that his editor, Feder, mangled the review, adding as much as two-thirds of it himself). Nonetheless, Garve's basic complaint that Kantian ideals do not apply in the real world remains, and it is repeated in Garve's later political interchanges with Kant. Beiser, *The Fate of Reason,* 175–76. See also van der Zande, "In the Image of Cicero," 438; and Kuehn, *Kant: A Biography,* 250–54.

9   Beiser, *Enlightenment, Revolution, and Romanticism.*

10   Garve, "Abhandlung über die Verbindung der Moral mit der Politik," cited in Beiser, *Enlightenment, Revolution, and Romanticism,* 311–16.

11   Kant, "Theory and Practice." Significantly, Kant did not dogmatically apply the categorical imperative to all questions of political ethics. He recognized that persuasion of absolute rulers and their ministers would require arguments beyond deductions from the moral law.

12   Beiser seems sympathetic to Garve's point in *Enlightenment, Revolution, and Romanticism* (see, e.g., 316 and 326). He nearly repeats Garve's misreading of Kant in the introduction to the book.

13   Kant, *Perpetual Peace,* 8:344–46; 318–19.

14   Later in this chapter I discuss Kant's account of the role of the philosopher in promoting international peace. Here I would like to stress that Kant explicitly offers himself as a source of fairly reliable political judgment, defending that role in the introductory paragraph and elsewhere.

15   Kant, *Perpetual Peace,* 8:343; 317. Skittles is an old form of bowling, in which players tried to knock down the most of nine pins with the fewest throws of so-called skittle balls.

16   Of course, as I discuss especially in chapter 5, Kant more than once uses the philosophical faculty as an example of a functioning source of reliable public judgment. But while important, in that Kant's ideal public sphere takes many of its key elements from the model of scholarship, professional philosophers taken narrowly are not Kant's best example of a judging public, as I argue in detail there.

17   Kant, *Perpetual Peace,* 8:348–49; 322.

18   Ibid., 8:349; 322; 354; 325.

19   Ibid., 8:357; 328.

20   Ibid., 8:358; 329. See Muthu, *Enlightenment Against Empire.*

21   The use of the term *supplement* in the Gregor translation for both "Ergänzung" and "Zusatz" is slightly misleading in this regard, since the reader might conclude that the first and second supplements are directly related to the "supplement" supposedly provided by cosmopolitan right to the other two kinds of right. Since, I argue, the form of the text suggests such a reading even without the false impression that the same word is employed in both contexts, this is not a grave error on Gregor's part.

22   The material context of international relations from Kant's point of view includes

membership in an absolutist state, which itself is embedded in a balance-of-power context, surrounded by potentially aggressive foreign states. Kant recognizes that rulers of states have an interest in the continued existence of their state (though he accords less respect to the continued existence of a particular regime).

23 Kant, *Perpetual Peace,* 8:357; 328.

24 Ibid., 8:343; 317.

25 Kant switches back and forth from various points of view with hardly any warning in this text, and indeed in all of his less formal political works. Here Kant signals the appropriation of the statesman's point of view with remarks about the dignity of the ruler, the need for security both within the state and from its enemies, and so forth.

26 Kant, *Perpetual Peace,* 8:369; 338.

27 Leslie Mulholland makes a similar observation but calls it "the need to change from the standpoint of the despot to that of the moral politician." Mulholland, *Kant's System of Rights,* 371.

28 Kant, *Perpetual Peace,* 8:347; 320.

29 Though not, Kant adds lightly, "*ad calendas graecas,* as Augustus used to promise" (8:347; 321). Klenner explains that Augustus is said to have used this expression to joke that something would never get done, since the Greek calendar, unlike the Roman one, had "no particular designation for the first day of the month." Klenner, notes to *Rechtslehre: Schriften zur Rechtsphilosophie,* 511.

30 Even commentators who put little emphasis on provisional right in general agree with my contention that international right for Kant is always in practice only provisional. See for example Mulholland, *Kant's System of Rights,* 367.

31 Kant, *Perpetual Peace,* 8:347; 320–21. On permissive laws in Kant generally, see Brandt, "Das Erlaubnisgesetz." See also Brandt, "Person und Sache."

32 In the subject headings to various articles of Kant's *Perpetual Peace,* I have provided a gloss in my own words of the articles' contents.

33 Kant, *Perpetual Peace,* 8:343; 317.

34 Cited in Georg Cavallar, "Kant's Judgment on Frederick's Enlightened Absolutism," 123–24.

35 Kant, *Perpetual Peace,* 8:350–51; 324.

36 Ibid., 8:360; 330–31.

37 Ibid., 8:344; 318. Howard Williams argues that here Kant is "obliquely" criticizing acquisition by war via a critique of "the milder forms of imperialism which he lists." The more straightforward reading, however, has Kant directly criticizing the treatment of a state as if it were personal property. This was a common practice among European rulers of Kant's time (more so earlier), and the practice stands in contradiction to even an idealized social contract justification of rule. See Kant's arguments against states as patrimony in *Rechtslehre,* 6:323ff.; 99ff. Williams, *Kant's Political Philosophy,* 249.

38 Quite a lot of scholarship has been devoted to testing this empirical hypothesis of Kant's. While there is still some disagreement, most scholars today believe that Kant's hypothesis that popular sovereignty will reduce wars of aggression is contradicted by

two centuries of nationalist warfare in Europe and elsewhere. Habermas points out that Kant did not foresee the phenomenon of nationalism, which made the newly democratic state "no more peaceful than its predecessor, the dynastic absolutist state." Habermas, "Kant's Idea of Perpetual Peace," 120. Nevertheless, a variant of Kant's hypothesis remains of interest to scholars in the form of Doyle's Law, which states that democracies tend not to go to war with each other. See Doyle, "Kant, Liberal Legacies, and Foreign Affairs," parts 1 and 2. One difficulty with the democratic peace hypothesis is that scholars' evaluations of it vary with the methodology they use to test it. Thus, as Green, Kim, and Yoon argue, pooled analysis tends to confirm the hypothesis, while fixed-effects regression does not. Green et al., "Dirty Pool."

39 Kant, *Perpetual Peace,* 8:347; 321.

40 Ibid., 8:345; 318.

41 Ibid., 8:345; 319.

42 Ibid., 8:374; 341.

43 Ibid., 8:374n.; 341n.

44 I treat preliminary article 5 last, reversing Kant's order to suit my argument.

45 Kant, *Perpetual Peace,* 8:346; 320.

46 Ibid., 8:346–47; 320.

47 See, for example, Francheschet, *Kant and Liberal Internationalism.*

48 See, for example, Howard Williams, who argues that had Kant understood the potential for international organization, he would not have had "to fall back on the idea of one true church and a benign nature or Providence to ensure the ultimate success of the project." Williams rightly criticizes Kant's reliance on teleology. Williams, *Kant's Political Philosophy,* 259.

49 Kant, *Perpetual Peace,* 8:346; 320.

50 Kant, *Groundwork,* 4:421; 73 (italics removed).

51 Williams, *Kant's Political Philosophy,* 246–47.

52 See for example those listed in Cavallar, "Kant's Society of Nations," 461.

53 "The rational idea of a *peaceful* . . . community of all nations on the earth that can come into relations affecting one another is not a philanthropic (ethical) principle but a principle *having to do with rights.* Nature has enclosed them all together within determinate limits (by the spherical shape of the place they live in, a *globus terraqueus*)." *Rechtslehre,* 6:352; 121. For an excellent account of the metaphysical implications of the concept of the *globus terraqueus* in Kant's political thought, see Flikschuh, *Kant and Modern Political Philosophy.*

54 Kant, *Perpetual Peace,* 8:349; 322.

55 See, for example, *Rechtslehre,* 6:350; 119.

56 Kant, *Perpetual Peace,* 8:349; 322.

57 Ibid., 8:351–52; 324. Gregor translates both "bürgerliche Verfassung" and "Konstitution" as "civil constitution," which is slightly misleading. By the latter phrase, Kant refers to the original compact by which a people is formed out of the state of nature, whereas the former is simply the type of state (republican or despotic). Since the "Kon-

stitution" is always ideal, and the "bürgerliche Verfassung" is always real, there is little room for confusion on account of Gregor's conflation, however. Legitimate confusion does arise from Kant's own usage, since apart from "bürgerliche Verfassung" as the form of government (despotic or republican) he also uses the plain term "Verfassung" to refer to the form of sovereignty (autocratic, aristocratic, or democratic). For example, he writes that a representative system is a necessary element of any government that is republican in spirit, no matter what its "Verfassung," by which he means whether it is a monarchy or not. *Perpetual Peace*, 8:353; 325.

58 Kant, *Perpetual Peace*, 8:352; 324. On Kant and Montesquieu, see LaVaque-Manty, *Arguments and Fists*, 50, 64.

59 Kant, *Perpetual Peace*, 8:352; 324. This distinction is not as far-fetched as it seems at first. Like Rousseau, Kant argues that there is a fundamental difference between the public opinion of the people at any given time (Rousseau calls this the "will of all"), which may be highly arbitrary, and the general will, which is based on practical reason. Thus direct representation of the actual desires of the people may contradict the general will, which is an expression of what a people with access to perfect political judgment would support. For both Kant and Rousseau, practical approximation of ideal political judgment is a difficult problem that takes up a large portion of their political-theoretical energies.

60 Kant, *Perpetual Peace*, 8:352; 325.

61 As Leslie Mulholland rightly argues, however, Kant's contention does not rest on his empirical assumption that republics do not start wars. Rather, only in a republic can the government be trusted to abide by its commitments, because only in a republic does public and not private will determine policy. Mulholland, however, overstates the case with the claim that Kant makes only the a priori argument about trustworthy commitments, whereas in fact Kant makes both the a priori and the empirical claims. Mulholland, *Kant's System of Rights*, 370.

62 Kant, *Perpetual Peace*, 8:350; 323–24. Kant's strong version of republicanism here is moderated in the next paragraph, where he allows for a kind of virtual republicanism.

63 Kant, *Perpetual Peace*, 8:353; 325.

64 In his late work *Conflict*, Kant explains that the right of self-legislation "is still always only an Idea of which the realization is restricted to the condition of accord of its means with the morality which the nation may not transgress; and this may not come to pass through revolution, which is always unjust. To rule autocratically and yet to govern in a republican way, that is, in the spirit of republicanism and on analogy with it—that is what makes a nation satisfied with its constitution." *Conflict*, 7:87n.; 157n.

65 Kant, *Perpetual Peace*, 8:354; 325.

66 Ibid., 8:357; 328.

67 Ibid., 8:356; 328.

68 Ibid., 8:355–56; 327.

69 Thus Habermas's argument for unmediated access of world citizens to world govern-

ment may be compelling on its own merits, but it is not, for the reasons just given, a Kantian claim. Habermas rightly notes that for Kant individuals and not states are the bearers of (what I would call conclusive) rights. He concludes, however, that Kant therefore "ought not allow the autonomy of citizens to be mediated through the sovereignty of their states." In an ideal world, cosmopolitan law might, as Habermas writes, "go over the heads of the collective subjects of international law [i.e., states] to give legal status to the individual subjects" ("Kant's Idea of Perpetual Peace," 128). Here, however, Kant argues from the point of view of a world that may move toward international legal security, but in which the only available sources of adjudication are in fact sovereign states. As Kant consistently argues, long-term goals, however lofty, cannot justify the provisional abandonment of basic rights to secure them. The foundation of legal order is the state-constructing social contract among individuals, which may not be violated even for the goal of perpetual peace.

70 Kant, *Perpetual Peace*, 8:357; 328.

71 "This homage that every state pays the concept of right (at least verbally) nevertheless proves that there is to be found in the human being a still greater, though at present dormant, moral predisposition . . . for otherwise the word *right* would never be spoken by states wanting to attack one another." Kant, *Perpetual Peace*, 8:356; 327.

72 Ibid., 8:355–56; 327.

73 Note that Kant's defense of the provisional right to property is based not on any absolute property right relating to individuals but on the general necessity of preserving the possibility of political progress toward republican government. Kantian political theory thus defies the traditional distinction between liberal rights and democratic general welfare.

74 Kant, *Conflict*, 7:90n.; 163n.

75 Kant, *Perpetual Peace*, 8:356; 328.

76 Ibid., 8:350–51; 323–24.

77 Kant in his early years pursued serious study of the classics, including Thucydides's *History of the Pelopponesian War* (Kuehn, *Kant: A Biography*, 48–49). He would, therefore, have had ready access to at least one historical example of democratic empire building.

78 Kant, *Perpetual Peace*, 8:357; 328.

79 Ibid.

80 See Muthu, "Justice and Foreigners."

81 Kant, *Perpetual Peace*, 8:359; 330.

82 Habermas reads this differently. See Habermas, "Kant's Idea of Perpetual Peace," 116, 117.

83 Kant, *Perpetual Peace*, 8:360; 330–31.

84 The European Court of Human Rights has a surprisingly strong track record, probably thanks to its association with a supranational quasi-state, the European Union. The relatively weak International Criminal Court, on the other hand, is associated with the less powerful United Nations.

85 See, for example, Francheschet, *Kant and Liberal Internationalism,* Habermas, "Kant's Idea of Perpetual Peace," 123–26, and Bohman, "The Public Spheres of the World Citizen," 181.

86 Though Bohman misses the Kantian distinction between provisional and conclusive right, he quite rightly argues that the "public sphere is meant to be a substitute for the limited effects of coercive civil law." See Bohman, "The Public Spheres of the World Citizen," 181–82.

87 Kant, *Perpetual Peace,* 8:365; 335.

88 See Habermas's description of Kant's failed attempt to substitute a hidden plan of nature for plausible moral motivation to enter into a world federation. Habermas, "Kant's Idea of Perpetual Peace," 119. Howard Williams argues that the two views—teleological and practical necessity—are compatible. Kant's pessimism about the success of humanly willed action leads him, Williams argues, to put faith in nature or providence as a sort of last resort. "His optimism about the future rests on his belief in Providence, so that even if public enlightenment and the skilful diplomacy of moral politicians fail in the task of bringing harmony to the international relations of states all is not lost." Williams, *Kant's Political Philosophy,* 244, 253. As I argue in chapter 2, Kant never loosened his strict rules, developed in the first *Critique,* on the status of knowledge gained according to various standards. Conclusions based on faith, even on rational faith in providence, had a much lower epistemological status for Kant than those based on practical (ethical) necessity.

89 Habermas agrees with me that moral motivation comes from practical reason itself, but he does not connect the public sphere with this problem of moving limited rational human beings not only to recognize the right but also to act on that recognition.

90 The agents in Kant's teleology certainly make use of their will, but only in the sense of "Willkür," or choice, and not in the sense of "Wille," or action according to rational principles. See Beck, "Kant's Two Conceptions of the Will in Their Political Context." The better account of progress in Kant, in which the mechanism is not natural inclinations but publicity, makes empirical use of ideal principles. Members of the public sphere, inspired by their judgment that reality falls short of the principles of political right they know in their hearts, speak out and offer criticism of current affairs. The motivation in this case is empirical, a feeling of enthusiasm, but it is inspired by ideal principles of right. The solution is akin to Kant's eventual position in his practical philosophy that individuals are inspired to overcome their baser inclinations by awe before the moral law. Both accounts are attempts to bridge the gap between freedom and nature.

91 Kant, *Perpetual Peace,* 8:366; 335. This statement contradicts the main tenor of Kant's political thought, in which he argues that the general will, as an ideal, is inaccessible directly but is mediated to practice by means of the public judgment of citizens. If Kant really thinks that the general will is "impotent in practice," then he would have to give up the main arguments in "What Is Enlightenment?" "Theory and Practice," the *Rechtslehre,* the rest of *Perpetual Peace,* and *Conflict of the Faculties,* at the very least. A few

pages later, in the first appendix to *Perpetual Peace*, Kant writes that "if we do not assume that pure principles of right have objective reality, that is, that they can be carried out," then we would have to conclude that even creation itself cannot be justified. No matter how willing Kant's present-day readers might be to take such a leap, Kant himself certainly does not agree with "such desperate conclusions" (8:380; 346). Lest the reader conclude that Kant believes that while practical reason may be carried out individually the general will still remains "revered but impotent," I call attention to Kant's discussion in the first appendix to *Perpetual Peace*. Here Kant anticipates the objection that even if the moral law is practical for all individuals, the collective unity required for the general will is empirically impossible. Yes, Kant replies, this unity will not arise of its own accord but will require the provisional assistance of "power" in order to form a collective whole from a fragmented many (8:371; 339).

92 Kant, *Perpetual Peace*, 8:366; 335.

93 See my discussion of this point in chapter 4, where I show that Kant cannot accept a Hobbesian version of social contract theory.

94 Kant, *Perpetual Peace*, 8:366; 335. Note that Kant uses the terms *public* and *private* here in the ordinary sense of "common" and "individual," rather than in the specialized senses he develops in "What Is Enlightenment," of public as "taking one's standards from reason alone" and private as "taking one's standards from some interest other than reason."

95 Rousseau's formula is: "Find the form of association which defends and protects with all common forces the person and goods of each associate, and by means of which each one, while uniting with all, nevertheless obeys only himself and remains as free as before." *Social Contract*, 148.

96 But see Habermas, "Kant's Idea of Perpetual Peace," 119, 121, 122.

97 See my argument in chapter 2 on strong teleology versus weak teleology in Kant.

98 Kant, *Perpetual Peace*, 8:367; 336.

99 Roughly, this is so because any human willing must have an object. A morally necessary object, such as perpetual peace, could not obligate us if it were impossible.

100 Kant, *Perpetual Peace*, 8:362; 332.

101 The term *Realpolitik* was coined by the publicist August Ludwig von Rochau (1810–1873) in his 1853 work, *Grundsätze der Realpolitik*. Rochau denied that questions of political legitimacy mattered, insisting instead on a standard of practical success or failure. As Rochau wrote in 1869, "Through its title [*Principles of Realpolitik*], this work placed itself squarely in opposition to political idealism" (204; my translation).

102 This section of Kant's essay could well have been subtitled "Against Garve," like the first section of "Theory and Practice."

103 See the Third Antinomy in *Critique of Pure Reason*, A444/B472–A457–B479; 484–89.

104 Kant, *Perpetual Peace*, 8:371; 339. Translation slightly altered. Gregor translates "der Praktiker" as "the practical man," which is correct but invites confusion, since gener-

ally Kant uses "practical" to refer only to action under the moral law. He says, for example, that "the self-seeking propensity of human beings . . . because it is not based on maxims of reason, must still not be called practice." 8:379; 346.

105 Kant, *Perpetual Peace*, 8:370; 338 (italics removed). Note that Kant does not accuse the practitioner of having immoral goals, or of being immoral himself. Even granting the best will and the right object (perpetual peace), argues Kant, political prudence will not succeed.

106 Ibid., 8:376; 343. See also *Conflict*, 7:86n.; 155n.

107 See especially chapters 1 and 5, on "What Is Enlightenment?" and *Conflict*.

108 Kant, *Perpetual Peace*, 8:377; 344.

109 See Kant, *Perpetual Peace*, 8:370; 339.

110 Kant, *Conflict*, 7:80; 143: "It was all very well for the Jewish prophets to prophesy . . . complete dissolution [that] awaited their state, for they themselves were the authors of this fate."

111 Kant, *Perpetual Peace*, 8:378; 345; 373; 341. For the metaphor of humankind as a machine, see chapter 1.

112 Ibid., 8:372; 340.

113 Ibid., 8:371; 339; 380; 346; 377; 344.

114 In a similar vein, Mika LaVaque-Manty has described Kant's political thought as providing the missing account of political legitimacy that would bridge Montesquieu's design for political institutions, on the one hand, and his almost naturalistic account of human activity, on the other. *Arguments and Fists*, 62.

115 Allen D. Rosen makes a similar point. Rosen, *Kant's Theory of Justice*, 184 and 196. Rosen is interested strictly in Kant's theory of the ideal state, arguing that Kantian liberalism is concerned not only with the right but also, if secondarily, with the good. He argues that Kant's ideal state is no minimalist state but one concerned with the promotion of social welfare. This is of course hard to square with Kant's frequent declarations that justice has nothing to do with welfare. But Rosen faces this challenge directly, arguing that Kant's theory of the ideal state is in the first instance concerned with justice but in the second instance is concerned with the ideal state as a human political institution, aimed at promoting the public happiness. Rosen's analysis of Kant's affirmative principle of publicity supports this claim (184ff.).

116 Kant, *Perpetual Peace*, 8:381; 347.

117 The formal principles of publicity are discussed most explicitly in Rawls, "Kantian Constructivism," 553 and passim; in Habermas, *Structural Transformation*, though Habermas also works out the logic of publicity-based justice in "Wahrheitstheorien"; and in Gutmann and Thompson, *Democracy and Disagreement*, chapter 3.

118 Kant, *Perpetual Peace*, 8:382–83; 348. By "transcendental" here Kant means that the principle is derived from removing all empirical elements in thought, leaving only the form that "transcends" the phenomenal world. Kant uses the term *transcendental* for formal principles that are rationally justifiable; the term *transcendent* usually has negative connotations of imaginary idealism.

119 Ibid., 8:381; 347. Note that Kant uses the weaker term for knowledge here (*erkennen* (cognize), as opposed to *wissen* (know).

120 Ibid., 8:383–84; 349.

121 Ibid., 8:384; 350.

122 Ibid., 8:386; 351.

123 Ibid., 8:385–86; 351.

124 See Bohman, "The Public Spheres of the World Citizen," 182–83.

125 Kant, *Perpetual Peace,* 8:369; 338.

126 Ibid., 8:369; 338.

CHAPTER 4 Provisional Right

1 Kant, *Rechtslehre,* 6:347; 485.

2 Gutmann and Thompson, "Why Deliberative Democracy is Different."

3 Mansbridge, "Using Power/Fighting Power: The Polity."

4 Kant, *Perpetual Peace,* 8:343–49; 317–22

5 Kant calls this transition the "continual approximation to the highest political good." Kant, *Rechtslehre,* 6:355; 492.

6 Kant himself contributed to this misunderstanding by airing his unrelated but certainly less-than-progressive points of view on such subjects as marriage. *Rechtslehre,* 6:277–80; 426–29.

7 For a different argument with a similar conclusion, see Laursen, *The Politics of Skepticism,* chapter 9.

8 Kant, *Rechtslehre,* 6:205; 365.

9 Note that Kant sets different limits to public discussion as he proceeds through his various conceptions of the role of publicity. For example, in "What Is Enlightenment?" Kant limits public deliberation to viewpoints transmitted in writing, "in the manner of a scholar," to the reading public. Elsewhere (for example, *Conflict*) he is more liberal.

10 This is especially important given the ideal nature of the perfect state: all really existing political institutions are outside it, though, as Kant will argue, it functions as a norm for them.

11 Kant frequently invokes a bipartite distinction between the state of nature, on the one hand, and the civil condition, on the other. Like Rousseau's, however, Kant's state of nature has multiple stages, including the conditions under which provisional right applies, but always excluding the conclusive rights that accompany the perfect civil condition.

12 The concept of provisional right belongs in the same class of bridging concepts as the concept of the public sphere in "What Is Enlightenment?" and the judging public in *Conflict.* (Kant's concepts of the formal principles of publicity in *Perpetual Peace* and of teleology in *Judgment* also belong in this category.) Note that none of these bridging concepts is successfully grounded in a deduction from a priori principles (though in a few cases, Kant does go through the motions). Even the formal principles of pub-

licity, presented as if they followed directly from the categorical imperative, are mentioned in *Perpetual Peace* and then dropped from Kant's usage almost immediately after he uses them to make a decidedly particular argument against a right of revolution. In previous and later refutations of the right of revolution, Kant uses more appropriate modes of argumentation—those without scientific certainty, based instead on assumptions about the active power of freedom in the world (something that can never be observed but may under limited circumstances be presumed).

13 In both his formal and informal works, Kant consistently stresses that successful transitions to the rule of law must be gradual, rather than revolutionary, transformations.

14 See this chapter's discussion of Kant's deduction of property rights for a more complete account of this topic.

15 Kant, *Rechtslehre*, 6:205; 365. Kant writes that "all examples (which only illustrate but cannot prove anything) are treacherous." *Rechtslehre*, 6:355; 491.

16 Kant provides some explanation of this lapse in the preface, where he writes that toward "the end of the book I have worked less thoroughly over certain sections than might be expected in comparison with earlier ones." *Rechtslehre*, 6:209; 368.

17 Ibid., 6:229–30; 386–87.

18 Ibid., 6:352; 489. On this trope, see Flikschuh, *Kant and Modern Philosophy*.

19 Ibid., 6:371; 505.

20 Ibid., 6:230; 387.

21 Ibid., 6:232; 389.

22 Ibid., 6:218–20; 383–85, and *Doctrine of Virtue* (second half of *The Metaphysics of Morals*), 6:383; 515. See Allison's lucid account of "respect," *Kant's Theory of Freedom*, 120–28.

23 Kant, *Rechtslehre*, 6:232; 389.

24 "Civil society" is used here in the older sense, as the opposite of the state of nature; only in the late eighteenth century did "civil society" come to mean an entity separate from the state. See chapter 1.

25 Allison, *Kant's Theory of Freedom*, 68.

26 "I ought never to act except in such a way that I could also will that my maxim should become a universal law." *Groundwork*, 4:402; 57.

27 Kant, *Rechtslehre*, 6:230; 387.

28 As will be seen shortly, in cases of equity, judgment is possible, but not the strict legal judgment required of *Recht*. Instead, general questions of right are appealed to the "court of conscience" (*Rechtslehre*, 6:235; 391), which is very similar to the court of public opinion that promotes political enlightenment without having anything to say about legal rights and wrongs under the prevailing system of justice (however iniquitous). Again, Kant's defense of the legal system against destabilizing forces, however just, echoes Hobbes' similar arguments in *Leviathan*: the sovereign may be iniquitous but never unjust. Hobbes of course goes further in his defense and allows less possibility for political enlightenment: truth, as defined by the sovereign, he argues, is never a destabilizing force (2:xviii).

29 Kant, *Rechtslehre*, 6:233–36; 390–92.

30 Ibid., 6:235; 392; 236; 392.

31 Rawls's distinction between procedural and distributive justice runs along the same lines. Rawls, *A Theory of Justice*.

32 Kant, *Rechtslehre*, 6:235; 391.

33 Private right, for Kant, is "the sum of laws that do not need to be promulgated." *Rechtslehre*, 6:210; 368. That is, private right exists without actual legislation; a people need not even be constituted as such before private right comes into play. By this, however, Kant does not mean that private right prevails in a state of nature. The contrary is the case: though it comes into force without explicit legislation on the part of any body, private right by its very nature implies the existence of a state of civil order. *Rechtslehre*, 6:256–57; 410.

34 Ibid., 6:260; 413; 261; 414.

35 Ibid., 6:258; 411. See Reinhard Brandt's discussion in "Person und Sache," 895 and passim.

36 Kant, *Rechtslehre*, 6:230; 387.

37 Gregor, introduction to Kant's *Metaphysics of Morals*, xiv.

38 Kant, *Rechtslehre*, 6:264; 416.

39 Ibid., 6:291; 438–39; 249–50; 403–04.

40 Kant, *Conflict*, 7:90; 163.

41 Allison, *Kant's Theory of Freedom*, 230. There are two distinct accounts of the relation between freedom and the categorical imperative in Kant's ethical works. Roughly speaking, in the *Groundwork* Kant takes freedom as a given and derives the necessity of the categorical imperative from it, while in *Critique of Practical Reason* he bases the necessary presumption of moral freedom on the brute fact of respect for the moral law. Philosophers concerned with the validity of the ethical deductions disagree about the relative successes of the two accounts, but the version from the second *Critique* is held by many to be the superior, if still flawed, account. Though many of the arguments from the *Groundwork* are incorporated into the *Rechtslehre*, the "fact of reason deduction" from the later work is the basis of the deduction of the postulate of practical reason in the *Rechtslehre*. See Allison, *Kant's Theory of Freedom*, chapters 12 and 13.

42 Kant, *Rechtslehre*, 6:205; 365.

43 Onora O'Neill's *Constructions of Reason*, for example, contains several chapters on the application of Kantian ethics to political questions.

44 Gregor, "Translator's Note on the Text of the Metaphysics of Morals," in *Practical Philosophy*, 355–59. Gregor translates the reconstructed version of the *Rechtslehre*.

45 Ibid.

46 Many writers on Kant's politics, and even on his theory of property rights, simply pass over this section. See, for example, Shell, *The Rights of Reason*. Those who do address it, find it wanting. Rosen, for example, refers to "at least two serious weaknesses," though

the failure of the deduction does not interfere with his argument about the consequences of Kantian views on justice. Rosen, *Kant's Theory of Justice*, 20n. My point of
view is similar: the deduction, by Kant's own standards, is not a success; however, the
system of rights based on the possibility of external property holding is still worthy of
consideration. After all, Kant's fellow contract theorists each justified private property
differently. A possible exception is Howard Williams, who uses the old version of the
text (which introduced land holding before addressing the possibility of having anything external as one's own), but whose comments suggest that he approves of Kant's
reasoning. Williams, *Kant's Political Philosophy*, 84–86.

47 A "deduction" in Kantian philosophy is an attempt to answer the question, How is something for which we have a concept really possible? Kant's deductions are attempts to
prove that certain aspects of life, such as theoretical knowledge, practical freedom, and
even property rights, are necessarily possible for us. Of course we have concepts of these
things, but it is not a given that just because we can conceive of them, they may be real. After all, we have concepts of imaginary things like unicorns.

48 Kant, *Rechtslehre*, 6:249; 403; 252; 406; 250; 404.

49 The following summary is based on Kant's deduction. *Rechtslehre*, 6:249–52; 403–07.

50 See Robert Paul Wolff's very interesting discussion of this point in his book chapter,
"The Completion of Kant's Moral Theory in the Tenets of the *Rechtslehre*," 39–62; see
especially 59. Wolff argues that Kant's ethics are incomplete without the categorical requirement to enter into civil society, and thus without the *Rechtslehre*. This is of course
the opposite of what Kant and most of his interpreters believe about the relationship
between politics and ethics. Wolff's fundamental point is well taken: Kant cannot make
the moral theory of the *Groundwork*, based as it is on the interaction of mutually con-
senting autonomous individuals, coherent without bringing in conclusions from social
contract theory. As I have argued myself, the two areas of endeavor—Kantian ethics
and traditional social contract theory—are not easy to reconcile. The result is a theory
which presumes rationally interested actors (such as those who necessarily acquire
property), but which denies that the particular interests which characterize these actors
can have any moral standing.

51 See Rosen's related remarks, *Kant's Theory of Justice*, 20.

52 Wolff, "Completion," 55.

53 Kant, *Rechtslehre*, 6:312; 455–56.

54 Even a state of nature without injustice, Kant writes, "would still be a state *devoid of justice* (*status iustitia vacuus*) in which when rights are *in dispute* (*ius controversum*), there
would be no judge competent to render a verdict having rightful force." *Rechtslehre*,
6:312; 456.

55 Of course, Hobbes's sovereign is legitimate in his terms, even though he is not answerable to the people or bound by any written constitution. For Hobbes, an arbitrary sovereign's adjudication may still be just.

56 Kant uses the word *rechtlich* here to describe the desired state of affairs. Gregor trans-

lates this literally as "rightful," which is correct, but which lacks the sense, present in the German, of "rule of law."

57 Kant, *Rechtslehre,* 6:306; 450–51.

58 Though Kant lists such societies at *Rechtslehre,* 6:306; 451, these prelegal societies are not relevant to the argument at hand except to bolster Kant's refutation of the idea, held by Gottfried Achenwall among others, that mere social organization—without general laws—constitutes an escape from the state of nature.

59 Kant, *Rechtslehre,* 6:372; 506.

60 Ibid., 6:313; 456–57.

61 Ibid., 6:255; 409. Italics removed.

62 Ibid., 6:237–38; 393–94.

63 Ibid., 6:255–56; 409. Hobbes, as usual, puts this problem beautifully: "For he that should be modest and tractable, and perform all he promises, in such time and place where no man else should do so, should but make himself a prey to others." *Leviathan,* part 1, ch. 15, 99.

64 Patrick Riley rightly calls Kant's use of the term *general will* here part of the "Rousseauian mood" of the *Rechtslehre.* Riley, "The Elements of Kant's Practical Philosophy," 12. As is well known, Kant credited Rousseau with pointing out the worthiness of human rights as an object of study. For Rousseau's influence on Kant, see Velkley, *Freedom and the End of Reason.*

65 Kant, *Rechtslehre,* 6:256; 409.

66 Ibid., 6:256–57; 410; 6:256; 410; 6:257; 410.

67 Hobbes, *Leviathan,* part 1, ch. 14, 80. See Brandt, "Person und Sache."

68 Kant, *Rechtslehre,* 6:347; 485.

69 Kant, "What Is Enlightenment?" 8:36; 18.

70 Kant, *Rechtslehre,* 6:257; 410.

71 Rousseau, *Discourse on the Origin of Inequality,* 71.

72 Kant, "Theory and Practice," 7:302; 301.

73 Kant, *Rechtslehre,* 6:347; 485. This formulation could stand as a general formulation of provisional right.

74 Ibid., 6:354; 491.

75 Ibid., 6:372; 505. From the appendix to the 1798 edition of the *Rechtslehre,* which responded to a review by Friedrich Bouterwek published in 1797.

76 Ibid., 6:317–26; 460–68; and passim.

77 Ibid., 6:317; 460; 319; 462. Kant's argument here is only a short step away from Hobbes's claim that even an arbitrary sovereign must be obeyed. However, unlike Hobbes, who would deny that arbitrary behavior on the part of sovereign power even constitutes an injustice, Kant allows expressive, if not active, resistance.

78 Ibid., 6:319; 462.

79 Ibid., 6:325; 467–68. See also 6:346; 484, where Kant writes of the sovereign's "duty" to the people.

80 Ibid., 6:343; 482. Recent works on Kant's international politics mainly agree that Kant does not have a consistent theory of international relations. As Mark F. N. Franke puts it, "Contrary to what generations of scholarship would have us believe, his theory cannot be reduced to any one theory of international relations." Franke, *Global Limits,* 195. See also Fransceschet, *Kant and Liberal Internationalism.*

81 Kant, *Rechtslehre,* 6:347; 485.

82 *Perpetual Peace* was published in 1795; the *Rechtslehre* was published in 1797.

83 Kant, *Rechtslehre,* 6:350; 487.

84 Ibid., 6:346; 484.

85 Ibid., 6:345–48; 483–85. See also chapter 4.

86 Ibid., 6:347; 485.

87 Interestingly, an ongoing debate over the use of assassination as a weapon by the present-day United States runs along the same lines as Kant's eighteenth-century claims. Assassination is prohibited by executive order (issued under the Ford administration after evidence about the CIA's bungled attempts to assassinate Cuban president Fidel Castro came to light). Years of frustration with the inability of the United States to bend former Iraqi dictator Saddam Hussein's regime to its will, however, led some to call for the reinstatement of assassination as a legal weapon of war, or even of foreign policy. The argument against such a policy shift stresses that the use of assassination, while it might succeed at achieving short-term policy objectives, would in the long run undermine more important aspects of international politics, including especially relations of trust with allies of the United States. Alasdair Palmer, "Assassination Could Save Time and Trouble," *Sunday Telegraph* (London), September 8, 2002; *Washington Post,* February 19, 1998, A22; *Washington Post,* October 7, 1990, D1; and Michael Kinsley, "We Shoot People, Don't We?" *Time,* October 23, 1989, 118.

88 Kant, *Rechtslehre,* 6:349; 487.

89 In the real world of provisional rather than conclusive right, of course, one must frequently resort to less enforceable arbitration, seeking the judgment, for example, of public opinion along with the legal judgment of sovereign power.

90 Kant, *Rechtslehre,* 6:350; 487–88; Klenner, ed., *Rechtslehre,* 480.

91 Though Kant was aware of the United States Constitution of 1787, I doubt that he or many (any?) of his European colleagues had an opportunity to read the debates in American newspapers between the Federalists and their opponents. One wonders whether Madison's argument against Montesquieu (that a large state is more likely to guarantee freedom than a small state, as it contains more diverse and overlapping interests than a small one) would have convinced Kant, especially since Kant himself argues that diversity preserves freedom in the international arena. See Dippel, *Germany and the American Revolution.*

92 Kant, *Rechtslehre,* 6:350; 487.

93 Ibid., 6:351; 488.

94 Ibid., 6:311; 455. This line of argument is similar to the one Kant will make against revolution; however universal, the desirable goal of revolutionary action, if it violates the

premises underlying such a goal (and any disruption of civil order would, according to Kant, violate the civil right to enjoyment of one's property on which all other political rights are based), it cannot be justified. In short, for Kant, civil rights come first, democracy (or at least the good of the whole), second.

95 Ibid., 6:354; 491.

96 As Michael Doyle has ably and thoroughly argued, many of today's important international institutions are constructed along Kantian lines: they adjudicate disputes and promote peaceful and prosperous interaction but forgo, so far as possible, interfering with national sovereignty. Doyle, "Liberalism and International Relations," 173–204.

97 Kant, *Rechtslehre*, 6:256; 409.

98 Kant, *Perpetual Peace*, 8:343; 317. In German this joke makes more sense, since the names of public houses often designate their place with the word "zu," which means both "toward" and simply "at" or "of."

99 I have used Reiss's more felicitous translation here. *Perpetual Peace*, in Reiss edition, 8:362–62; 108–09 (331–32 in the Gregor edition).

100 Kant, *Rechtslehre*, 6:255–57; 409–11.

101 Ibid., 6:350; 487.

102 Ibid., 6:355; 491.

103 Thus Kant, even as he opposes any actions that would disrupt civil order, stalwartly defends the right to "reason publicly" about matters of state. Kant, *Rechtslehre*, 6:372; 505–06. See also my ensuing section on revolution.

104 Kant, *Perpetual Peace*, 8:370; 339.

105 Kant, "Theory and Practice," 8:279; 282; 280–81; 282–83.

106 Ibid., 8:290; 291.

107 Ibid., 8:276–77; 280.

108 Ibid., 7:313; 309.

109 See for example Rosen, *Kant's Theory of Justice*.

110 Kant, *Rechtslehre*, 6:320; 463.

111 Ibid., 6:347; 485.

112 Ibid., 6:355; 491–92. Kant exhibits a keen understanding of the importance of those political moments in which the rules, and not just ordinary issues of the day, are up for grabs. In one of his discussions of the French Revolution, Kant remarks that Louis XVI made a "very serious error in judgment" in calling the Estates General, since once the original legislative (i.e., the people) is constituted in assembly, the legislative power reverts to them. *Rechtslehre*, 6:341–42; 481. The framers of the U.S. Constitution understood this as well when they made it very hard to call new conventions to propose amendments to their recently constructed handiwork. See also Arendt, *On Revolution*.

113 On this topic, see Aretin, ed., *Der aufgeklärte Absolutismus*. See also Langer, *Reform nach Prinzipien*.

114 See, for example, "What Is Enlightenment?" 8:36–42; 17–22; "Theory and Practice," 8:304; 302; *Conflict*, 7:86n.; 155n.; 92; 167.

115 Kant, *Rechtslehre*, 6:372; 505–06.

116 Kant, "Theory and Practice," 8:304; 302.

117 In some places, though not in the *Rechtslehre*, Kant makes the argument that naturally occurring, apparently contingent, and possibly violent changes can, as if by an invisible hand, lead to political progress. I discuss this line of reasoning, which is not especially convincing, nor made with much conviction by Kant, in chapters 2 and 3.

118 Kant, *Rechtslehre*, 6:318; 461. Kant specifies that only inquiries with a "practical aim in view" should be banned, leaving open the possibility of legitimate *scholarly* inquiry into the origins of constituted regimes.

119 Kant, *Rechtslehre*, 6:319; 462.

120 Ibid., 6:346, 484.

121 For example, *Rechtslehre*, 6:319; 462: "The presently existing legislative authority ought to be obeyed, whatever its origin."

122 I discuss Kant's argument against divided sovereignty by means of infinite regress in the earlier section on revolution. See *Rechtslehre*, 6:319–20; 462–64.

123 Ibid., 6:325; 467–68; 345–46; 484; 6:346; 484.

124 Ibid., 6:345; 483; 6:345; 483; 6:345–46; 484.

125 Ibid., 6:347; 485. Kant quotes Cicero's "Pro Milone": "In times of war the laws are silent," though he does not endorse this position. For a general refutation of this point of view, see Walzer, *Just and Unjust Wars.*

126 This is, of course, the principle of provisional right. *Rechtslehre*, 6:347; 485

127 Ibid., 6:347; 485.

128 Ibid., 6:345–46; 484.

129 For a similar argument, see Kuehn, *Kant: A Biography*, 13–15 and passim.

130 Writers tend either to synthesize a unified theory by picking and choosing from all of Kant's works, as Howard Williams does in *Kant's Political Philosophy*, or to select one of Kant's books as the key to what is assumed to be his existing, but unwritten, political thought (see my discussion in the introduction and chapter 2).

131 He used the phrase only once, to the best of my knowledge. Since Kant tends to "float" some of his less certain ideas in print, and since this thread is not taken up again, I think it is safe to assume that Kant was not satisfied with the comparison. I have argued similarly with regard to Kant's formal "principles of publicity" in chapter 3.

132 Riley, *Will and Political Legitimacy*, 125–62.

133 Yack, *The Longing for Total Revolution*, 106.

134 Gregor, *Laws of Freedom*, 18.

135 Kant, preface to the first edition of *Critique of Pure Reason*, Avii–xxii; 99–105.

136 Kant, *Rechtslehre*, 6:215–16; 370–71.

137 The status of practical knowledge has been the subject of a great deal of philosophical debate. Kant's clearest statement on the subject is found in the note to preface to *Critique of Practical Reason*, where he writes that "whereas freedom is indeed the *ratio essendi* of the moral law, the moral law is the *ratio cognoscendi* of freedom. For, had not the moral law *already* been distinctly thought in our reason, we should never consider

ourselves justified in *assuming* such a things as freedom. . . . But were there no freedom, the moral law would *not be encountered* at all in ourselves." 5:5; 140.

138 Kant, *Conflict,* 7:79; 141.

CHAPTER 5 **The Judging Public**

1 Keck and Sikkink, *Activists Beyond Borders.*

2 Ibid., 13.

3 Ibid., 30.

4 Ibid., 202 and passim.

5 See, for example, Rawls, *Political Liberalism;* Gutmann and Thompson, *Democracy and Disagreement;* Habermas, *Between Facts and Norms.*

6 Keck and Sikkink, *Activists Beyond Borders,* 205. See Rawls, *Political Liberalism.*

7 Keck and Sikkink, *Activists Beyond Borders,* 205.

8 Haas, "Introduction: Epistemic Communities and International Policy Coordination."

9 This chapter addresses only the introduction and the second part of *Conflict,* on the faculty of law. Part 2 was written three or four years before its publication as part of *Conflict* in 1798. Klenner, ed., *Rechtslehre,* 530. Mary Gregor, in the introduction to her English translation of *Conflict,* says that the essay was likely written in 1795. Two things matter for my purposes: first, that part 2 of *Conflict* was written at the same time as or shortly after *Theory and Practice* and, second, that Kant's introductory essay to *Conflict* was written at least three years later. Gregor, "Translator's Introduction" to *Conflict,* xxiii.

10 Kant, *Conflict,* 7:85; 153; translation from the Reiss edition, 182.

11 Fehér, "Practical Reason in the Revolution," 167–68.

12 Kant does not defend this position in *Conflict,* merely accepting as doctrine his conclusion from *Perpetual Peace* that republican governments are naturally averse to war. Kant, *Perpetual Peace,* 8:350; 323. In *Conflict,* he is careful to specify that republican governments would avoid aggressive wars, not defensive ones.

13 Kant, *Conflict,* 7:86n.; 155n.

14 Kant, "What Is Enlightenment?" 8:39; 20.

15 Kant, *Conflict,* 7:86–87; 155–57.

16 See Gregor, "Translator's Introduction," Klenner's notes to his edition of the *Rechtslehre,* and Brandt, "Zum 'Streit der Fakultäten.'"

17 Klenner, ed., *Rechtslehre,* 523. See also Kuehn, *Kant: A Biography,* 379–80.

18 Kant, *Conflict,* 7:6–10; 11–19.

19 Ibid., 7:10; 19.

20 See Kuehn, *Kant: A Biography,* 366–72.

21 Gregor, "Translator's Introduction," xxi. Kant had some interesting and peculiar ideas about "rational," that is, nonempirical and noninvasive, medicine; for example, he argued that controlled breathing promotes health. See also Kuehn, *Kant: A Biography,* 406.

22 Kant, *Conflict,* 7:11; 21.

23 Gregor cites a 1793 letter of Kant's on the conflict. Gregor, "Translator's Introduction," vii.

24 Kant employs such a technique with far more subtlety in the early essay "What Is Enlightenment?"; see chapter 1.

25 Kant, *Conflict*, 7:19–20; 27–29.

26 Ibid., 7:34; 57.

27 See, for example, O'Neill, "Reason and Politics in the Kantian Enterprise," in her *Constructions of Reason*. See also Saner, *Kant's Political Thought*.

28 Commentators eager to establish political concerns at the center of Kant's work frequently cite his use of judicial metaphor in the *Critiques*. They do not mention, however, that he also uses a number of other, less evocative metaphors, such as the metaphor of battle used at B774–75 and throughout his work.

29 Kant, *Critique of Pure Reason*, Bxxxv; 119.

30 Ibid., B779–80; 649–50. The primacy of the *practical* is another matter: when Kant wrote, in the preface to the second edition of *Critique of Pure Reason*, that he had to deny knowledge to make room for faith, he meant it. Even as the strict limits on theoretical knowledge remain firm in Kant's mature theory, they may be superseded in practice through the use of postulates that are, Kant claims, at least practically (if not theoretically) necessary. *Critique of Pure Reason*, Bxxx; 117.

31 Ibid., B766–85; 643–52. I am grateful to an anonymous reader for Yale University Press for pointing out that Kant's use of the term *Luftfechter* (literally, "air-fencer") in this passage refers to something more like shadowboxing than fencing; as Kant says, "Both parties beat the air, and wrestle with their own shadows, since they go beyond the limits of nature, where there is nothing that they can seize and hold with their dogmatic grasp." *Critique of Pure Reason*, B784; 652; translation from the Norman Kemp Smith edition, 604. See also Reinhard Brandt's interesting discussion of the state of nature metaphor and Kant's early physical theories of attraction and repulsion, and of the natural emergence of order out of chaos. Brandt, "Zum 'Streit der Fakultäten.'"

32 He does defend the philosophical faculty against state interference. Kant argues that "free teachers of right, i.e., the philosophers" are the natural sources of enlightened reason for the people and ought on that account to be allowed to flourish unencumbered by state interference, which would deprive them of the source of their authority—their allegiance to truth. *Conflict*, 7:89; 161; translation from the Reiss edition, 186.

33 Ibid., 7:80; 143; translation from the Reiss edition, 178.

34 First, after outlining three possible visions of human history, all of which must be incorrect, Kant returns to the possibility of progress in history as the most plausible. Second, after claiming that "direct experience" cannot solve the problem of progress, Kant concludes that "indirect experience" can do so. Kant, *Conflict*, 7:81–84; 145–51.

35 Kant's conflation of two very distinct modes of argumentation in *Conflict* has led numerous readers astray. In *Kant's Political Philosophy*, for example, Howard Williams writes that Kant argues in *Conflict* that violent struggles "can usually be expected to hamper the progress of a nation towards a rational form of constitution since they will

lead to the undermining of all order and right." It is certainly true that Kant opposed any "undermining of all order and right," and that he advocated reform over revolution. But these claims are part of Kant's synthetic account of progress, one that includes moral willing as a cause in the world. In his accounts of the purposiveness of nature, however, Kant argues that while war is immoral, over the long run the very experience of violent struggle brings humankind closer to perfect political organization. As I argue throughout this book, Kant's strong teleological claims are among his weakest arguments. Nonetheless, the reader ought to recognize them as a separate account from his far better, agency-centered account of politics.

36 Kant, *Conflict,* 7:79–80; 141–43: "But how is a history a priori possible? Answer: if the diviner himself creates and contrives the events which he announces in advance."

37 Descartes' ontological proof of the existence of God is of course more complicated than this sketch indicates. Like his predecessor St. Anselm, Descartes began with the problematic premise that imperfect beings like ourselves cannot have ideas of perfection without these ideas being given by something perfect.

38 Kant, "Theory and Practice," 8:309; 306.

39 "There must be some experience in the human race which, as an event, points to the disposition and capacity of the human race to be the cause of its own advance toward the better." Kant, *Conflict,* 7:84; 151.

40 Ibid., 7:83; 149.

41 Ibid., 7:83; 149.

42 Ibid., 7:84; 151; translation emended.

43 Why, one might ask at this point, could we not have knowledge of moral willing while denying its effectiveness (that is, could moral willing turn out to be strictly epiphenomenal)? Kant offers two arguments against this objection. First, qua willing, moral willing has an object that must be possible. Second, and more interestingly from my perspective, the mechanism of the judging public, through which moral willing is applied to concrete human events, ensures that such willing has an effect, at least over the long run.

44 Kant, *Conflict,* 7:84; 151.

45 Ibid., 7:87; 157; 85; 153.

46 See Kuehn, *Kant: A Biography,* 340–43, 392.

47 Heinrich Heine, *Zur Geschichte der Religion und Philosophie in Deutschland* (1835); cited in Brandt, "Zum 'Streit der Fakultäten,'" 39.

48 In part 1 of *Conflict,* for example, Kant writes: "This conflict [of faculties] is quite compatible with an agreement of the learned and civil community in maxims which, if observed, must bring about a constant progress of both ranks of the faculties toward greater perfection, and finally prepare the way for the government to remove all restrictions that its choice has put on freedom of public judgment." Kant, *Conflict,* 7:35; 59.

49 Ibid., 7:86n.; 155n.

50 Ibid., 7:85–93; 153–69. However, no people may be declared categorically unready for freedom. See Kuehn, *Kant: A Biography,* 372.

51 Kant, *Conflict,* 7:91; 165; translation altered.

52 Ibid., 7:89; 161.

53 Kant, *Critique of Pure Reason,* B766–67; 643.

54 See my discussion in chapter 1.

55 Kant, *Conflict,* 7:85; 153; 86; 155.

56 Kant, *Critique of Pure Reason,* B774; 647.

57 Kant, *Conflict,* 7:86–87; 155–57. Kant carefully distinguishes among sympathy, enthusiasm, and emotion (*Affekt,* translated as "passion" by Gregor). As he does with the *Triebfeder* problem, Kant has some difficulty accounting for motivation in the case of purely universalistic inspiration. The problem of moral motivation in the case of the categorical imperative is solved (at least to the satisfaction of some) by Kant's account of the awe one feels before the moral law. Here, similarly, Kant argues that "true enthusiasm is always directed exclusively towards the *ideal,*" even as "all *Affekt* as such is blameworthy." For a general account of moral motivation in Kant, see Ameriks, *Kant and the Fate of Autonomy,* 317–24.

58 Kant, *Conflict,* 7:88; 159.

59 Ibid., 7:89; 161; translation from the Reiss edition, 186.

60 See Kant's discussion in *Critique of Pure Reason,* B774; 647.

61 Kant certainly experienced political interference with the search for truth at his own University of Königsberg. See Kuehn, *Kant: A Biography,* especially chapter 2.

62 Kant, *Conflict,* 7:90; 163; translation from the Reiss edition, 187.

63 Kant's confusion between representative legitimacy in the state and publicity in civil society (in the modern sense) is echoed by present-day confusion over the meaning of "deliberative" in relation to democracy. While most students of American politics use "deliberative" to denote reasoning *by elected officials,* students of political theory tend to look for deliberation among members of civil society. I am grateful to Harvey Tucker of Texas A&M University for pointing this out to me.

64 Kant, *Conflict,* 7:91; 165.

65 Ibid., 7:93; 169; translation from the Reiss edition, 189.

66 To inform Kant of the political climate facing scholarly publication, his student Kiesewetter wrote that Frederick William had "seen Jesus again." *Philosophical Correspondence,* 11:264–66; 173.

67 Kant, *Conflict,* 7:93; 169.

68 Levinger, "Kant and the Origins of Prussian Constitutionalism." Though Frederick William II and Wöllner were both gone before *Conflict* was published, Kant first presented the essay that became part 2 to the government censor under their regime. Kuehn, *Kant: A Biography,* 403.

69 Kant, *Conflict,* 7:79; 141.

70 Ibid., 7:92; 167. Kant lists Plato, More, Harrington, and "Allais" (actually, Denis Veiras, a Huguenot political novelist and author of the utopian work "The History of the Sevarambians"; see Laursen, "Liars and Unbelief in the Forgotten Utopia") as examples of fruitless constitution building.

71 Kant considers this possibility here, of course, and does not reject it. But I argue that the third alternative is more consistent with his argument, and also more plausible philosophically. See also my argument on teleological history in chapter 2, on *Judgment*.

72 Kant, *Conflict*, 7:91–92; 165–67.

73 Ibid., 7:91; 165.

74 Ibid., 7:88–89; 159–61.

75 At issue here is not whether one is justified in presuming physical cause and effect but whether one is justified in presuming the necessity of transcendental causes of phenomena.

76 Allison, *Kant's Theory of Taste*, 206.

77 Kant, *Conflict*, 7:86n.; 155n.; and Gregor's note, 219.

78 Kant, *Conflict*, 7:90–91; 163–65; translation from the Reiss edition, 187.

79 As Kant argues here and elsewhere, welfare is an appropriate goal for individuals and rulers, but it has nothing to do with public right. "But welfare possesses no principle either for him who receives it or for him who dispenses it . . . inasmuch as what matters in welfare is the material of the will, which is empirical, and which is thus unfit for the universality of a rule." *Conflict*, 7:87n.; 157n. For a different interpretation, see Rosen, *Kant's Theory of Justice*, 192–96.

80 Kant, *Conflict*, 7:91; 165. The need to separate judgment from power also explains Kant's use of the metaphor of the drama in his primary example of the functioning public sphere in *Conflict*. The sympathetic public partisans of the revolution are described as spectators viewing a stage on which concrete political actions are played out. No one would expect (at least not in the eighteenth century!) the audience to change the course of the drama at hand. But their judgments over time might well come to change the course of future dramatic production.

81 Ibid., 7:33; 55.

82 Ibid., 7:92; 167.

83 Ibid., 7:92n.; 167n. Kant draws a similar conclusion in the *Rechtslehre:* "The attempt to realize this idea [of constitutional government] should not be made by way of revolution. . . . But if it is attempted and carried out by gradual reform in accordance with firm principles, it can lead to continual approximation of the highest political good." Kant, *Rechtslehre*, 6:355; 124.

84 See chapter 1.

85 Kant, *Conflict*, 7:93; 169. There are clear similarities between Kant's view and later accounts of the political system of "enlightened absolutism" and its internal contradictions. As Gianfranco Poggi has observed, the policies of enlightened absolutism "revealed and often unwittingly fostered the start of a remarkable change in the internal configuration and political significance of civil society. In the long run, such change would transform the system of rule by realizing the civil society's demand for an active, decisive role in the political process." Poggi, *The Development of the Modern State*, 79; see also 79–85.

86 Kant, *Conflict*, 7:87n.; 157n.

87 Kant, *Perpetual Peace*, 8:380; 347; translation from the Reiss edition, 125.

Conclusion

1   See, for an introduction, Marc Lynch, "Globalization and International Democracy."

2   Greater respect for the marketplace, however, emphatically does not entail limiting government to a nightwatchman state. See Rosen, *Kant's Theory of Justice*, chapter 5.

3   Not that Kantian provisional politics is the only theory to focus on process. See both Rawls and Habermas on procedural norms.

4   Rousseau, *Social Contract*, especially 3:15.

5   Nor, *pace* Rosen, are there positive Kantian requirements for market interventions aimed at welfare as a good. In a particular society, however, there may well be good Kantian reasons for state intervention in the economic marketplace in order to realize maximum substantive citizenship.

6   Marshall, *Class, Citizenship, and Social Development*; Rees, "T. H. Marshall and the Progress of Citizenship"; and Dahrendorf, "Citizenship and Social Class."

7   Klausen, "Social Rights Advocacy and State Building"; Kymlicka and Norman, "Return of the Citizen."

8   Klausen, "Social Rights Advocacy and State Building," 245.

9   Ibid., 247, 253–59.

10 Ibid., 246.

11 As Klausen notes: "The tendency to obfuscate the difference between redistributive policy and citizenship can be traced directly to Marshall." Ibid., 250.

12 Rees, "T. H. Marshall and the Progress of Citizenship," 22.

13 Dahrendorf, "Citizenship and Social Class," 37. Italics mine.

14 See Kymlicka, *Politics in the Vernacular*, which contains a number of responses to critics of his *Multicultural Citizenship*.

15 See the introduction to this chapter and the preceding chapters. In Kantian political theory, conclusive right includes those principles that are true for all limited rational beings; for Kant, conclusive right includes, for example, the categorical imperative. Provisional right, on the other hand, is the rule of political right in the specific context of always imperfect actual states. The rule of provisional right is roughly: act such that you promote the possibility of progress.

16 Klausen, "Social Rights Advocacy and State Building," 252.

17 For example, Glendon, *Rights Talk*.

18 Martin Luther King Jr. "Beyond Vietnam."

19 Isaac, *The Poverty of Progressivism*, 40.

20 Putnam, *Bowling Alone*.

21 Putnam, with Leonardi and Nanetti, *Making Democracy Work*.

22 Among the other factors that did not make significant differences to governmental success were party politics, ideology, affluence, social stability, and population movements.

23 Putnam, "The Prosperous Community," and "Unsolved Mystery."

24　Putnam and Goss, introduction, *Democracies in Flux*, 6.

25　Skocpol, *Diminished Democracy*, 12.

26　Skocpol and Fiorina, eds., *Civic Engagement in American Democracy*.

27　Though Putnam is much less interested than Skocpol in organizational-level change, he does acknowledge the importance of what Skocpol calls the shift from membership to management. Putnam divides political activity into declining old-style activities, such as voting, party activism, youth activism, and local meeting attendance, on the one hand, and rising new-style activities, such as check writing, litigation, mailing list membership organizations, and listening to talk radio. He writes that "these rising forms of political engagement rest on a constricted notion of citizenship—citizen as disgruntled claimant, not citizen as participant in collective endeavor to define the public interest." Putnam, "Unsolved Mystery, the Tocqueville Files."

28　Wuthnow, "Mobilizing Civic Engagement."

29　Skocpol, *Diminished Democracy*, 124.

30　Ibid., 177.

31　Ibid., 243.

32　In fact, as Putnam points out, the rise of mass media, particularly television, is not a primarily political phenomenon, but it has had impressive political repercussions. Putnam, "Unsolved Mystery."

33　Both Putnam and Skocpol stress that recognition of the fundamental role played by civil society in public life in no way obviates the important role that the state may play in public welfare. In fact, as Skocpol's work has documented both historically and cross-nationally, the state has played and should continued to play a critical role in the development of social institutions supporting citizenship. See, for example, Skocpol, *Protecting Mothers and Soldiers*.

34　This is why heirs to Kant's ethics tend to focus on the courts as arbitrators of meaningful political questions, while the heirs to Kant's politics would focus instead on institutions and processes that restrict or promote citizens' capacities for self-rule. The appointed panels making decisions for international trade regimes, the devices like base-closure commissions used to get around representational failure, governmental and nongovernmental agencies devoted to ensuring inclusive access to the levers of everyday power (for example, Legal Services Corp., such as it is), electoral reforms designed to represent citizens on the basis of participation rather than inheritance, stakeholder schemes for resolving environmental disputes, micro-lending agencies that encourage citizen autonomy, and so forth: these are the locations of interest to the Kantian political theorist, because these are the places where citizens either get or lose the capacity to determine their fates themselves.

35　See Shapiro, *Democratic Justice*, 39–45. See also Jung and Shapiro, "South Africa's Negotiated Transition."

36　Ann Orloff, for example, cites Marshall when she argues that to achieve genuine autonomy, women must be able to maintain a household without married support. However, she laments the fact that most of Marshall's successors ignore gender issues in the development of social citizenship. Orloff, "Gender and the Social Rights of Citizenship."

37 For a similar argument applying to citizens generally, see Klausen, "Social Rights Advocacy and State Building."

38 Fraser, "Gender Equity and the Welfare State," 219.

39 Fraser, "After the Family Wage," 599–600; cited in Orloff, "Gender in the Welfare State," 73.

40 See also Baer, *Our Lives Before the Law.*

41 The relevant passage is Kant, *Rechtslehre,* 6:313–15; 91–92, sec. 46.

42 Kaplan, "Was Democracy Just a Moment?"

43 Dahrendorf, "Citizenship and Social Class," 26.

SELECTED BIBLIOGRAPHY

WORKS BY IMMANUEL KANT

The Preussischen Akademie der Wissenschaften edition, *Kants gesammelte Schriften*, is the standard edition of Kant's writings. Citations of Kant's work include the volume and page numbers from this edition, usually followed by the page numbers of the relevant translation.

Other German-Language Editions

Schriften zur Anthropologie, Geschichtsphilosophie, Politik, und Pädagogik. In *Werke in Sechs Bänden*, vol. 6. Edited by Wilhelm Weischedel. Frankfurt am Main: Insel-Verlag, 1964.

Kritik der praktischen Vernunft und Grundlegung zur Metaphysik der Sitten. Edited by Wilhelm Weischedel. Frankfurt am Main: Suhrkamp, 1974.

Rechtslehre: Schriften zur Rechtsphilosophie. Edited by Herman Klenner. Berlin: Akademie-Verlag, 1988.

English-Language Editions

Critique of Pure Reason (1781, first edition; 1787, second edition). Translated by Paul Guyer and Allen W. Wood. Cambridge: Cambridge University Press, 1998.

Prolegomena to Any Future Metaphysics That Will Be Able to Come Forward as a Science. In *Philosophy of Material Nature* (1783). Edited by J. W. Ellington. Indianapolis: Hackett, 1985.

"An Answer to the Question: What Is Enlightenment?" (1784). In *Immanuel Kant: Practical Philosophy.* Translated and edited by Mary J. Gregor. Cambridge: Cambridge University Press, 1996.

Groundwork of the Metaphysics of Morals (1785). In *Immanuel Kant: Practical Philosophy.* Translated and edited by Mary J. Gregor. Cambridge: Cambridge University Press, 1996.

Critique of Practical Reason (1788). In *Immanuel Kant: Practical Philosophy.* Translated and edited by Mary J. Gregor. Cambridge: Cambridge University Press, 1996.

Critique of Judgment (1790). Translated by Werner S. Pluhar. Indianapolis: Hackett, 1987.

"On the Common Saying: That May Be Correct in Theory, but It Is of No Use in Practice" (1793). In *Immanuel Kant: Practical Philosophy.* Translated and edited by Mary J. Gregor. Cambridge: Cambridge University Press, 1996.

Toward Perpetual Peace: A Philosophical Sketch (1795). In *Immanuel Kant: Practical Philosophy.* Translated and edited by Mary J. Gregor. Cambridge: Cambridge University Press, 1996.

The Metaphysics of Morals (1797). In *Immanuel Kant: Practical Philosophy.* Translated and edited by Mary J. Gregor. Cambridge: Cambridge University Press, 1996.

The Conflict of the Faculties (1798). Translated by Mary J. Gregor. Lincoln: University of Nebraska Press, 1979.

Critique of Pure Reason. Translated by Norman Kemp Smith. New York: St. Martin's Press, 1929.

Groundwork of the Metaphysics of Morals. Translated and edited by H. J. Paton. 3d ed. New York: Harper & Row, 1956.

Kant on History. Edited by Lewis White Beck. New York: Bobbs-Merrill, 1963.

Kant: Philosophical Correspondence, 1759–99. Edited by Arnulf Zweig. Chicago and London: University of Chicago Press, 1967.

Anthropology from a Practical Point of View. Translated by Victor Lyle Dowdell. Edited by Hans H. Rudnick. Carbondale: Southern Illinois University Press, 1978.

Metaphysical Foundations of Natural Science. In *Philosophy of Material Nature.* Edited by J. W. Ellington. Indianapolis: Hackett, 1985.

Kant: Political Writings. Edited by H. Reiss. 2d ed. Cambridge: Cambridge University Press, 1991.

The Metaphysics of Morals. Edited by Mary J. Gregor. Cambridge: Cambridge University Press, 1996.

The Cambridge Edition of the Works of Immanuel Kant: Practical Philosophy. Translated and edited by Mary J. Gregor. Cambridge: Cambridge University Press, 1996.

OTHER SOURCES

Alexander, Herbert E., and Anthony Corrado. *Financing the 1992 Election.* Armonk, N.Y.: M. E. Sharpe, 1995.

Allison, Henry E. *Idealism and Freedom: Essays on Kant's Theoretical and Practical Philosophy.* Cambridge: Cambridge University Press, 1996.

———. *Kant's Theory of Freedom.* Cambridge: Cambridge University Press, 1990.

———. *Kant's Theory of Taste: A Reading of the Critique of Aesthetic Judgment.* Cambridge: Cambridge University Press, 2001.

———. *Kant's Transcendental Idealism: An Interpretation and Defense.* New Haven and London: Yale University Press, 1983.

———. *Lessing and the Enlightenment: His Philosophy of Religion and its Relation to Eighteenth-Century Thought.* Ann Arbor: University of Michigan Press, 1966.

———. "On a Presumed Gap in the Derivation of the Categorical Imperative." *Philosophical Topics* 19 (1991): 1–15.

Ameriks, Karl. *Kant and the Fate of Autonomy: Problems in the Appropriation of the Critical Philosophy.* Cambridge: Cambridge University Press, 2000.

Arendt, Hannah. *Between Past and Future: Eight Exercises in Political Thought.* New York: Penguin Books, 1993.

————. *Lectures on Kant's Political Philosophy.* Edited by R. Beiner. Chicago and London: University of Chicago Press, 1982.

————. *On Revolution.* New York: Viking, 1963.

Aretin, Karl Otmar Freiherr von, ed. *Der aufgeklärte Absolutismus.* Cologne: Kiepenheuer & Witsch, 1974.

Ashcraft, Richard. *Revolutionary Politics and Locke's Two Treatises of Government.* Princeton: Princeton University Press, 1986.

Atkinson, R. F. "Kant's Moral and Political Rigorism." In *Essays on Kant's Political Philosophy,* edited by H. Williams. Cardiff: University of Wales Press, 1992.

Baer, Judith A. *Our Lives Before the Law: Constructing a Feminist Jurisprudence.* Princeton: Princeton University Press, 1999.

Bahr, Ehrhard. "Nachwort." In *Was ist Aufklärung? Thesen und Definitionen,* edited by E. Bahr. Stuttgart: Reclam, 1974.

Bartholomew, Amy. "Constitutional Patriotism and Social Inclusiveness: Justice for Immigrants?" Paper presented at the 2001 meeting of the American Sociological Association, Anaheim, California, August 2001.

Batscha, Zwi, ed. *Materialen zu Kants Rechtsphilosophie.* Frankfurt am Main: Suhrkamp, 1976.

Baumann, Peter. "Zwei Seiten der Kantischen Begründung von Eigentum und Staat." *Kant-Studien* 85 (1994): 147–59.

Baxley, Anne Margaret. "Does Kantian Virtue Amount to More Than Continence?" *Review of Metaphysics* 56 (March 2003): 559–86.

Becher, Ursula A. J. *Politische Gesellschaft: Studien zur Genese bürgerlicher Öffentlichkeit in Deutschland.* Vol. 59, *Veröffentlichungen der Max-Plank-Instituts für Geschichte.* Göttingen: Vandenhoeck & Ruprecht, 1978.

Beck, Lewis White. "Kant's Two Conceptions of the Will in Their Political Context." In *Kant and Political Philosophy: The Contemporary Legacy,* edited by R. Beiner and W. J. Booth. New Haven and London: Yale University Press, 1993.

Behler, Ernst. "Die Auffassung der Revolution in der deutschen Frühromantik." In Peter V. Hohendahl, Herbert S. Lindenberger, and Egon Schwartz, eds., *Essays on European Literature: In Honor of Liselotte Dieckmann.* St. Louis: Washington University Press, 1972.

Beiner, Ronald, and William James Booth, eds. *Kant and Political Philosophy: The Contemporary Legacy.* New Haven and London: Yale University Press, 1993.

Beiser, Frederick C., trans. and ed. *The Early Political Writings of the German Romantics.* Cambridge: Cambridge University Press, 1996.

————. *Enlightenment, Revolution, Romanticism: The Genesis of Modern German Political Thought.* Cambridge: Harvard University Press, 1992.

————. *The Fate of Reason: German Philosophy from Kant to Fichte.* Cambridge: Harvard University Press, 1987.

Bell, Daniel. *East Meets West: Human Rights and Democracy in East Asia.* Princeton: Princeton University Press, 2000.

Beyerhaus, Gisbert. "Kants 'Programm' der Aufklärung aus dem Jahre 1784." *Kant-Studien* 26 (1921): 1–16.

Bielefeldt, Heiner. "Autonomy and Republicanism: Immanuel Kant's Philosophy of Freedom." *Political Theory* 25 (1997): 524–58.

Biester, Johann Erich [E. v. K.]. "Vorschlag, die Geistlichen nicht mehr bei Vollziehung der Ehen zu bemühen." In *Was Ist Aufklärung?: Beiträge aus der Berlinischen Monatsschrift,* edited by N. Hinske. Darmstadt: Wissenschaftliches Buchgesellschaft, 1977.

Birtsch, Günter. "The Berlin Wednesday Society." In *What Is Enlightenment?: Eighteenth-Century Answers and Twentieth-Century Questions,* edited by J. Schmidt. Berkeley: University of California Press, 1996.

Bittner, Rüdiger. "What Is Enlightenment?" In *What Is Enlightenment?: Eighteenth-Century Answers and Twentieth-Century Questions,* edited by J. Schmidt. Berkeley: University of California Press, 1996.

Bödeker, Hans Erich, ed. *Aufklärung der Politisierung—Politisierung der Aufklärung.* Hamburg: F. Meiner Verlag, 1987.

————. "Prozesse und Strukturen politischer Bewußtseinsbildung der deutschen Aufklärung." In *Aufklärung der Politisierung—Politisierung der Aufklärung,* edited by H. E. Bödeker. Hamburg: F. Meiner Verlag, 1987.

Bohman, James. "Citizenship and Norms of Publicity: Wide Public Reason in Cosmopolitan Societies." *Political Theory* 27 (1999): 176–202.

————. "The Public Spheres of the World Citizen." In *Perpetual Peace: Essays on Kant's Cosmopolitan Ideal,* edited by J. Bohman and M. Lutz-Bachmann. Cambridge, Mass.: MIT Press, 1997.

Bohman, James, and Matthias Lutz-Bachmann, eds. *Perpetual Peace: Essays on Kant's Cosmopolitan Ideal.* Cambridge: MIT Press, 1997.

Bohman, James, and William Rehg, eds. *Deliberative Democracy.* Cambridge, Mass.: MIT Press, 1997.

Booth, William James. *Interpreting the World: Kant's Philosophy of History and Politics.* Toronto: University of Toronto Press, 1986.

————. "The Limits of Autonomy: Karl Marx's Kant Critique." In *Kant and Political Philosophy: The Contemporary Legacy,* edited by R. Beiner and W. J. Booth. New Haven and London: Yale University Press, 1993.

————, et al., eds. *Politics and Rationality.* Cambridge: Cambridge University Press, 1993.

Brandt, Reinhard. "Das Erlaubnisgesetz, oder: Vernunft und Geschichte in Kants Rechtslehre." In *Rechtsphilosophie der Aufklärung: Symposium Wolfenbüttel 1981,* edited by Reinhard Brandt. Berlin, 1982.

————. "Person und Sache: Hobbes' 'jus omnium in omnia et omnes' und Kants Theorie des Besitzes der Willkür einer anderen Person im Vertrag." *Deutsche Zeitschrift für Philosophie* 47 (1999): 887–910.

————. "Zum 'Streit der Fakultäten.'" In *Kant Forschungen,* edited by R. Brandt and W. Stark. Hamburg: Felix Meiner Verlag, 1987.

Brandt, Reinhard, and Berndt Ludwig. Exchange on the question, "Will die Natur unwiderstehlich die Republik?" *Kant-Studien* (1997–1998): 88–89.

Brunner, Otto, Werner Conze, and Reinhart Koselleck, eds. *Geschichtliche Grundbegriffe: Historisches Lexikon zur politischen-sozialen Sprache in Deutschland.* 8 vols. Stuttgart: Klett-Cotta, 1972–.

Buchwalter, Andrew. "Hegel's Concept of Virtue." *Political Theory* 20 (1992): 548–83.

Büsch, Otto, and Walter Grab, eds. *Die demokratische Bewegung in Meitteleuropa im ausgehenden 18. und frühen 19. Jahrhundert: Ein Tagungsbericht.* Vol. 29, *Einzelveröffentlichungen der Historischen Kommission zu Berlin.* Berlin: Colloquium-Verlag, 1980.

Busch, Werner. *Die Entstehung der kritischen Rechtsphilosophie Kants 1762–1780.* Berlin: Kant-Studien Ergänzungshefte, 1979.

Buzás, Ladislaus. *German Library History, 800–1945.* Translated by William D. Boyd, with Irmgard H. Wolfe. Jefferson, N.C., and London: McFarland, 1986.

Calhoun, Craig, ed. *Habermas and the Public Sphere.* Cambridge, Mass.: MIT Press, 1992.

Cassirer, Ernst. *Kant's Life and Thought.* Translated by James Haden. New Haven and London: Yale University Press, 1981.

————. *Rousseau, Kant, Goethe: Two Essays.* Translated by James Gutmann, Paul Oskar Kristeller, and John Herman Randall Jr. New York: Harper and Row, 1963.

Cavallar, Georg. *Kant and the Theory and Practice of International Right.* Cardiff: University of Wales Press, 1999.

————. "Kant's Judgment on Frederick's Enlightened Absolutism." *History of Political Thought* 14 (1993): 103–32.

————. "Kant's Society of Nations: Free Federation or World Republic?" *Journal of the History of Philosophy* 32 (1994): 461–82.

————. *Pax Kantiana: Systemisch-historische Untersuchungen des Entwurfs 'Zum ewigen Frieden' (1795) von Immanuel Kant.* Vienna: Böhlau, 1992.

Caygill, Howard. "Enthusiasm." In *A Kant Dictionary,* edited by H. Caygill. Oxford: Blackwell, 1995.

Clarke, Michael. "Kant's Rhetoric of Enlightenment." *Review of Politics* 59 (1997): 53–73.

Cohen, Ted, and Paul Guyer, eds. *Essays in Kant's Aesthetics.* Chicago and London: University of Chicago Press, 1982.

Cronin, Ciaran. "Kant's Politics of Enlightenment," *Journal of the History of Philosophy* 41 (2003): 51–80.

Curran, James. "Rethinking the Media as a Public Sphere." In *Communication and Citizenship: Journalism and the Public Sphere in the New Media Age,* edited by P. Dalhgren and C. Sparks. London and New York: Routledge, 1991.

Dahl, Robert Alan. *Dilemmas of Pluralist Democracy: Autonomy versus Control.* New Haven and London: Yale University Press, 1982.

Dahlgren, Peter. "Introduction." In *Communication and Citizenship: Journalism and the Public Sphere in the New Media Age,* edited by P. Dalhgren and C. Sparks. London and New York: Routledge, 1991.

Dahrendorf, Ralf. "Citizenship and Social Class." In Martin Bulmer and Anthony M. Rees, eds., *Citizenship Today: The Contemporary Relevance of T. H. Marshall.* London: University College London Press, 1996.

Dann, Otto, ed. *Lesegesellschaften und bürgerliche Emanzipation: Ein europäischer Vergleich.* Munich: C. H. Beck, 1981.

Darnton, Robert, and Daniel Roche, eds. *Revolution in Print: The Press in France: 1775–1800.* Berkeley: University of California Press, in cooperation with the New York Public Library, 1989.

Davidovitch, Adina. "How to Read *Religion within the Limits of Reason Alone.*" *Kant-Studien* 85 (1994): 1–14.

Davis, Kevin R. "Kantian 'Publicity' and Political Justice." *History of Philosophy Quarterly* 8 (1991): 409–21.

———. "Kant's Different Publics and the Justice of Publicity." *Kant-Studien* 83 (1992): 170–84.

Dippel, Horst. *Germany and the American Revolution, 1770–1800: A Sociohistorical Investigation of Late Eighteenth-Century Political Thinking.* Translated by Bernard A. Uhlendorf. Chapel Hill: University of North Carolina Press, 1977.

Dodson, Kevin E. "Autonomy and Authority in Kant's *Rechtslehre.*" *Political Theory* 25 (1997): 93–111.

Doyle, Michael W. "Kant, Liberal Legacies, and Foreign Affairs," parts 1 and 2. *Philosophy and Public Affairs* 12 (1983): 205–235; 323–353.

———. "Liberalism and International Relations." In *Kant and Political Philosophy: The Contemporary Legacy,* edited by R. Beiner and W. J. Booth. New Haven and London: Yale University Press, 1993.

Egert, Ilonka. "Die 'Berlinische Monatsschrift' (1783–1796) in der deutschen Spätaufklärung." *Zeitschrift für Geschichtswissenschaft* 39 (1991): 130–52.

Eisenstein, Elizabeth L. *The Printing Press as an Agent of Change: Communications and Cultural Transformations in Early Modern Europe.* 2 vols. Cambridge: Cambridge University Press, 1979.

Engelsing, Rolf. *Sozial- und Wirtschaftsgeschichte Deutschlands.* 3d ed. Göttingen: Vandenhoeck & Ruprecht, 1983.

Euler, Werner, and Gideon Stiening. "'. . . und nie die Pluralität widersprach'? Zur Bedeutung von Immanuel Kants Amtsgeschäften." *Kant-Studien* 86 (1995): 54–69.

Fehér, Ferenc. "Practical Reason in the Revolution: Kant's Dialogue with the French Revolution." *Social Research* 56 (1989): 161–85.

Fishkin, James. *Democracy and Deliberation: New Directions for Democratic Reform.* New Haven and London: Yale University Press, 1991.

Fleischacker, Samuel. *A Third Concept of Liberty: Judgment and Freedom in Kant and Adam Smith.* Princeton: Princeton University Press, 1999.

———. "Values Behind the Market: Kant's Response to the *Wealth of Nations.*" *History of Political Thought* 17 (1996): 379–407.

Flikschuh, Katrin. *Kant and Modern Political Philosophy.* Cambridge: Cambridge University Press, 2000.

Förster, Eckart, ed. *Kant's Transcendental Deductions: The Three 'Critiques' and the 'Opus postumum.'* Edited by E. Förster. Stanford: Stanford University Press, 1989.

Franceschet, Antonio. *Kant and Liberal Internationalism: Sovereignty, Justice, and Global Reform.* New York: Palgrave Macmillan, 2002.

Franke, Mark F. N. *Global Limits: Immanuel Kant, International Relations, and Critique of World Politics.* Albany: State University of New York Press, 2001.

Fraser, Nancy. "After the Family Wage: Gender Equity and the Welfare State," *Political Theory* 22 (1994): 591–618.

———. "Gender Equity and the Welfare State: A Postindustrial Thought Experiment." In *Democracy and Difference: Contesting the Boundaries of the Political,* edited by Seyla Benhabib. Princeton: Princeton University Press, 1996.

Gadamer, Hans-Georg. "On the Possibility of a Philosophical Ethics." In *Kant and Political Philosophy: The Contemporary Legacy,* edited by R. Beiner and W. J. Booth. New Haven and London: Yale University Press, 1993.

Galston, William A. *Kant and the Problem of History.* Chicago and London: University of Chicago Press, 1975.

———. "What Is Living and What Is Dead in Kant's Practical Philosophy." In *Kant and Political Philosophy: The Contemporary Legacy,* edited by R. Beiner and W. J. Booth. New Haven and London: Yale University Press, 1993.

Garber, Jörn, ed. *Kritik der Revolution: Theorie des deutschen Frühkonservatismus 1790–1810.* Vol. 1. Kronberg: Scriptor, 1976.

———, ed. *Revolutionäre Vernunft: Texte zur jakobinischen und liberalen Revolutionsrezeption, 1790–1810.* Kronberg: Scriptor, 1974.

Gay, Peter. *The Enlightenment: An Interpretation.* 2 vols. New York: Knopf, 1966–1969.

Glendon, Mary Ann. *Rights Talk: The Impoverishment of Political Discourse.* New York and Toronto: Free Press, 1991.

Goetschel, Willi. *Constituting Critique: Kant's Writing as Critical Practice [Kant als*

Schriftsteller]. Translated by Eric Schwab. Durham: Duke University Press, 1994.

Green, Donald P., Soo Yeon Kim, and David H. Yoon. "Dirty Pool." International Organization 55, no. 2 (spring 2001): 441–68.

Gregor, Mary J. Introduction and notes to her translation. In *Immanuel Kant: The Conflict of the Faculties [Der Streit der Fakultäten,]* edited by M. J. Gregor: Abaris Books, 1979.

———. "Kant on 'Natural Rights.'" In *Kant and Political Philosophy: The Contemporary Legacy,* edited by R. Beiner and W. J. Booth. New Haven and London: Yale University Press, 1993.

———. *Laws of Freedom: A Study of Kant's Method of Applying the Categorical Imperative in the* Metaphysik der Sitten. Oxford: Blackwell, 1963.

Grier, Michelle Gilmore. "Kant's Doctrine of Transcendental Illusion." Ph.D. dissertation, Department of Philosophy, University of California, San Diego, La Jolla, California, 1993.

Gutmann, Amy, and Dennis Thompson. *Democracy and Disagreement.* Cambridge, Mass.: Belknap Press of Harvard University Press, 1996.

———. "Why Deliberative Democracy Is Different," *Social Philosophy and Policy* 17 (winter 2000): 161–80.

Haas, Peter M. "Epistemic Communities and International Policy Coordination." *International Organization* 46 (1992): 1–35.

Habermas, Jürgen. *Between Facts and Norms: Contributions to a Discourse Theory of Law and Democracy.* Translated by William Rehg. Cambridge, Mass.: MIT Press, 1998.

———. "Kant's Idea of Perpetual Peace, with the Benefit of Two-Hundred Years' Hindsight." In *Perpetual Peace: Essays on Kant's Cosmopolitan Ideal,* edited by J. Bohman and M. Lutz-Bachmann. Cambridge, Mass.: MIT Press, 1997.

———. *Knowledge and Human Interests.* Translated by Jeremy J. Shapiro. Boston: Beacon Press, 1971.

———. "Morality and Ethical Life: Does Hegel's Critique of Kant Apply to Discourse Ethics?" In *Kant and Political Philosophy: The Contemporary Legacy,* edited by R. Beiner and W. J. Booth. New Haven and London: Yale University Press, 1993.

———. *The Structural Transformation of the Public Sphere: An Inquiry into a Category of Bourgeois Society.* Translated by Thomas Burger, with Frederick Lawrence. Cambridge, Mass.: MIT Press, 1989.

———. "Wahrheitstheorien." In *Wirklichkeit und Reflexion: Walter Schulz zum 60. Geburts tag,* edited by Helmut Farhenbach. Pfüllingen: Neske, 1973.

Hartung, Fritz. "Der aufgeklärte Absolutismus." In *Der aufgeklärte Absolutismus,* edited by Karl Otmar Freiherr von Aretin. Cologne: Kiepenheuer & Witsch, 1974.

Heider-Markel, Donald P., and Kenneth J. Meier. "The Politics of Gay and Lesbian

Rights: Expanding the Scope of Conflict." *Journal of Politics* 58 (1996): 332–49.

Heine, Heinrich. *Zur Geschichte der Religion und Philosophie in Deutschland.* edited by Wolfgang Harich. Frankfurt am Main: Insel Verlag, 1966.

Henrich, Dieter, ed. *Kant-Gentz-Rehberg: Über Theorie und Praxis.* Frankfurt am Main: Suhrkamp, 1967.

———. "On the Meaning of Rational Action in the State." In *Kant and Political Philosophy: The Contemporary Legacy,* edited by R. Beiner and W. J. Booth. New Haven and London: Yale University Press, 1993.

———. *The Unity of Reason: Essays on Kant's Philosophy,* edited by R. Velkley. Cambridge, Mass.: Harvard University Press, 1994.

Herman, Barbara. *The Practice of Moral Judgment.* Cambridge: Harvard University Press, 1993.

Hinske, Norbert, ed. *Was Ist Aufklärung?: Beiträge aus der Berlinischen Monatsschrift.* 2d ed. Darmstadt: Wissenschaftliches Buchgesellschaft, 1977.

Hirschman, Albert O. *The Passions and the Interests: Political Arguments for Capitalism before Its Triumph.* Princeton: Princeton University Press, 1977.

———. *The Rhetoric of Reaction: Perversity, Futility, Jeopardy.* Cambridge, Mass.: Harvard University Press, 1991.

Hobbes, Thomas. *Leviathan.* Edited by E. Curley. Indianapolis: Hackett, 1994 [1651].

Höffe, Otfried. *Immanuel Kant.* Munich: C. H. Beck, 1983.

Hölderlin, Friedrich. *Essays and Letters on Theory.* Translated by Thomas Pfau. Albany: SUNY Press, 1988.

Holmes, Stephen. *Benjamin Constant and the Making of Modern Liberalism.* New Haven and London: Yale University Press, 1984.

Hölscher, Lucien. "Öffentlichkeit." In *Geschichtliche Grundbegriffe: Historisches Lexikon zur politisch-sozialen Sprache in Deutschland,* edited by Otto Brunner, Werner Conze, and Reinhart Koselleck. Stuttgart: Klett-Cotta, 1972–1989.

Horkheimer, Max. "Kant und die Wissenschaften." In *Immanuel Kant zu Ehren,* edited by J. Koppe and R. Malter. Frankfurt am Main: Suhrkamp, 1974.

Howard, Dick. "Kant's System and (Its) Politics." *Man and World* 18 (1985): 79–98.

Hume, David. *Political Essays.* Edited by Knud Haakonssen. Cambridge: Cambridge University Press, 1994.

Isaac, Jeffrey C. *The Poverty of Progressivism: The Future of American Democracy in a Time of Liberal Decline.* Lanham, Md.: Rowman & Littlefield, 2003.

———. "The Strange Silence of Political Theory." *Political Theory* 23 (1995): 636–52.

Ivison, Duncan. "The Secret History of Public Reason: Hobbes to Rawls." *History of Political Thought* 18 (1997): 125–47.

Jung, Courtney, and Ian Shapiro. "South Africa's Negotiated Transition: Democracy, Opposition, and the New Constitutional Order." In Shapiro, *Democracy's Place.*

Kaplan, Robert D. "Was Democracy Just a Moment?" *Atlantic Monthly* 280, no. 6 (December 1997): 55–72.

Keane, John. "Despotism and Democracy: The Origins and Development of the Distinction Between Civil Society and the State, 1750–1850." In *Civil Society and the State: New European Perspectives,* edited by J. Keane. London and New York: Verso, 1988.

Keck, Margaret E., and Kathryn Sikkink. *Activists Beyond Borders: Advocacy Networks in International Politics.* Ithaca and London: Cornell University Press, 1998.

Kelly, George Armstrong. *Idealism, Politics and History.* Cambridge: Cambridge University Press, 1969.

Kersting, Wolfgang. "Kant's Concept of the State." In *Essays on Kant's Political Philosophy,* edited by Howard Williams. Cardiff: University of Wales Press, 1992.

———. *Wohlgeordnete Freiheit: Immanuel Kants Rechts- und Staatsphilosophie.* Berlin: Walter de Gruyter, 1984.

King, Martin Luther Jr. "Beyond Vietnam." Address given at Riverside Church, April 4, 1967. In "Martin Luther King, Jr. Papers Project at Stanford University": http://www.stanford.edu/group/King/publications/speeches/Beyond _Vietnam.pdf.

Kitcher, Patricia. *Kant's Transcendental Psychology.* New York: Oxford University Press, 1990.

Klausen, Jytte. "Social Rights Advocacy and State Building: T. H. Marshall in the Hands of Social Reformers." *World Politics* 47 (1995): 244–67.

Kneller, Jane, and Sidney Axinn, eds. *Autonomy and Community: Readings in Contemporary Kantian Social Philosophy.* Albany: SUNY Press, 1998.

Knippenberg, Joseph M. "The Politics of Kant's Philosophy." In *Kant and Political Philosophy: The Contemporary Legacy,* edited by R. Beiner and W. J. Booth. New Haven and London: Yale University Press, 1993.

Knudsen, Jonathan. "On Enlightenment for the Common Man." In *What Is Enlightenment?: Eighteenth-Century Questions and Twentieth-Century Answers.* Edited by J. Schmidt. Berkeley: University of California Press, 1996.

Kopitzsch, Franklin. "Die Aufklärung in Deutschland: Zur ihren Leistungen, Grenzen und Wirkungen." *Archiv für Sozialgeschichte* 23 (1983): 1–21.

Korsgaard, Christine M. *Creating the Kingdom of Ends.* Cambridge: Cambridge University Press, 1996.

———. "Kant's Formula of Universal Law." *Pacific Philosophical Quarterly* 66 (1985): 24–47.

Koselleck, Reinhart. *Critique and Crisis: Enlightenment and the Pathogenesis of Modern Society.* Oxford: Berg, 1988.

———. *Futures Past.* Translated by Keith Tribe. Cambridge: MIT Press, 1985.

————. "Linguistic Change and the History of Events." *Journal of Modern History* (1989): 649–66.

————. "Geschichtliche Grundbegriffe" and introduction. In *Geschichtliche Grundbegriffe: Historisches Lexikon zur politisch-sozialen Sprache in Deutschland*, edited by Otto Brunner, Werner Conze, and Reinhart Koselleck. Stuttgart: Ernst Klett Verlag, 1972–1989.

Kuehn, Manfred. *Kant: A Biography.* Cambridge: Cambridge University Press, 2001.

————. *Scottish Common Sense in Germany, 1768–1800.* Montreal and Kingston: McGill-Queen's University Press, 1987.

Kymlicka, Will. *Politics in the Vernacular: Nationalism, Multiculturalism, and Citizenship.* Oxford: Oxford University Press, 2001.

————. "Three Forms of Differentiated Citizenship in Canada." In *Democracy and Difference: Contesting the Boundaries of the Political*, edited by Seyla Benhabib. Princeton: Princeton University Press, 1996.

Kymlicka, Will, and Wayne Norman. "Return of the Citizen: A Survey of Recent Work on Citizenship Theory." *Ethics* 104 (1994): 352–81.

La Mettrie, Julian Offray de. *Man a Machine and Man a Plant.* Translated by Richard A. Watson and Maga Kybalka. Indianapolis: Hackett, 1994.

LaVaque-Manty, Mika. *Arguments and Fists: Political Agency and Justification in Liberal Theory.* New York and London: Routledge, 2002.

La Vopa, Anthony J. "Conceiving a Public: Ideas and Society in Eighteenth-Century Europe." *Journal of Modern History* 61 (1992): 79–116.

————. "The Politics of Enlightenment: Friedrich Gedike and German Professional Ideology." *Journal of Modern History* 62 (1990): 34–56.

Langer, Claudia. *Reform nach Prinzipien: Untersuchungen zur politischen Theorie Immanuel Kants.* Stuttgart: Klett-Cotta, 1986.

Laursen, John Christian. "Kant and Schlözer on the French Revolution and the Rights of Man in the Context of Publicity." In *Revolution and Enlightenment in Europe.* Edited by Timothy O'Hagen. Aberdeen: Aberdeen University Press, 1991.

————. "Liars and Unbelief in the Forgotten Utopia: Denis Veiras' *History of the Severambians* at the Roots of Modernity." In *La Vie Intellectuelle aux Refuges Protestantes*, edited by Jens Häseler and Antony McKenna. Paris: Honoré Champion, 1999.

————. "Pierre Bayle and the Elitism of the Republic of Letters (Then and Now)." Paper delivered at the Center for European Studies, Universidad de Nevarra, Spain, 1999.

————. *The Politics of Skepticism in the Ancients, Montaigne, Hume, and Kant.* Leiden and New York: E. J. Brill, 1992.

————. "Publicity and Cosmopolitanism in Late Eighteenth-Century Germany." *History of European Ideas* 16 (1993): 117–22.

———. "Scepticism and Intellectual Freedom: The Philosophical Foundations of Kant's Politics of Publicity." *History of Political Thought* 10 (1989): 439–55.

———. "The Subversive Kant: The Vocabulary of 'Public' and 'Publicity.'" *Political Theory* 14 (1986): 584–603.

Lefèbvre, Georges. "Der aufgeklärte Despotismus." In *Der aufgeklärte Absolutismus.* Edited by Karl Otmar Freiherr von Aretin. Cologne: Kiepenheuer & Witsch, 1974.

Lessing, Gotthold Ephraim. *Die Erziehung des Menschengeschlechts, und andere Schriften.* Edited by H. Thielicke. Stuttgart: Reclam, 1965.

Lestition, Steven. "Kant and the End of Enlightenment in Prussia." *Journal of Modern History* 65 (1993): 57–112.

Levinger, Matthew. "Kant and the Origins of Prussian Constitutionalism." *History of Political Thought* 19 (1998): 241–63.

Locke, John. *Two Treatises of Government.* Edited by Mark Goldie. London: Everyman Press, 1993.

Lynch, Marc. "Globalization and International Democracy." *International Studies Review* 2, no. 3 (December 2000): 91–101.

Macedo, Stephen. *Deliberative Politics: Essays on Democracy and Disagreement.* New York and Oxford: Oxford University Press, 1999.

Madison, James, et al. *The Federalist Papers.* Edited by Clinton Rossiter. New York: Mentor, 1961.

Malter, Rudolf. "Königsberger Gesprächskultur im Zeitlater der Aufklärung: Kant und sein Kreis." *Aufklärung* 7 (1992): 7–23.

Mandeville, Bernard. *The Fable of the Bees.* Edited by Phillip Harth. Harmondsworth: Penguin, 1989.

Mansbridge, Jane. "Using Power/Fighting Power: The Polity." In *Democracy and Difference: Contesting the Boundaries of the Political,* edited by Seyla Benhabib. Princeton: Princeton University Press, 1996.

Marshall, T. H. *Class, Citizenship, and Social Development: Essays.* Garden City, N.Y.: Doubleday, 1964.

Maurer, Michael. *Aufklärung und Anglophilie in Deutschland, Veröffentlichungen des Deutsches Historischen Instituts London.* Göttingen and Zurich: Vandenhoeck & Ruprecht, 1987.

McCarthy, Thomas. "Kantian Constructivism and Reconstructivism: Rawls and Habermas in Dialogue." *Ethics* 105 (1994): 44–63.

Mellin, G. S. A. "Enthusiasmus." In *Encylopädisches Wörterbuch der Kritischen Philosophie,* edited by G. S. A. Mellin. Jena and Leipzig: Friedrich Frommann, 1799.

Mill, John Stuart. *On the Logic of the Moral Sciences.* Chicago and La Salle, Ill.: Open Court Classics, 1987.

Mulholland, Leslie. *Kant's System of Rights.* New York: Columbia University Press, 1990.

Munzel, G. Felicitas. *Kant's Conception of Moral Character: The 'Critical' Link of Morality, Anthropology, and Reflective Judgment.* Chicago and London: University of Chicago Press, 1999.

Muthu, Sankar. *Enlightenment Against Empire.* Princeton: Princeton University Press, 2003.

———. "Justice and Foreigners: Kant's Cosmopolitan Right." *Constellations* 7, no. 1 (2000): 23–45.

Nisbet, H. B. "*Was ist Aufklärung?:* The Concept of Enlightenment in Eighteenth-Century Germany." *Journal of European Studies* 12 (1982): 77–95.

O'Neill, Onora. *Constructions of Reason: Explorations of Kant's Practical Philosophy.* Cambridge: Cambridge University Press, 1989.

Orloff, Ann. "Gender and the Social Rights of Citizenship." *American Sociological Review* 58 (1990): 303–28.

———. "Gender in the Welfare State." *Annual Reviews of Sociology* 22 (1996): 51–78.

Oz-Salzberger, Fania. *Translating the Enlightenment: Scottish Civic Discourse in Eighteenth-Century Germany.* Oxford: Clarendon Press, 1995.

Pagden, Anthony. "Introduction." In *The Languages of Political Theory in Early-Modern Europe,* edited by A. Pagden. Cambridge: Cambridge University Press, 1987.

Peter, Klaus, ed. *Die politische Romantik in Deutschland.* Stuttgart: Reclam, 1988.

Phillipson, Nicholas, and Quentin Skinner, eds. *Political Discourse in Early Modern Britain.* Cambridge: Cambridge University Press, 1993.

Pitkin, Hanna Fenichel. *Wittgenstein and Justice: On the Significance of Ludwig Wittgenstein for Social and Political Thought.* Berkeley: University of California Press, 1972.

Pocock, J. G. A. "The Concept of a Language and the *métier d'historien:* Some Considerations on Practice." In *The Languages of Political Theory in Early-Modern Europe,* edited by A. Pagden. Cambridge: Cambridge University Press, 1987.

———. *Politics, Language, and Time.* Chicago and London: University of Chicago Press, 1989.

———. *The Machiavellian Moment: Florentine Political Thought and the Atlantic Republican Tradition.* Princeton: Princeton University Press, 1975.

Poggi, Gianfranco. *The Development of the Modern State: A Sociological Introduction.* Stanford: Stanford University Press, 1978.

Puder, Martin. "Kant und die französische Revolution." *Neue Deutsche Hefte* 20 (1973): 10–46.

Putnam, Robert D. *Bowling Alone: The Collapse and Revival of American Community.* New York: Simon & Schuster, 2000.

———. "The Prosperous Community." *The American Prospect* 4, no. 13 (March 1993): 35–42.

———. "Unsolved Mystery, the Tocqueville Files." *The American Prospect* 7, no. 25 (March 1996): 26–28.

Putnam, Robert D., and Kristin A. Goss. "Introduction." In *Democracies in Flux: The Evolution of Social Capital in Contemporary Society.* Oxford: Oxford University Press, 2002.

Putnam, Robert D., with Robert Leonardi and Raffaella Y. Nanetti. *Making Democracy Work: Civic Traditions in Modern Italy.* Princeton: Princeton University Press, 1993.

Rawls, John. "Justice as Fairness: Political not Metaphysical." *Philosophy and Public Affairs* 14 (1985): 223–51.

———. "Kantian Constructivism in Moral Theory." *Journal of Philosophy* 77 (1980): 515–73.

———. *Lectures on the History of Moral Philosophy.* Cambridge, Mass.: Harvard University Press, 2000.

———. *Political Liberalism.* 2d ed. New York: Columbia University Press, 1996.

———. "Themes in Kant's Moral Philosophy." In *Kant and Political Philosophy: The Contemporary Legacy,* edited by R. Beiner and W. J. Booth. New Haven and London: Yale University Press, 1993.

———. *A Theory of Justice.* Cambridge, Mass.: Harvard University Press, 1971.

Rayner, Jeremy. "On *Begriffsgeschichte.*" *Political Theory* 16 (1988): 496–501.

———. "On *Begriffsgeschichte* Again." *Political Theory* 18 (1990): 306–07.

Reath, Andrews. "Hedonism, Heteronomy and Kant's Principle of Happiness." *Pacific Philosophical Quarterly* 70 (1989): 42–72.

———. "Kant's Theory of Moral Sensibility: Respect for the Moral Law and the Influence of Inclination." *Kant-Studien* 80, no. 3 (1989): 284–302.

Rees, Anthony M. "T. H. Marshall and the Progress of Citizenship." In *Citizenship Today: The Contemporary Relevance of T. H. Marshall,* edited by Martin Bulmer and Anthony M. Rees. London: University College London Press, 1996.

Reiss, Hans. Review of Schmidt, ed., *What Is Enlightenment? Eighteenth-Century Answers and Twentieth-Century Questions. Political Theory* 27 (1999): 236–73.

Richter, Melvin. *The History of Political and Social Concepts: A Critical Introduction.* New York: Oxford University Press, 1995.

———. "Understanding *Begriffsgeschichte.*" *Political Theory* 17 (1989): 296–301.

Riedel, Manfred. "Gesellschaft, bürgerliche." In *Geschichtliche Grundbegriffe: Historisches Lexikon zur politisch-sozialen Sprache in Deutschland,* edited by Otto Brunner, Werner Conze, and Reinhart Koselleck. Stuttgart: Klett-Cotta Verlag, 1972–1989.

———. "Transcendental Politics? Political Legitimacy and the Concept of Civil Society in Kant." *Social Research* 48 (autumn 1981): 588–614.

Riem, Andreas. "Aufklärung ist ein Bedürfnis des menschlichen Verstandes." In *Was ist Aufklärung? Thesen und Definitionen,* edited by E. Bahr. Stuttgart: Reclam, 1974.

Riley, Patrick. "The Elements of Kant's Practical Philosophy." In *Kant and Political*

Philosophy: The Contemporary Legacy, edited by R. Beiner and W. J. Booth. New Haven and London: Yale University Press, 1993.

————. *Kant's Political Philosophy.* Totowa, N.J.: Rowman and Littlefield, 1983.

————. *Will and Political Legitimacy: A Critical Exposition of Social Contract Theory in Hobbes, Locke, Rousseau, Kant, and Hegel.* Cambridge, Mass.: Harvard University Press, 1982.

Rimmerman, Craig A., Kenneth D. Wald, and Clyde Wilcox, eds. *The Politics of Gay Rights.* Chicago: University of Chicago Press, 2000.

Risse, Thomas, Stephen C. Ropp, and Kathryn Sikkink, eds. *The Power of Human Rights: International Norms and Domestic Change.* Cambridge: Cambridge University Press, 1999.

Rochau, August Ludwig von. *Grundsätze der Realpolitik: Angewendet auf die staatlichen Zustände Deutschlands.* Frankfurt am Main: Ullstein, 1972.

Rosen, Allen D. *Kant's Theory of Justice.* Ithaca: Cornell University Press, 1993.

Rosenberg, Hans. *Bureaucracy, Aristocracy and Autocracy: The Prussian Experience, 1660–1815.* Boston: Beacon Press, 1958.

Rousseau, Jean-Jacques. *The Confessions.* Translated by J. M. Cohen. London: Penguin, 1953.

————. *Discourse on the Origin of Inequality.* In *Basic Political Writings.* Edited by D. A. Cress. Indianapolis: Hackett, 1987.

————. *Emile: or On Education.* Translated by Allan Bloom. New York: Basic Books, 1979.

Sandel, Michael J. *Liberalism and the Limits of Justice.* 2d ed. Cambridge: Cambridge University Press, 1998.

Saner, Hans. *Kant's Political Thought: Its Origin and Development.* Translated by E. B. Ashton. Chicago: University of Chicago Press, 1973.

Schattschneider, E. E. *The Semi-Sovereign People.* New York: Reinholt & Winston, 1960.

Schmidt, James. "Civility, Enlightenment, and Society: Conceptual Confusions and Kantian Remedies." *American Political Science Review* 92 (1998): 419–27.

————. "The Question of Enlightenment: Kant, Mendelssohn, and the *Mittwochgesellschaft.*" *Journal of the History of Ideas* 50 (1989): 269–91.

————. "What Enlightenment Was: How Moses Mendelssohn and Immanuel Kant Answered the *Berlinische Monatsschrift.*" *Journal of the History of Philosophy* 30 (1992): 77–101.

————, ed. *What Is Enlightenment?: Eighteenth-Century Answers and Twentieth-Century Questions.* Berkeley: University of California Press, 1996.

Schudson, Michael. *The Good Citizen: A History of American Civic Life.* New York: Free Press, 1998.

————. *The Power of News.* Cambridge, Mass.: Harvard University Press, 1995.

Schuhmann, Alfred. "Kants Stellungnahme zu Politik und Presse." Dissertation, Department of Philosophy, Ludwig-Maximilians-Universität, Munich, 1928.

Shapiro, Ian. *Democracy's Place.* Ithaca and London: Cornell University Press, 1996.

———. *Democratic Justice.* New Haven and London: Yale University Press, 1999.

———. "Enough of Deliberation: Politics Is about Interests and Power." In *Deliberative Politics: Essays on Democracy and Disagreement,* edited by Stephen Macedo. New York and Oxford: Oxford University Press, 1999.

Shell, Susan Meld. *The Embodiment of Reason: Kant on Spirit, Generation, and Community.* Chicago and London: University of Chicago Press, 1996.

———. *The Rights of Reason: A Study of Kant's Philosophy and Politics.* Toronto: University of Toronto Press, 1980.

Shklar, Judith N. "Alexander Hamilton and the Language of Political Science." In *The Languages of Political Theory in Early-Modern Europe,* edited by A. Pagden. Cambridge: Cambridge University Press, 1987.

———. *Freedom and Independence: A Study of the Political Ideas of Hegel's Phenomenology of Mind.* Cambridge: Cambridge University Press, 1976.

Sieburg, Heinz-Otto. "The French Revolution as Mirrored in the German Press and in Political Journalism (1789–1801)." *History of European Ideas* 13 (1991): 509–24.

Silber, John R. "Kant's Conception of the Highest Good as Immanent and Transcendent." *Philosophical Review* 68, no. 4 (1959): 469–92.

Skinner, Quentin. *The Foundations of Modern Political Thought.* 2 vols. Cambridge: Cambridge University Press, 1978.

———. *Reason and Rhetoric in the Philosophy of Hobbes.* Cambridge: Cambridge University Press, 1996.

Skocpol, Theda. *Diminished Democracy: From Membership to Management in American Civic Life.* Norman: University of Oklahoma Press, 2003.

———. *Protecting Mothers and Soldiers.* Cambridge, Mass.: Harvard University Press, 1992.

Skocpol, Theda, and Morris Fiorina, eds. *Civic Engagement in American Democracy.* Washington, D.C.: Brookings Institution Press, 1999.

Smith, Adam. *The Wealth of Nations.* Books 1 to 3. London: Penguin, 1986.

Stark, Werner. "Kant und Kraus: Eine übersehene Quelle zur Königsberger Aufklarung." In *Kant Forschungen,* edited by R. Brandt and W. Stark. Hamburg: Felix Meiner Verlag, 1987.

Strawson, P. F. *The Bounds of Sense.* London: Methuen, 1966.

Strum, Arthur. "A Bibliography of the Concept *Öffentlichkeit.*" *New German Critique* (61): 161–202, 1994.

Stuke, Horst. "Aufklärung." In *Geschichtliche Grundbegriffe: Historisches Lexikon zur politisch-sozialen Sprache in Deutschland,* edited by Otto Brunner, Werner Conze, and Reinhart Koselleck. Stuttgart: Klett-Cotta, 1972–1989.

Taylor, Charles. "Kant's Theory of Freedom." In *Philosophy and the Human Sci-*

ences: Philosophical Papers 2, edited by C. Taylor. Cambridge: Cambridge University Press, 1985.

————. "The Motivation behind a Procedural Ethics." In *Kant and Political Philosophy: The Contemporary Legacy,* edited by R. Beiner and W. J. Booth. New Haven and London: Yale University Press, 1993.

Timmons, Mark, ed. *Kant's Metaphysics of Morals: Interpretive Essays.* Oxford: Oxford University Press, 2002.

Tribe, Keith. "The *Geschichtliche Grundbegriffe* Project: From History of Ideas to Conceptual History." *Comparative Studies in Society and History* 31 (1989): 180–84.

————. "Translator's Introduction." In Reinhart Koselleck, *Futures Past.* Cambridge, Mass.: MIT Press, 1985.

Trouille, Mary. "La femme mal mariée: Mme. d' Epinay's Challenge to *Julie* and *Emile.*" *Eighteenth Century Life* 20, no. 1 (1996): 42–66.

Van De Pitte, Frederick P. *Kant as Philosophical Anthropologist.* The Hague: Nijhoff, 1971.

Van der Zande, Johan. "In the Image of Cicero: German Philosophy Between Wolff and Kant." *Journal of the History of Ideas* 56, no. 3 (1995): 419–42.

Velkley, Richard L. "The Crisis of the End of Reason in Kant's Philosophy and the 'Remarks' of 1764–1765." In *Kant and Political Philosophy: The Contemporary Legacy,* edited by R. Beiner and W. J. Booth. New Haven and London Yale University Press, 1993.

————. *Freedom and the End of Reason: On the Moral Foundations of Kant's Critical Philosophy.* Chicago and London: University of Chicago Press, 1989.

Vierhaus, Rudolf, and Mitarbeitern des Max-Planck-Instituts für Geschichte, eds. *Frühe Neuzeit—Frühe Moderne: Forschungen zur Vielschichtigkeit von Übergangsprozessen.* Göttingen: Vandenhoeck & Ruprecht, 1992.

Viroli, Maurizio. "The Concept of *Ordre* and the Language of Classical Republicanism in Jean-Jacques Rousseau." In *The Languages of Political Theory in Early-Modern Europe,* edited by A. Pagden. Cambridge: Cambridge University Press, 1987.

Vorländer, Karl. *Immanuel Kant: Der Mann und das Werk.* 2 vols. Leipzig: F. Meiner, 1924.

Wegert, Karl H. "Political Engagement and the German Intelligensia, 1789–1800." *Canadian Journal of History* 22 (1987): 297–314.

Walzer, Michael. *Just and Unjust Wars: A Moral Argument with Historical Illustrations.* New York: Basic Books, 1977.

Williams, Howard, ed. *Essays on Kant's Political Philosophy.* Cardiff: University of Wales Press, 1992.

————. "Kant's Optimism in His Social and Political Theory." In *Essays on Kant's Political Philosophy,* edited by H. Williams. Cardiff: University of Wales Press, 1992.

————. *Kant's Political Philosophy.* Oxford: Basil Blackwell, 1983.

Wolff, Robert Paul. *The Autonomy of Reason.* New York: Harper and Row, 1973.

————. "The Completion of Kant's Moral Theory in the Tenants of the *Rechtslehre.*" In *Autonomy and Community: Readings in Contemporary Kantian Social Philosophy,* edited by Jane Kneller and Sidney Axinn. Albany: SUNY Press, 1998.

Wood, Allen. *Kant's Ethical Thought.* Cambridge: Cambridge University Press, 1999.

Wood, Gordon S. "Conspiracy and the Paranoid Style: Causality and Deceit in the Eighteenth Century." *William and Mary Quarterly* 3 (1982): 401–41.

Wuthnow, Robert. "Mobilizing Civic Engagement: The Changing Impact of Religious Involvement." In *Civic Engagement in American Democracy,* edited by Theda Skocpol and Morris Fiorina. Washington: Brookings Institution Press, 1999.

Yack, Bernard. *The Longing for Total Revolution: Philosophic Sources of Social Discontent from Rousseau to Marx and Nietzsche.* Berkeley: University of California Press, 1992.

————. "The Problem with Kantian Liberalism." In *Kant and Political Philosophy: The Contemporary Legacy,* edited by R. Beiner and W. J. Booth. New Haven and London: Yale University Press, 1993.

Yovel, Yirmiyahu. *Kant and the Philosophy of History.* Princeton: Princeton University Press, 1980.

Zammito, John H. *The Genesis of Kant's 'Critique of Judgment.'* Chicago and London: University of Chicago Press, 1992.

————. *Kant, Herder and the Birth of Anthropology.* Chicago and London: University of Chicago Press, 2002.

Zöllner, Friedrich. "Ist es rathsam, das Ehebündniß nich ferner durch die Religion zu sanciren?" In *Was ist Aufklärung?: Beiträge aus der Berlinischen Monatsschrift,* edited by N. Hinske. Darmstadt: Wissenschaftliches Buchgesellschaft, 1977.

INDEX